LIKE ROLLING THUNDER

LIKE ROLLING THUNDER

The Air War in Vietnam
1964–1975

Ronald B. Frankum Jr.

ROWMAN & LITTLEFIELD PUBLISHERS, INC.
Lanham • Boulder • New York • Toronto • Oxford

ROWMAN & LITTLEFIELD PUBLISHERS, INC.

Published in the United States of America
by Rowman & Littlefield Publishers, Inc.
A wholly owned subsidiary of
The Rowman & Littlefield Publishing Group, Inc.
4501 Forbes Boulevard, Suite 200, Lanham, Maryland 20706
www.rowmanlittlefield.com

PO Box 317
Oxford
OX2 9RU, UK

Distributed by National Book Network

British Library Cataloguing in Publication Information Available

Library of Congress Cataloging-in-Publication Data
Frankum, Ronald Bruce, 1967–
Like rolling thunder : the air war in Vietnam, 1964–1975 / Ronald B.
  Frankum Jr.
    p. cm. — (Vietnam, America in the war years ; v. 3)
  Includes bibliographical references and index.
  ISBN 0-7425-4302-1 (alk. paper)
    1. Vietnamese Conflict, 1961–1975—Aerial operations, American. 2. United
States. Air Force—History. I. Title. II. Series.

DS558.8 .F75 2004
959.704'348—dc22

                                                              2003019265

Printed in the United States of America

∞™ The paper used in this publication meets the minimum requirements of
American National Standard for Information Sciences—Permanence of Paper
for Printed Library Materials, ANSI/NISO Z39.48-1992.

Acknowledgments

This work would not have been possible without the timely and efficient assistance of several individuals. Sherri Lynn Brouillette diligently read early chapter versions and offered suggestions and comments to make the final product a much better one. Dr. Richard Verrone, oral historian for the Vietnam Project at Texas Tech University, read many of the final chapters and provided the insight and editorial advice needed for a work that covers so much in so little space. The Vietnam Project at Texas Tech University and its director, Dr. James Reckner, gave support and some quiet time to gather the information and analysis within these pages. I also wish to thank Millersville University for its assistance at the end of this project, which enabled me to complete the work in a timely manner.

Especially important to this work and many of those that will follow was the Virtual Vietnam Archive (www.vietnam.ttu.edu), which, at the time of this writing, contains over 500,000 pages of documents on the war. It is an indispensable resource for anyone interested in studying the war. Jeannine Swift, archivist at the National Archives and Records Administration at College Park, Maryland, was of great assistance in wading through documents on the air war and ensuring the quick declassification of a number of those used in the chapters on North and South Vietnam and Laos.

This volume covers a most significant time in U.S. history and examines some of the major events of the wars in Vietnam, Laos, and Cambodia. The individuals above made the work possible and better, but I, alone, accept fault for any errors or omissions. Writing on U.S. involvement in Southeast Asia is a challenge to any historian, but the new discoveries are the greatest reward and well worth the effort.

About the Author

Ronald B. Frankum Jr. earned his Ph.D. from Syracuse University and is currently an assistant professor of history at Millersville University of Pennsylvania. He served as associate director for the Vietnam Center at Texas Tech University and is author of *Silent Partners: The United States and Australia in Vietnam, 1954–1968* (2001) and coauthor of *The Vietnam War for Dummies* (2002).

Contents

List of Maps and Illustrations

MAPS

ILLUSTRATIONS

List of Tables

Acronyms and Abbreviations

AAA	antiaircraft artillery
ADVON	Advanced Echelon
AF	Air Force
AFB	Air Force base
AHC	Assault Helicopter Company
AIRA	air attaché
APC	Accelerated Pacification Campaign
ARRG	Aerospace Rescue and Recovery Group
ARRS	Aerospace Rescue and Recovery Squadron
ARS	Aerospace Rescue Squadron
ARVN	Army of the Republic of Vietnam (South Vietnamese Army)
AW	automatic weapons
CBU	Cluster Bomb Unit
CIDG	Civilian Irregular Defense Group
CINCPAC	Commander in Chief, Pacific
CTZ	Corps Tactical Zone
DMZ	De-Militarized Zone
DRV	Democratic Republic of Vietnam (North Vietnam)
ECM	electronic counter measures
ELINT	electronic intelligence
EOGB	electro-optically guided bomb
FAC	forward air controller
FANK	Forces Armées Nationales Khmer
JCS	Joint Chiefs of Staff
KIA	killed-in-action
LGB	laser-guided bomb
LOC	lines of communication
LORAN	long-range navigation
MAAG	Military Assistance Advisory Group
MACV	Military Assistance Command, Vietnam
MAW	Marine Air Wing
MiG	Mikoyan-Gurevich aircraft (used by the DRV)

MR	Military Region (for Laos)
NATO	North Atlantic Treaty Organization
NVA	North Vietnamese Army (People's Army of Vietnam)
OPLAN	operating plan
PACAF	Pacific Air Force
POL	petroleum, oil, and lubricants
POW	prisoner of war
PPS	Petroleum Products Storage
PRC	People's Republic of China
QRF	Quick Reaction Force
RAAF	Royal Australian Air Force
RLA	Royal Laotian Army
RLAF	Royal Laotian Air Force
RLG	Royal Laotian Government
RTAFB	Royal Thai Air Force Base
RVN	Republic of Vietnam (South Vietnam)
SAC	Strategic Air Command
SAM	surface-to-air missile
SAR	search-and-rescue
SIOP	Single Integrated Operational Plan
TAC	Tactical Air Command
TFS	Tactical Fighter Squadron
TFW	Tactical Fighter Wing
USAF	United States Air Force
USMC	United States Marine Corps
USN	United States Navy
VNAF	Vietnamese Air Force (South Vietnam)
WIA	wounded in action

Introduction

Aircraft played a pivotal and unprecedented role in the Vietnam War, and its use helped to shape the U.S. military and political strategy and tactics in Southeast Asia. In this prominent role, both the plane and the helicopter replaced, in most cases, equipment used in previous wars. Aircraft transported troops and supplies into Southeast Asia; between the battlefields it supplemented, or replaced, the ship, train, truck, and jeep. The firepower of the aircraft dominated the battlefield. It acted as artillery as well as additional automatic weapons (AW) fire that functioned as a multiplier for troop strength, allowing American forces to operate in much smaller units against an unknown and elusive enemy. Helicopters became ambulances to evacuate the dead and wounded while planes transported these casualties of war home or to places of safety. Aircraft transformed the way the United States fought in Southeast Asia because Vietnam, Laos, and Cambodia presented new challenges and required new techniques in conducting war.

The Vietnam War demonstrated the advantages of aircraft in war while exposing the limits of air power, which was only as effective as the decision makers, the geography, and the enemy would make it. In Vietnam, air power was often held back by political, historical, or cultural considerations. When restrictions were eased, the use of aircraft showed some surprisingly advantageous results. For the effective use of air power, the opponent had to have a strategy and tactics that were conducive to air strike damage. In Vietnam the North Vietnamese and their Viet Cong ally did not always conform to this condition. When they did, as will be discussed in the chapter on the 1972 Eastertide Offensive, air power had devastating results. In Laos the nature of the war and the terrain and climate of the region dictated the use of aircraft, although American air assets allowed the United States to do much more than had earlier been believed. However, geography and climate were not unique to Laos. Throughout Southeast Asia, both influenced the use of air power.

The diverse geography of Southeast Asia was a significant factor in the conduct of the air war. The differences in topography, climate, and soil created a variety of landscapes that posed unique challenges to the United States.* The climate in Southeast Asia is based upon the monsoon winds, which determine cloud coverage and precipitation levels. Rather than the usual four seasons—winter, spring, summer, and fall—southwest and northeast monsoons govern Southeast Asia. The winter northeast monsoon is caused by the cool, dry air over the Asian continent that is forced toward the warmer air over the Indian Ocean; the trend reverses in the summer as warm, moist air moves inland from the ocean. The summer, southwest monsoon season brings significant rainfall to the interior of Vietnam, Laos, and Cambodia with cloud coverage prevalent over the Red River Delta in the north and central highlands. There are few cloudless days that call for the cancellation of many air missions. The transition from the summer to winter monsoon season is quick and often associated with heavy thunderstorms and typhoons in the center of Vietnam around the Gulf of Tonkin. The winter monsoon season produces less precipitation outside the central region but brings in a concentration of clouds, fog, and light drizzle or rain. This effect, known as the Crachin, is prevalent around Hanoi and presented great problems to the air war over North Vietnam. The climate over Laos is also affected by these monsoon seasons with the dry season associated with the winter northeast monsoon and the wet season with the southwest monsoon. The weather in Laos was so influential that it determined who held the military initiative and how the United States utilized its air assets.

The topography of Vietnam determined the course of all aspects of the air war. Long, flat stretches of rice paddies dominate the Mekong and Red River Deltas with patches of rain forest and mangroves. The Annamite Chain towers over the interior landscape of Vietnam from the Chinese border to just north of Saigon and divides the two Vietnams from Laos and Cambodia. In addition to the rugged terrain, triple canopy and monsoon jungle cover the landscape. This jungle environment made it difficult to conduct reconnaissance and challenged munitions makers to devise new weapons to penetrate the canopy. In contrast with the Annamite chain is the soft, sandy coastal region that lines the entire shoreline of Vietnam while the Mekong Delta in the south and the Red River Delta in the north offered low, flat, and wet terrain over hundreds of square miles. The diversity of climate and geography in Southeast Asia dictated how the war was

---

*For more information on the geography of Southeast Asia, see CHECO Report, Louis Seig, "Impact of Geography on Air Operations in SEA—Special Report" (June 11, 1970).

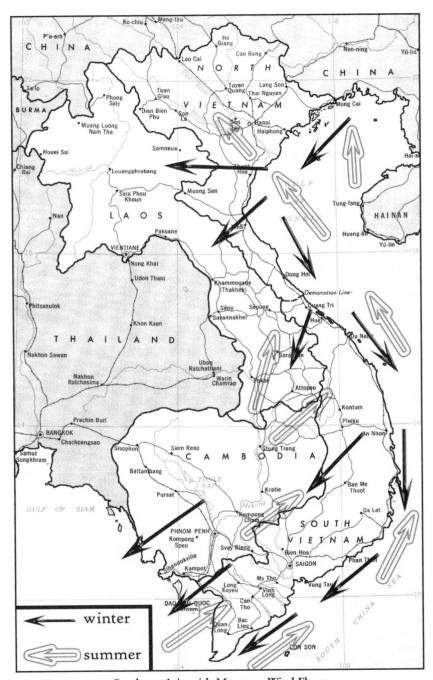

Southeast Asia with Monsoon Wind Flows

fought; it influenced the aircrafts and weapons used on the battlefield and determined strategy and tactics.

The decision on when and where to employ air power in Southeast Asia proved complicated as each branch of the Armed Forces claimed authority over similar areas and types of missions. Previous to 1964, the Air Force Section of the Military Assistance Advisory Group, Vietnam (MAAG) controlled the air over Vietnam but, with increased U.S. involvement and the transformation of MAAG into the Military Assistance Command, Vietnam (MACV), decisions on how to allocate air power became more contested. The heart of the controversy was directly related to the struggle within the United States Armed Forces that had intensified during World War II, when the modern Air Force came into existence and both its offensive and defensive roles emerged.

In May 1964 the 2nd Air Division established a command post in Southeast Asia to coordinate the increasing number of reconnaissance flights over Laos. The problem of command and control was further complicated when United States Navy (USN) aircraft, operating from Task Force 77 in the China Sea, also became involved in the reprisal air strikes over the Democratic Republic of Vietnam (DRV) in August 1964. The commander of the 2nd Air Division reported to the commander of MACV, becoming the Deputy Commander, MACV, and to the Commander in Chief of the Pacific Air Force (PACAF), which caused some confusion and tension for those who had the expertise and authority to direct air strikes in Vietnam, Laos, and Cambodia. The problem did not become a major one until the United States made the decision to escalate its air campaign against the DRV. MACV insisted that it should coordinate this activity through the 2nd Air Division while PACAF argued that operations outside of counterinsurgency, especially air operations over the DRV, fell under its control. When the Marines landed at Da Nang in February 1965, following closely behind the Marine Air Group, another problem emerged as Marine air assets reported directly to the Marine Commander. It was agreed that the 2nd Air Division would retain control of Marine air operations with MACV in command of ground troops, but the USAF did not want the Marine Air Group in Da Nang because of its limited capacity. Eventually the USAF squadrons were transferred to Bien Hoa to make room for the upgraded Marine Air Wing, but this move did not stop the Marines from circumventing the command and control structure in place in Vietnam. Often, the Marines would conduct sorties outside of the 2nd Air Division authority, preferring to work with Army of the Republic of

Command and Control Structure in Southeast Asia, 1965

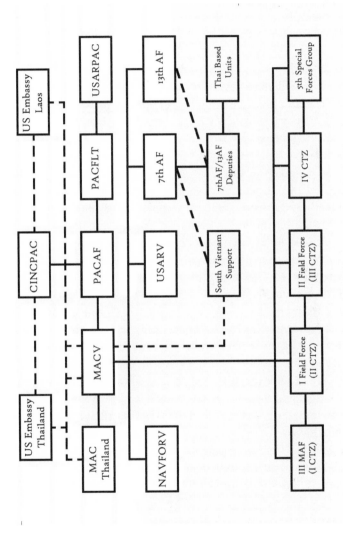

Source: CHECO Reports, Kenneth Sams, "Command and Control—1965—Continuing Report" (December 15, 1966), and Robert M. Burch, "Command and Control—1966–1968—Continuing Report" (August 1, 1969).

Vietnam (ARVN) units in the area to identify targets of opportunity in I Corps Tactical Zone (CTZ).

When U.S. air strikes expanded beyond the Vietnamese borders into Laos, PACAF again argued that it was the logical organization to direct the air campaign because it had the expertise. Including MACV in the decision-making process, according to PACAF, would only add another echelon that would delay the execution of the air war. MACV, however, maintained that since the majority of aircraft flying in Laos originated from South Vietnam, it should control how these aircraft were used just as it controlled how they were deployed over South Vietnam. The U.S. ambassador to Laos, William Sullivan, rejected MACV and PACAF direct control of air strikes in Laos, insisting instead that all missions go through the embassy to limit the political damage associated with a bombing campaign. The U.S. ambassador to Thailand, Graham Martin, wanted access to the decision-making process for all American air assets that left Thailand on sorties ending in Vietnam and Laos. Add to the mix the Strategic Air Command (SAC), which controlled reconnaissance over North Vietnam and the B-52 air sorties, and the Army Aviation units that entered the country in 1965 to support the escalating ground war, and it is easy to see how complicated the situation had become.

In order to create an efficient and clear line of authority for the air war in Southeast Asia, PACAF recommended a complete reorganization of the command and control. The plan, which was approved on July 8, 1965, created a working model for future command and control issues. The 2nd Air Division reported directly to PACAF, and the 13th Air Force took over the operation of bases in Thailand to separate the U.S. interests in Thailand from the Vietnamese conflict. The deputy commander of the 2nd Air Division worked with the 13th Air Force and the ambassador to coordinate Thai-originated flights over Laos and Vietnam. MACV controlled air operations with South Vietnam, and the USAF and USN divided air coverage of the DRV by route packages with the USN operating closer to the shoreline and the USAF operating inland. The USAF worked with the embassy in Laos on target selection in northern Laos while the southern Laotian region still had a mixture of USAF, USN, and MACV command and control.

On April 1, 1966, the 7th Air Force was established to replace the 2nd Air Division, which had overseen the escalation of air assets in South Vietnam and coordinated air operations despite the fact that it answered to both MACV and PACAF and had some of its air assets in Thailand. The 7th Air Force upgraded the 2nd Air Division and simplified the control and command by assigning it to PACAF, although the commander of the 7th did report directly to the Commander, MACV and the Commander in Chief, PACAF. The creation of the 7th Air Force paved the way for a larger air commitment to Southeast Asia under a coordinated command and control structure.

The difficulties in this structure were not the cause of the failure of air power in Southeast Asia. In fact, the complicated chain of command demonstrated that despite bickering and internal disagreements on who should be in charge, the various air assets of the United States Armed Forces were able to coordinate a sophisticated air war over the two Vietnams, Laos, and Cambodia. One might even question whether the air war was a failure when all air operations are taken into account.

As the following chapters indicate, there were several different types of air operations in Southeast Asia during the decade of intense American involvement in Vietnam. Some air campaigns, such as the first sustained bombing of the DRV, Operation ROLLING THUNDER, achieved modest success in their overall failure while other air campaigns, such as Operation BARREL ROLL in northern Laos and LINEBACKER I during the 1972 DRV invasion into South Vietnam, provided the firepower that turned defeat into stalemate or victory. In judging the air war in Southeast Asia and drawing up a ledger of victories, successes, and failures, this book includes noncombatant air sorties (a sortie equals one aircraft on one mission).

The U.S. air assets had some remarkable achievements during the conflict. Reconnaissance, search-and-rescue (SAR), tactical airlift, and medical evacuation techniques underwent unprecedented transformations as they confronted the challenges of war. Technological advancements, also discussed in this book, represent some of the greatest successes of the air war. On the other hand, failures in U.S. military strategy and tactics in combating an enemy that fought under a different set of rules and regulations also came to the surface.

Just as command and control presented some difficult challenges for the U.S. air war in Southeast Asia, so does the organization of the history of that period in time. In the past, the Vietnam War has been examined chronologically as well as thematically. Both methods provide good models for the study of the war but neither, alone, is acceptable for the examination of the air war. This book merges the two models and synthesizes the various historical debates over how the air war was conducted. The book begins with a chronological description of the early U.S. involvement in Vietnam. Air power had a specific use until 1964, namely, reconnaissance and training of Vietnamese pilots. From there, as the ground and air war escalated, the book takes on a thematic approach that examines the separate air campaigns in North Vietnam, South Vietnam, Laos, and Cambodia. There are many common elements in each of these air campaigns that require some cross-referencing between chapters in order to avoid duplication.

The book departs from the thematic approach in chapter 6, which examines the last significant air campaign of the war, the response to the 1972 Eastertide Offensive. Combining the two models of history has its pitfalls, but in order to consolidate so much diverse history and intrigue, such an approach is warranted. *Like Rolling Thunder* also makes some assumptions. The U.S. military strategy and tactics are not belabored except as they directly apply to the air campaigns. Indeed, several good works, listed in the Bibliographical Essay, provide an overview of the war. Because the study of the Vietnam War is not a simple exercise, only one very important aspect of the conflict is examined here as a supplement to other volumes in the Vietnam Series by Rowman & Littlefield.

The air war in Southeast Asia was unlike any that the United States had ever experienced. It is probable that the nation will never again use its air assets in the same way as it did in Vietnam, Laos, and Cambodia. Technology has seen to this, as have the lessons learned from America's longest war.

CHAPTER **One**

THE EARLY AIR WAR

THE UNITED STATES RECOGNIZED THE GOVERNMENTS OF VIETNAM, Laos, and Cambodia on February 7, 1950, soon after the French government created the Associated States from its Indochina colony. At the time, the French had been involved in nearly five years of conflict with Vietnamese nationalists intent on ousting France from Southeast Asia. At the end of World War II, the United States focused its national security policy on communism in the Soviet Union and its growing threat to Europe. While Washington officials had been cognizant of the Vietnamese people and their plight against French colonialism, Indochina did not register high on the priority list of foreign policy concerns. The Truman administration chose to support France, whose strength in Europe was more strategic to U.S. interests than the independence of the Associated States. After the formal recognition of the three countries, President Harry S. Truman asked the National Security Council to compose a memorandum outlining the government's position toward Indochina and the possible influence of communism in the region. National Security Council paper 68, which Truman approved in March 1950, discussed the Indochina situation as it related to the emerging Cold War between Washington and Moscow. One possible concern for the United States was the need to protect the security of Indochina while also preventing the spread of communism in Southeast Asia. The paper concluded by calling on the

1

Departments of State and Defense to develop programs to protect American security interests in Indochina.

For Vietnam, the most strategic of the three countries because of its location, large population, and natural resources, this policy study signaled the beginning of twenty-five years of military and political involvement there and in the region. Shortly after the June 25, 1950, invasion of South Korea by forces of North Korea, which Washington had identified as firmly in the Communist camp, the United States established a military presence in Vietnam in the form of MAAG. The advisory group had the responsibility of coordinating American assistance to the French Union Forces fighting against the Viet Nam Doc Lap Dong Minh Hoi (known as the Viet Minh), who had the support of the Soviet Union and the People's Republic of China (PRC). In November 1950, MAAG established an Air Force Section to handle the increasing role of the United States Air Force (USAF) in Indochina. MAAG remained in Vietnam until June 1964 when it was integrated into MACV, which had been created on February 8, 1962. During this early period of the air war, the Air Force Section assisted in the training of the Republic of Vietnam Air Force (VNAF) and coordinated U.S. air assets in Indochina. The Air Force Section maintained this assistance during the French war in Indochina and continued to support, after 1954, South Vietnam's struggle against the Viet Minh—South Vietnamese insurgents labeled by the southern regime as Viet Cong—and North Vietnamese.

In 1950 the French Air Force in Vietnam consisted of a variety of older model aircraft that had been the mainstay of the British and Free French Air Force during World War II as well as a number of captured German transports. These surplus aircraft performed well in Vietnam even though the French had a difficult time in maintaining them. The lack of spare parts hampered their air operations. One of France's earliest requests was more modern aircraft for their operations in Indochina. MAAG's first significant move after its formation was replacing the French aircraft. The United States provided forty F-6F fighters, supplanting the Supermarine Spitfires, the workhorse of the British Royal Air Force during World War II. This fighter force was augmented in 1951 with eighty F-8F fighters. The United States also replaced the captured German JU-52 transport aircraft with C-47 transports and introduced surplus World War II B-26 bombers to provide close air support for the French Union Forces engaged against the Viet Minh. While the ongoing Korean War restricted the number of aircraft provided by the United States to the French in Indochina, the upgrades gave the French more firepower than they could have brought to the battlefield on their own. After the MAAG commitment and delivery of American aircraft, the French more than doubled the number of weekly sorties in Vietnam.

B-26 Invader. *Douglas Pike Collection, The Vietnam Archive, Texas Tech University*

France's Air Force controlled the skies over Indochina during the nine years of its war with the Viet Minh between 1945 and 1954. Air power provided the French with an advantage, but it did not guarantee victory, nor did any amount of U.S. military assistance to the French Union Forces fighting in Indochina. Because of the lack of spare parts and technicians, the French became increasingly dependent upon the Air Force Section of MAAG. Washington leveraged this need with advice on how to handle the Viet Minh. In the administration's Cold War strategy, Truman needed a strong France in Europe to bolster its defenses. He played into French concerns in Indochina that the loss of the colonies would result in the collapse of the government in Paris. While the United States used its military assistance to France in Indochina to influence the conduct of the war, the French used the Cold War to continue American assistance in its colonial struggle.

In accordance with this relationship, General Henri Navarre, commander of the French Union Forces in Indochina, developed a plan to force the Viet Minh to commit to a battle against the consolidated French forces in northern Vietnam. In order to gather his forces, Navarre requested U.S. air transports and, after initially rejecting a loan of C-119 transport aircraft, accepted twenty-five C-47 transports in December 1953. The cornerstone of the general's plan was Dien Bien Phu, a small outpost in the northwestern part of Vietnam. Navarre turned the outpost into a fortress with the goal of cutting off Viet Minh forces traveling between northern Laos and Vietnam along Highway 19, the only major road in the region. Dien Bien Phu was in a strategic, though isolated, location. After the Viet Minh cut the roads leading into the valley, the French were compelled to resupply the fortress by air. By January 1954 the French Union Forces required twenty C-119 and fifty C-47 transport sorties per day to maintain an adequate supply level. After various ground relief efforts failed to reopen the highway leading into Dien Bien Phu and the Viet Minh captured the only usable airstrip in the valley in March, the situation became critical for the French. Their air power provided an equalizer to the Viet Minh artillery, but as the battle raged, the French had a difficult time in maintaining their sortie rate due to attrition from Viet Minh antiaircraft artillery (AAA) and wear and tear.

At the request of the Paris government, Washington loaned a number of B-26 bombers and twelve additional C-119 transports to the French but rejected the use of American pilots, as the United States could not risk casualties. Through the Air Force Section of MAAG the USAF sent an additional 200 technicians to Hanoi to service the aircraft and keep the French fleet in the air. Nonmilitary American pilots volunteered to fly some of the sorties to reach the 170 tons of ammunition and thirty-two tons of food required per day at Dien Bien Phu. These Civil Air Transport pilots were veterans of World War II and employed by the Central Intelligence Agency to assist in the international struggle against communism. These men not only flew some missions to Dien Bien Phu but also released a number of French pilots to the battle by flying other air routes throughout Indochina. The civilian pilots filled the obvious French need and allowed the United States to contribute to the defense of Dien Bien Phu without having to publicly acknowledge its involvement.

The USAF contributed 1,800 airlift sorties in Indochina, or 13,000 flying hours, to allow the French enough resources to focus on Dien Bien Phu. Despite the increased American assistance, the effort was not enough to alter the outcome of the battle. The Viet Minh surrounded

Navarre's forces at Dien Bien Phu and began to slowly eliminate them through battlefield casualties and squalid living conditions. As the situation became more perilous, French political and military leaders began requesting additional American aid to avoid defeat at Dien Bien Phu. A loss of this magnitude would have disastrous results for the future of the French in Indochina, whose people were already war-weary with the colonial conflict.

General Paul Ely, commander in chief of the French Union Forces, met with the chairman of the Joint Chiefs of Staff (JCS), Admiral Arthur Radford, and expressed a strong desire for a massive U.S. bombing campaign around the fortress at Dien Bien Phu to relieve the beleaguered French forces. From these meetings a plan was developed in which the United States would deploy sixty B-29 bombers to attack the Viet Minh hiding in the hills surrounding the French. The plan, known as Operation VULTURE, was not well received in Washington because few government leaders believed that air power alone could save Dien Bien Phu. While the plan met resistance in the United States, the idea of helping the French in Indochina received a boost when Secretary of State John Foster Dulles proposed a plan, United Action, to combat the Communist forces in Indochina. United Action called for the United States to intervene in Indochina to assist the French against the Viet Minh. One prerequisite of the military operation was the active cooperation of America's allies, specifically the United Kingdom. In addition to the caveat not to intervene in Indochina alone, the United States also had concerns about the ability of the French Air Force to handle the addition of U.S. aircraft requested by Ely. The French did not have enough pilots to fly the bombers, nor did they have the technical staff to maintain the fleet. American personnel would be required to fly and maintain the aircraft for the French, which might lead to accusations by the Chinese Communists that Washington was intensifying the war. The Truman administration did not want the overt involvement of the Chinese in Indochina, as had been the case in the Korean War.

Another flaw with the concept of Operation VULTURE was the requirement to include fighter escorts for the B-29 bombers. The bombers were vulnerable to the threat of Chinese interceptors and required fighter escorts, which meant an additional presence of American personnel in Indochina to fly the fighters. Operation VULTURE would have significantly increased the size of the American commitment to Vietnam and drawn the United States further into the conflict. President Dwight D. Eisenhower, who took office in January 1953, maintained that it was not practical for his administration to escalate its involvement unless American allies also joined in the fight. When the United Kingdom refused to become more involved, United Action fell apart, and Operation VULTURE ceased to be a viable option to save the French at Dien Bien Phu. The fortress fell on May 7, 1954, and weakened the French position at the Geneva Conference, where the participants had been discussing the political and military situation in Asia. The conference, which was to begin its Indochina phase on May 8, changed from a negotiating session on the Indochina situation to one that finalized the end of nearly 100 years of French rule in Indochina. On July 21 representatives from Paris and from the Viet Minh signed an accord that ended the war and made arrangements for the French to leave Indochina.

The Geneva Agreements divided Vietnam into two temporary countries along the 17th parallel and provided for a general election within two years to unify them. The northern part of Vietnam was named the DRV, headed by Ho Chi Minh. The southern part eventually took the name the Republic of Vietnam (RVN—South Vietnam) and was first led by the last Nguyen emperor, Bao Dai, until Ngo Dinh Diem forced him out of power in 1955. Several other key elements of the 1954 Geneva Agreements affected the role of the United States in supporting South Vietnam as that country struggled against the Viet Minh and the DRV. Perhaps most important, the Geneva Agreements restricted the quantity and type of assistance that Washington could give to South Vietnam. During the early years of the Diem regime, most of the American aid went to the creation of ARVN and other ground forces fighting against the Viet Minh or to the preparation of a Korea-like invasion from the North. The VNAF was not a top priority for the United States.

The South Vietnamese government faced the threat of what was primarily perceived as a ground conflict, and it required assistance and advice on how to build up ARVN. After Diem consolidated power, the VNAF had one squadron of F-8F fighters, two squadrons of C-47 transports, two squadrons of L-19 observation aircraft, and one H-18 helicopter unit. To operate these aircraft, the VNAF had 4,140 personnel, the majority of whom had limited experience, including the technicians and pilots. The French continued to participate in the training of the VNAF until May 1957 when the USAF took over. The USAF advisers quickly learned that while the Vietnamese pilots were capable of flying their aircraft, they needed training and experience in combat. In order to transform the VNAF into an effective fighting force, the USAF needed to reorganize and retrain the Vietnamese personnel.

One of the immediate needs of the VNAF was a more modern Air Force. The F-8F was designed as an air-to-air fighter. While it could provide some ground support for ARVN troops engaged with the Viet Cong—the armed insurgent movement that formed in the South as the successor to the Viet Minh—it could not carry a wide assortment of bombs. The F-8F, a propeller-driven aircraft, had reached its prime during World War II and was ready for retirement. Replacement parts were sometimes difficult to obtain, and Vietnamese technicians had a hard time keeping the aircraft in operating condition. As a result, the United States agreed to provide the USN's AD-6 fighter/bomber to the Vietnamese. The AD-6, renamed the A-1 Skyraider, was also propeller driven and was

A-1 Skyraider. *Douglas Pike Collection, The Vietnam Archive, Texas Tech University*

capable of carrying a heavy load of armaments. The A-1 started its service in Vietnam in the late 1950s and continued to operate throughout the duration of the war. It earned a solid reputation as a ground support aircraft with the ability to remain in the air after sustaining significant battle damage and to loiter over the target area for a long duration. The A-1 became one of the central aircraft of the VNAF. In addition to the A-1, the United States upgraded the South Vietnamese helicopter force with the addition of the H-34. The H-34 allowed for air mobility while the A-1 provided the firepower to give ARVN a significant advantage in engagements with the Viet Cong.

There were fewer than 1,000 American military personnel in Vietnam when Eisenhower turned over the White House to John F. Kennedy in January 1961, even though the 1954 Geneva Agreements restricted American numbers to one-half that amount. These personnel advised the South Vietnamese government and ARVN on how to fight the war against the Viet Cong and against the soldiers of the North Vietnamese Army (NVA). It was during Kennedy's first year that the United States chose to become more involved in the struggle for Southeast Asia. American personnel increased dramatically from the Eisenhower era with newer and more efficient weapons readily available in Vietnam. The USAF, whose personnel in Vietnam reached over 400 by the end of 1961, continued to increase the number of aircraft available for the VNAF and ARVN in an effort to counter the rising number of NVA and Viet Cong soldiers fighting south of the 17th parallel. By the end of the Kennedy administration, there were over 4,600 USAF personnel in the RVN advising the VNAF in aerial operations.

U.S. Military Strength in Vietnam during the Kennedy Administration

	December 31, 1961	December 31, 1962	December 31, 1963
USAF	421	2,422	4,630
U.S. Army		7,885	10,119
USN		454	757
USMC		536	483
TOTAL Approximately 1,000 including MAAG personnel		11,297	15,989

Source: CHECO Report, Donald F. Martin and Carl O. Clever, "CHECO—Part I—Summary—October 1961–December 1963" (May 31, 1964), Chart I-1.

At the end of 1961, Kennedy made the decision to expand assistance to South Vietnam under a unified command, MACV, which was eventually established on February 8, 1962. In January 1962, Secretary of Defense Robert S. McNamara emphasized the president's commitment to improving the U.S. counterinsurgency forces to fight in small wars and insurgencies. He called for the use of South Vietnam as a proving and training ground for tactics, techniques, and weapons. The discussion on air power deployment in Vietnam occurred before Kennedy's decision to increase U.S. involvement. On May 11, 1961, the JSC developed a plan to send additional forces to Vietnam. In response the military Commander in Chief, Pacific (CINCPAC), Admiral Harry D. Felt, recommended that any ground forces introduced into Vietnam needed to be accompanied by Army aviation units, specifically B-57 aircraft for border reconnaissance and close support and F-102 fighters to counter the DRV MiG threat.[1] The JCS ordered Army aviation units to South Vietnam on October 17, 1961, to conduct ground support sorties and assist in the training of the VNAF under Project Jungle Jim. Between November and December 1961, Detachment 2A of the 4400th Combat Crew Training Squadron arrived in Vietnam to train and assist ARVN and the VNAF. To support this squadron, the 13th Air Force established the 2nd Advanced Echelon (ADVON) with four detachments—three in South Vietnam and one in Thailand. The 2nd Air Division replaced the 2nd ADVON on October 8, 1962, under the command of Brigadier General Rollen H. Anthis, who was also the chief of the Air Section in MAAG. This move created two organizational structures to oversee the air war in Vietnam. The USAF forces reported to the 2nd Air Division while the Army air assets reported to the United States Army senior corps advisers.

The chain of command during the early years of the air war ran up from the commander of MACV, General Paul D. Harkin (February 1962–June 1964) and General William C. Westmoreland (June 1964–June 1968), to the CINCPAC to the JCS. To assist in the day-to-day operations of the air war, the USAF had experienced officers at each level to provide assistance and carry out orders that dealt with the use of American and South Vietnamese air power. The commander of MACV coordinated the four different air components acting in Vietnam. As more aircraft were introduced into the country in 1962, the organizational structure remained the same. As noted above, the USAF reported to the commander of the 2nd Air Division. The Army aviation and United States Marine Corps (USMC) aviation chain of command ran through the United States Army senior corps advisers, and the VNAF reported to ARVN, who answered to the Vietnamese Joint General Staff. To further complicate matters, the use of air power by the USAF and VNAF was controlled by the Air Operations Center of the Tactical Air Control System. The Army and USMC aviation units were under the control of the Army Air Request Net. While these control centers operated separately, there was a high degree of coordination between them, which allowed for combined action between different units.

The aircraft introduced into Vietnam under Project Jungle Jim were placed within Operation FARM GATE, the official name of the U.S. operation to introduce its air assets into South Vietnam. While the initial mission of Project Jungle Jim was the training of VNAF personnel, it quickly expanded as VNAF needs were assessed. The U.S. air assets involved in the operation included eight T-28, four RB-26, and four SC-47 aircraft, all of which had VNAF markings on them. The T-28 was an armed, propeller-driven aircraft used to train the VNAF pilots in combat operations. The RB-57 aircraft, a modified B-57, was flown in reconnaissance in Laos and North Vietnam while the SC-47 aircraft, a modified C-47, was used for surveillance inside South Vietnam. Approximately 150 Air Force personnel were provided under the operation. American advisers recognized that VNAF personnel required more hands-on experience in the air to further improve their support of ground troops. As a result, American personnel engaged in combat operations even though such activity was not a part of the original order.

In December 1961, ARVN and American advisers participated in their first joint operation against the Viet Cong strongholds in War Zone D, northeast of Saigon. Washington ordered American personnel to keep their exposure to danger to a minimum. Precautions were put in place, but pilots and trainers could not avoid taking risks to achieve the desired results. U.S. forces were ordered not to fire on NVA/Viet Cong troops unless they were first attacked. This rule of engagement resulted in unnecessary risks as American pilots and personnel had to wait until they were fired on before they could respond. It was important to maintain this public position, despite the consequences, to preserve the appearance that the United States was in Vietnam only to advise and train. The Kennedy administration continued to maintain that the DRV was in violation of the 1954 Geneva Agreements. This argument would have no meaning if the DRV could prove that Washington also violated the agreements that it had promised to respect. In late December, American pilots were allowed to engage in combat missions if a VNAF pilot was also aboard or if the VNAF could not complete the mission. This subtle change brought more American personnel into combat situations with a real chance of significant casualty rates.

As the United States became more involved in the war in Vietnam in 1962, its air component became increasingly significant. American air assets in Vietnam provided ARVN with a distinct advantage in mobility and firepower, and Washington recognized that the VNAF would play a significant role in the struggle against the Viet Cong. FARM GATE missions increased despite the fact that the presence of the personnel and aircraft violated the 1954 Geneva Agreements, which the Kennedy administration had pledged to support but had not signed. As the war intensified, USAF and United States Army personnel stepped up VNAF training and built up the infrastructure needed to support air operations in South Vietnam. At Tan Son Nhut Air Base immediately to the north of Saigon, a Tactical Air Control System provided for early warning against possible DRV air strikes. The United States also established additional facilities at Da Nang and Pleiku. Initially, these radar facilities were manned and maintained by American personnel. Because the existing infrastructure in South Vietnam needed improvement, U.S. military personnel surveyed it as well as potential areas for airfields and military bases.

In February 1962, just as MACV had been established, the VNAF experienced a serious obstacle to continued growth when two of its pilots in A-1 fighters strafed and bombed Ngo Dinh Diem's presidential palace in Saigon in a failed assassination attempt. Diem, who was already expressing concerns about the increased U.S. military presence in Vietnam and the growing independence of his forces, made it more difficult for the expansion of the VNAF. He recognized that there were a growing number of officers who opposed his rule and who sought, in private circles, a change in government. The VNAF, which was already facing obstructions in its training and ability to maintain its aircraft, had additional political problems and less support from Saigon.

Throughout 1962 another problem that continually plagued the Kennedy administration was the inability of the VNAF to work with ARVN. VNAF aircraft flew ground support in less than 10 percent of ARVN operations. Recognizing this deficiency, the USAF placed special emphasis on stepped-up training and equipment in order to increase VNAF's ability to provide support. In April the USAF sent thirty pilots to fly with the 1st Transportation Group. The American pilots were on call twenty-four hours per day and flew 25,000 hours during their time in Vietnam. The Dirty Thirty, as they became known after a reporter remarked about their always-dirty uniforms, flew with VNAF pilots in C-47 transports to train them. The constant presence of USAF pilots increased the VNAF's effectiveness. The more experienced VNAF pilots made the transition from C-47 to fighter aircraft while the USAF pilots allowed for the release of a number of VNAF pilots for other air missions over South Vietnam and additional training in fighters.

As well as pilots and USAF advisers, the United States provided more helicopters to assist in ARVN airlift and convoy protection along the major roadways in South Vietnam. The Viet Cong presented a constant threat to ARVN convoys. After a significant ambush near Ben Cat on April 9 that killed twenty-three South Vietnamese and two Americans, the United States started to conduct air coverage to protect the vulnerable trucks. After implementation of the new program, the Viet Cong did not attempt even one ambush for the remainder of the year. The success of this project led many within American military circles to believe that air power held the key to victory in South Vietnam. The UH-1A, named the Iroquois but known as the Huey, was one of the helicopters introduced into South Vietnam and would become one of the icons of the Vietnam War. When the helicopters began taking ground fire from Viet Cong antiaircraft artillery and automatic weapons, the United States introduced armed helicopters into South Vietnam. For the remainder of the Kennedy administration, Washington concentrated on training the VNAF and providing the necessary personnel and equipment to supplement the VNAF effort against the Viet Cong.

By the end of 1963 the VNAF had been built up to 681 aircraft, thereby representing a fivefold increase from the first days of the Kennedy administration. The 681 total in the VNAF was comparable with the numbers of aircraft in the air forces of Taiwan (617), Indonesia (556), and North Korea (525).

U.S. and VNAF Air Strength in
Vietnam during the Kennedy Administration

	December 1961	*December 1962*	*December 1963*
USAF	35	63	117
VNAF	70	154	219
U.S. Army	40	200	325
USMC		20	20
Total	145	437	681

Source: CHECO Report, Donald F. Martin and Carl O. Clever, "CHECO—Part I—Summary—October 1961–December 1963" (May 31, 1964), Chart I-2.

In June 1964 the JCS asked CINCPAC to develop a list of targets in the DRV for possible air strikes. This request was in response to the increased involvement of North Vietnamese troops in South Vietnam and the DRV's support for the Viet Cong. A list of ninety-four targets emerged after examination of existing intelligence and aerial photography. This list would eventually be the one from which the United States would pick targets to hit after North Vietnam intensified its activities in South Vietnam. The first use for the list came in August 1964 when the North Vietnamese attacked a USN destroyer engaged in an intelligence-gathering mission off the coast of North Vietnam.

In the fall of 1963, President Kennedy authorized the use of American personnel to gather intelligence on North Vietnamese coastal defenses. The operatives also supported South Vietnamese missions designed to harass North Vietnamese villages and offshore naval facilities directly above the 17th parallel. These two missions were Operational Plan 34A (OPLAN 34A) and DeSoto. OPLAN 34A supported clandestine operations along the southern coast of North Vietnam while the DeSoto missions employed USN ships to conduct electronic intelligence (ELINT) operations to gather information about North Vietnamese radar and air defense installations. Hanoi interpreted both operations as overt acts of aggression. However, Washington justified them by arguing that the North Vietnamese used the areas to stage the movement of personnel and supplies south of the 17th parallel to support the southern insurgency against the South Vietnamese government. The United States viewed this movement as a clear violation of the 1954 Geneva Agreements.

In 1962 the Department of Defense pushed for the intensification of covert actions in Southeast Asia to combat the increased activities of the NVA/Viet Cong. To counter North Vietnamese infiltration into South Vietnam, Air Force Chief of Staff General Curtis E. LeMay advocated bombing the hub cities of Tchepone in Laos, a stopping point along what would become the Ho Chi Minh Trail (a series of footpaths and trails in Laos linking North and South Vietnam), and Vinh, the nearest large city to the north of the 17th parallel. After a series of studies and reports from Vietnam, the United States reached a compromise. It agreed to increase clandestine operations against North Vietnam, supported by MACV and the Central Intelligence Agency station chief in South Vietnam. The OPLAN 34A mission started in early November 1963 and continued through the early part of 1964 with some success. The mission had the full support of the new leader of South Vietnam, General Nguyen Khanh, who advocated pushing the war north. OPLAN 34A, a psychological success for the South Vietnamese, who had limited capabilities to take the war to the north, deployed U.S. naval craft and American, or neutral country, pilots transporting small teams of South Vietnamese commandos during the night to inflict as much damage as possible on coastal supply depots, radar installations, and artillery positions. The commandos also kidnapped or eliminated North Vietnamese soldiers in their effort to disrupt the flow of personnel and supplies south, to place political pressure on the North Vietnamese. A July 30–31, 1964, OPLAN 34A raid, which coincided with a DeSoto mission, would forever change the course of the U.S. war in Vietnam.

The July 30–31 OPLAN 34A mission called for an assault against the Hon Me and Hon Nieu islands in the Gulf of Tonkin. Four Norwegian-built fast patrol boats attacked the islands but caused minor damage. The boats returned safely to Da Nang, but the USS *Maddox*, which had monitored the raid, attracted the attention of the North Vietnamese naval forces around the islands. On August 2 the *Maddox*, while conducting a DeSoto mission in international waters, spotted five P-4 North Vietnamese torpedo boats approaching at high speed. Three of the P-4 boats moved to intercept and engage the *Maddox*. They continued on their attack course even after the destroyer fired three warning shots. When the torpedo boats came within range of the 5-inch guns of the *Maddox*, it opened fire. Four F-8 fighters from the carrier USS *Ticonderoga* joined in to support the *Maddox*. Two torpedo boats broke off their attack after suffering some damage, and the third boat was immobilized and sunk.

Undeterred, President Lyndon B. Johnson ordered the destroyer USS *C. Turner Joy* to support the *Maddox* and continue the DeSoto mission but at a greater distance from the North Vietnamese coast. On August 4 the two destroyers reported that they were under attack by unidentified vessels, presumably more P-4 torpedo boats. Both DRV and American accounts agree that the first attack took place, although investigations of a second one proved inconclusive. Historians have offered strong evidence to support the conclusion that a second attack never took place. Johnson, his cabinet, and those leading the advisory effort in Vietnam did not have the benefit of hindsight and treated the second attack as real. Johnson used the attack as a catalyst for the escalation of the war against North Vietnam and called the incident a legal justification for increased U.S. participation.

In response to the incident in the Gulf of Tonkin, Congress passed the Gulf of Tonkin Resolution on August 7, 1964. The resolution granted Johnson authority "to take all necessary measures to repel any armed attack against the forces of the United States and to prevent further aggression." In effect, it gave the president a blank check to deploy whatever force he deemed necessary to defend American forces and installations in Vietnam against attack and to assist the South Vietnamese in their war against North Vietnam. The Gulf of Tonkin Resolution was as close as the United States ever came to declaring war on North Vietnam. It provided the framework for an increased war presence and helped initiate a new phase in the air war.

President Johnson ordered Operation PIERCE ARROW in direct response to the attack on the U.S. forces. Under the air operation, USN planes targeted the four DRV patrol boat bases and the oil storage facility at Vinh, from which the attacks originated, destroying 25 percent of the facility. Washington considered the operation successful despite the fact that one pilot, Lieutenant Everett Alvarez, was shot down and captured, and another, Richard Sather, was killed. Alvarez, the first Navy prisoner of war, spent the next eight years in North Vietnam.

The Viet Cong did not heed the warning meant for them via PIERCE ARROW and continued to step up pressure against American forces in Vietnam. In September 1964 a reported attack on a DeSoto mission nearly led to another air strike, which was called off at the last moment. The Viet Cong launched a mortar attack on November 1 against the base at Bien Hoa, which housed many of the U.S. aircraft. Johnson chose not to send American aircraft against the DRV in response to this attack. On December 24 the Viet Cong again struck at American personnel by bombing the Brinks Hotel in Saigon, which also served as an Armed Forces bachelor officers' quarters. Johnson refused to respond militarily to this attack despite the fact that air assets were in place to conduct dedicated air reprisals against North Vietnam for any NVA/Viet Cong action.

While these events were cause enough to launch another air strike against North Vietnam, it was a February 7, 1965, Viet Cong mortar attack on Camp Holloway, near Pleiku in the Central Highlands, that served as the final catalyst. Eight Americans were killed, another 128 were wounded, sixteen helicopters were destroyed, and another eight fixed-wing aircraft were damaged or destroyed. Johnson had expected the next reprisal to be in response to another attack on a DeSoto patrol in the Gulf of Tonkin, but he used the Camp Holloway assault to order a retaliatory air strike against North Vietnam, named FLAMING DART. The FLAMING DART mission had three options based upon the ninety-four targets earlier identified:

- Air strikes on the Dong Hoi barracks (target 33), Vit Thu Lu barracks (target 36), and Chap Le barracks (target 39)
- Air strikes on the Chanh Hoa barracks (target 24) and Vu Con barracks (target 32)
- Air strikes on the Thanh Hoa bridge (target 14) and Quang Ke Naval Base (target 74)[2]

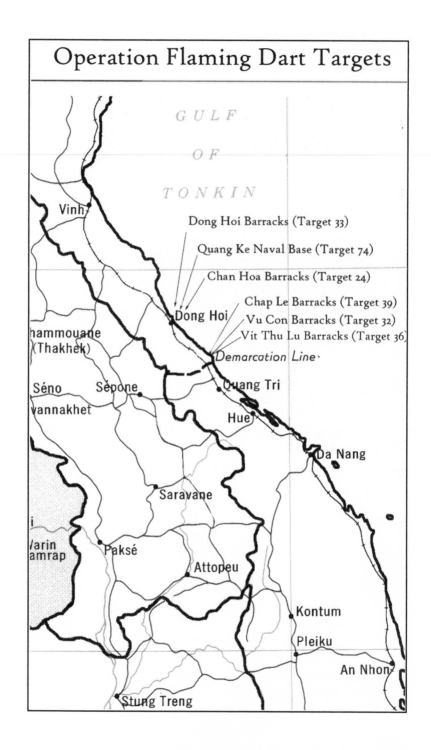

Operation Flaming Dart Targets

GULF

OF

TONKIN

Vinh

Dong Hoi Barracks (Target 33)

Quang Ke Naval Base (Target 74)

Chan Hoa Barracks (Target 24)

Chap Le Barracks (Target 39)

Dong Hoi — Vu Con Barracks (Target 32)

Vit Thu Lu Barracks (Target 36)

Demarcation Line

hammouane (Thakhek)

Séno   Sépone   Quang Tri

vannakhet   Hue

Da Nang

Saravane

i

/arin amrap   Paksé

Attopeu

Kontum

Pleiku

An Nhon

Stung Treng

The first FLAMING DART mission, executed by the VNAF, included all of the first option and the Vu Con barracks from the second option. On February 7, twenty-four A-4C and nine A-4E aircraft, all from the USN, supported by another thirty aircraft, attacked the Dong Hoi barracks (target 33), headquarters of the 325th NVA Division, and four of its battalions. Using a combination of 250-pound bombs, 2.75 rockets, Zuni rockets, and 20-mm ammunition, the A-4s destroyed sixteen buildings and damaged another six. One A-4E was destroyed by antiaircraft artillery fire, and another seven were damaged. Poor weather conditions forced the cancellation of the other three air strikes. Early the next morning the VNAF launched thirty A-1H and A-1E aircraft, led by Air Vice Marshal Nguyen Cao Ky and supported by an American F-100 jet aircraft, against the Chap Le barracks (target 39). After the VNAF dropped nearly 100,000 pounds of ordnance and the USAF added another 30,000 pounds targeted at flak suppression, reconnaissance aircraft conducting a bomb damage assessment estimated that at least 95 percent of the buildings were destroyed. While several aircraft were hit by small-caliber gunfire, no planes were shot down. The reprisal air strikes not only were a military operation but also had a political component. While RVN and U.S. aircraft struck North Vietnam, Soviet Premier Alexei N. Kosygin was meeting in Hanoi with government officials about increased Soviet support for the North Vietnamese war. It might have been more than a coincidence that the United States chose to respond to this Viet Cong attack rather than to the earlier, equally damaging one for its political effect with the Soviet Union. Whatever Washington's motive, the North Vietnamese chose to ignore and not to deal with the potential U.S. threat.

Increased NVA/Viet Cong activity encouraged CINCPAC to recommend to the JCS continued air strikes against North Vietnam. The air strikes had a positive effect on South Vietnamese morale, and the presence of American aircraft offered a real warning to the North Vietnamese and their allies, even if the DRV refused to deal with it. Preparations were begun to move a Marine Light Anti-Aircraft Missile battalion to Da Nang and the Army's 173nd Airborne Brigade to the Saigon area. The battalion served as a deterrent to possible North Vietnamese air strikes against the South while the brigade would protect American aircraft stationed in South Vietnam. Washington transferred additional aircraft, including ten tactical fighter squadrons and thirty B-52 bombers, to the Southeast Asian theater of operations. The lull after the first round of FLAMING DART missions did not last very long. On February 10 the Viet Cong attacked an American billet in Qui Nhon, killing twenty-three and wounding another twenty-one Americans. Another round of FLAMING DART missions, led by nearly 100 USN aircraft, struck the Chanh Hoa barracks (target 24), destroying twenty buildings but losing two A-4s and one F-8. The VNAF struck the Vu Con barracks (target 32). This would be the last FLAMING DART operation as a new, systematic bombing campaign against North Vietnam was set in motion.

The early air war in Southeast Asia emphasized specific tasks. The U.S. commitment to South Vietnam was in the training and buildup of the VNAF. Washington was content to continue a consistent level of interaction with the VNAF as long as the military and political situation remained the same. When the Viet Cong intensified its military action against the South Vietnamese government and NVA forces moved south of the 17th parallel, the United States was faced with a decision to either escalate or withdraw from Southeast Asia. It chose to remain faithful to South Vietnam and increase its involvement to combat what it perceived to be a growing Communist threat to the region.

The role of air power also underwent a transformation with the new American strategy. The United States expanded its training and modernization of the VNAF and introduced new mission sorties to assist South Vietnam against the NVA and Viet Cong. American assistance to Laos also underwent a transformation as combat support flights supplemented reconnaissance and SAR sorties. The United States had helped to design a VNAF that would be effective against an insurgency, but it was not intended to sustain a bombing campaign, nor did it have the personnel or aircraft to fulfill the requirements of an Air Force supporting its armed forces in war. The United States would take over this role, at the same time training the VNAF to eventually assume those responsibilities. Before the VNAF could function at this level, the United States invested its assets in the air campaigns over North and South Vietnam, Laos, and Cambodia. The American air war, in the fight for Southeast Asia, had begun in earnest.

NOTES

1. For more information on the MiG and DRV air defense, see chapter 2.
2. CHECO Report, SEA CHECO Team, "ROLLING THUNDER—March–June 1965—Continuing Report" (March 28, 1966), 4–13.

CHAPTER Two

A GRADUAL RESPONSE
THE AIR WAR OVER NORTH VIETNAM, 1965–1968

O N FEBRUARY 12, 1965, THE JCS FORWARDED TO SECRETARY OF DE-
fense Robert McNamara an air campaign program to increase
the pressure upon the Democratic Republic of Vietnam (North
Vietnam) to stop the infiltration of personnel and supplies into the RVN.
The eight-week program called for a separate strike by the United States
and South Vietnam on two days per week at preselected areas from the
94-target list generated earlier by the JCS. The United States would provide all of the logistics and air support for the strikes, including flak suppression, Combat Air Patrol, and reconnaissance for the air campaign,
which was titled ROLLING THUNDER. Operation ROLLING THUNDER would
become one of the largest air campaigns in U.S. history with much controversy and mixed results.

The political considerations for the eight-week program continued to
drive target selection and bombing mission. Early in ROLLING THUNDER,
the JCS wanted to connect the overt air campaign over the DRV as
retaliation to NVA/Viet Cong action in South Vietnam.[1] As the air campaign progressed, the need to associate ROLLING THUNDER with NVA/Viet
Cong attacks diminished. The early political considerations were due to
fear of the reaction that the Soviet Union and the People's Republic of
China might have to U.S. attacks against North Vietnam. There was no
question that the DRV would immediately begin to counter the American

sorties by escalating the war in South Vietnam, but the JCS hoped that the gradual nature of the air war would delay Soviet or PRC reaction. Of immediate concern in the planning stages was the introduction of Chinese volunteers and Soviet surface-to-air missile (SAM) weapons. It was the opinion of the JCS that the eight-week program would demonstrate to the DRV that the United States would punish any support for the insurgency in the South. Continued support for the Viet Cong would result in more intensified efforts against DRV targets north of the 19th parallel. The result, it was hoped, would be the end of DRV support for the Viet Cong and a peaceful resolution to the conflict.

Two air campaigns supported Operation ROLLING THUNDER during its tenure:

- IRON HAND: The main objective was to identify and eliminate SAM sites. These missions were flown in conjunction with ROLLING THUNDER sorties and could switch over to ROLLING THUNDER targets if no IRON HAND targets presented themselves.
- BLUE TREE: The main objective was to gather intelligence to support ROLLING THUNDER missions. These missions covered all of North Vietnam, except for the restricted areas around Hanoi and on the Chinese border, and were designed to work with IRON HAND.

The eight-week ROLLING THUNDER campaign had several objectives in addition to increasing pressure on the North Vietnamese. The air campaign was designed to cut the supply lines between Hanoi and Vinh—railways, roads, bridges, and water transport—as well as to eliminate the radar and communication stations. The Pentagon had a limited number of aircraft available for the operation. In South Vietnam there were eighteen F-100s and eighteen F-105s at Da Nang and eight B-57s in Bien Hoa. In Thailand the USAF had eighteen F-105s at Korat and eighteen F-100s at Takhli. When ROLLING THUNDER missions were on the drawing board, the Royal Thai government refused permission to use its airfields to launch bombing raids over North Vietnam, although by the end of February the United States gained approval. Despite the increase in operable aircraft, early strikes were limited because of the number of aircraft. General Nguyen Khanh, chairman of the Armed Forces Council and leader of South Vietnam, was very supportive of ROLLING THUNDER and wanted to proceed with the VNAF portion of the air campaign before the United States was prepared to begin. By February 17, Khanh had selected three targets—the

Vu Con Army barracks, the Dong Hoi bridge, and the Huu Hung ferry. He was persuaded to wait until the United States could coordinate the attack for maximum effect. Only later did Washington learn that Khanh wanted to attack the bridge because Ho Chi Minh was said to have been present for the dedication ceremonies held on February 18.[2]

ROLLING THUNDER was delayed by both weather and political intrigue in South Vietnam. A crisis developed in Saigon on February 20 when Khanh was ousted from power. The air campaign was again postponed with the reorganization of the new South Vietnamese government and the need to switch out the VNAF aircraft that had been loaded with ordnance more suitable for the coup d'état than for bombing the North. The first ROLLING THUNDER strike took place on March 2: ROLLING THUNDER V, which involved 160 aircraft. Forty-four U.S. F-105s from Thailand joined forty F-100s and twenty B-57s from Da Nang and Takhli to converge on the Xom Bang ammunition depot. After dropping more than 120 tons of bombs, the strike force damaged nearly 75 percent of the facility. On the same day the VNAF struck the naval base at Quang Khe. On each mission, aircraft suffered damage: four over Xom Bang and two over Quang Khe. The majority of the destruction and damage to aircraft occurred during suppression strikes against antiaircraft artillery positions, which caused a reexamination of procedures on how to attack these weapons. Other lessons learned included the need to decrease communications before the strikes so as not to give away intentions as well as to limit the number of aircraft over a target to reduce exposure to AAA and small-arms fire. The first air strike was militarily successful but, like so many that would follow, failed to achieve the political goals desired by the United States.

Before the first ROLLING THUNDER sorties executed their missions, the United States made plans to deal with the international reaction to the air strikes. The great concern was how the Soviets and Chinese would respond, and the first targets were selected with the objective of not pushing the Chinese toward overt aggression in Vietnam. Neither Washington nor Saigon announced the commencement of ROLLING THUNDER, although Soviet Foreign Minister Andrei Gromyko condemned the strikes in a letter of protest to Washington.[3] To the surprise of McNamara and Secretary of State Dean Rusk, the air strikes stirred less international reaction than anticipated. This result encouraged Johnson administration officials but did not cause any deviation from the planned gradual approach.

Both U.S. and VNAF aircraft took to the skies again on March 14, 1965, when twenty VNAF A-1H aircraft struck the Hon Gioi military barracks on Tiger Island, followed the next day by 137 USAF and USN aircraft against the Phu Qui ammunition depot. After these two missions the JCS expanded the air campaign so that the weekly strikes against the DRV could occur at any time. The JCS modified the ROLLING THUNDER campaign to include aircraft stationed in Thailand and to provide random armed reconnaissance, more intense Combat Air Patrol, and flak suppression. By March 19, ROLLING THUNDER missions took place on a daily basis usually with a number of aircraft sufficient to impose maximum damage. USAF, USN, and VNAF aircraft struck NVA supply depots, barracks, and petroleum, oil, and lubricants (POL) sites. One major concern about ROLLING THUNDER was the ability of the DRV to track U.S. and RVN aircraft over its territory. Starting on March 22, the missions began to concentrate on radar installations south of the 20th parallel in an effort to eliminate the DRV's early warning system. By making the DRV blind, American officials believed that greater bombing efficiency would result, which in turn would signal to the Soviets and Chinese that the United States was serious about defending South Vietnam.

The success of this round of missions resulted in a JCS decision to end the requirement of joint or concurrent U.S. and VNAF missions. Satisfied that ROLLING THUNDER was proceeding as planned, the U.S. military moved to ease other restrictions placed on the joint operation, eliminate unnecessary communication, and streamline the process of choosing targets. CINCPAC wanted to maintain control of the escalation of ROLLING THUNDER while keeping the option for a cessation of the air campaign.

ROLLING THUNDER continued to target the transportation choke points in the DRV with the objective of severely limiting the NVA's ability to supply and replenish its troops in the South. One particularly difficult target was the main bridge at Thanh Hoa that handled railway and road traffic. The USAF first struck the bridge on April 3 with thirty-one F-105s, with another fifteen F-105s and nineteen F-100s in support. Despite over 95 tons of bombs and several hundred 2.75 rockets, the bridge still stood at the end of the day. The USN was more successful against a similar bridge in the Thanh Hoa region, using MK-82, a low-level 500-pound bomb with pop-out fins, and MK-83, a free-fall, non-guided 1,000-pound ordnance. The USAF struck the Thanh Hoa bridge the next day and dropped 144 tons of bombs that resulted in some damage. Again, at the end of the day the bridge remained serviceable. The attacks on the Thanh Hoa bridge brought some criticism of U.S. tactics, as the 239 tons of bombs dropped should have been enough to destroy the bridge three times over. The attacks over the two days resulted in six aircraft lost, including two F-105s that were shot down by Soviet-built MiG jet fighters. The heavily defended bridge would remain a thorn in Washington's side for much of the war.

During the second week of April, the United States concentrated on the railroad bridges at Tam Da and Qui Vinh and the bridge at Kim Cuong. The air strikes succeeded in destroying spans on each of the bridges as well as a secondary target, the bridge at Khe Kiem. The movement of supplies through these choke points did not lessen despite the concentration of air power. As the United States would learn throughout the war, the DRV was resourceful in its day-to-day operations and easily adapted to or overcame on-the-spot obstacles. Transport units moved supplies through the choke points by human and animal power while ferries and nearby fords served when the bridges were being repaired. The bridges in the southern part of Vietnam were relatively new, and those who lived in the region remembered the time when the bridges did not exist. It was not difficult for the locals to make the adjustment when the bridges were down. This is not to say that the damage—the United States had destroyed fourteen bridges by April 20—did not affect the DRV. American intelligence estimated that the DRV had to divert a significant amount of resources to maintain the flow of supplies south and to repair the spans. More assets diverted to restoring the bridges meant fewer committed to the slowly developing DRV war machine.

As the end of April approached, the weather over North Vietnam improved. Thus, the United States could intensify ROLLING THUNDER, which was about to begin its second phase of destroying lines of communication (LOC). At the beginning of this phase, U.S. and VNAF aircraft had struck at most of the radar installations, barracks, and ammunition and supply depots south of the 20th parallel. The last primary target was communications. The strategy behind phase II was to deny the Viet Cong the support from, and contact with, the DRV, which would force the Viet Cong to live off the land, thus alienating the villagers in the South who had only enough food and supplies to maintain their own families. Phase II ignored the ample targets north of the 20th parallel. Attacking these targets worried some military strategists because of the MiG threat and possible Chinese intervention. As ROLLING THUNDER progressed, the United States made plans to increase its available aircraft in the Southeast Asian theater to include a second USAF F-105 squadron, a USMC F-4B squadron, and B-57 bombers. These additional aircraft supplemented the ROLLING THUNDER missions as well as Operation BARREL ROLL in northern Laos; Operation STEEL TIGER, the interdiction of the Ho Chi Minh Trail in southern

Laos; and ARC LIGHT missions, the use of B-52 bombers carrying a combination load of 500-, 1,000-, and 2,000-pound munitions.

Starting with the April 23, 1965, phase of ROLLING THUNDER, CINC-PAC proposed a widening of the air campaign above the 20th parallel as well as an intensification of the bombings between the 17th and 20th parallels. PACAF wanted to demonstrate to the DRV that it should not consider the area safe sanctuary and desired to hit the ample targets to disrupt the strategic facilities previously left untouched. Some of the targets on this list included the POL depots at Hanoi and Haiphong and the airfields at Gia Lam and Phuc Yen, home of the majority of MiG jet fighters. These recommendations were discussed at the secretary of defense's Honolulu Conference on April 20, 1965. McNamara was not happy with the results of ROLLING THUNDER, even though the armed reconnaissance seemed to be producing some positive results. Admiral Ulysses S. G. Sharp, Commander in Chief, Pacific, proposed increasing these sorties to an average of twenty-four per day, although he disagreed with McNamara on the success of this type of mission over Laos. During the conference, McNamara argued that ARC LIGHT missions were too infrequent while ROLLING THUNDER, BARREL ROLL, and STEEL TIGER sorties were too many. He proposed adding more squadrons to the Southeast Asian theater to meet the needs of ground support within South Vietnam.

As ROLLING THUNDER gained momentum, Washington officials adopted a plan to gradually reduce the air campaign's publicity as the number of sorties rose. This was primarily done to lessen Soviet and Chinese reactions but also to present an image to the international community that the air strikes were not an extraordinary measure in the war. Within Washington, some political and military officials began to debate the effectiveness of the air campaign and how it should proceed past the initial eight-week program. Outside Washington, the Johnson administration presented a unified front: ROLLING THUNDER was a restrained air campaign to show the DRV that the United States was intent on stopping North Vietnamese assistance to the insurgency. McNamara, and with him Assistant Secretary of State for Far Eastern Affairs William Bundy, Ambassador Maxwell Taylor, Chairman of the JCS General Earle Wheeler, Admiral Sharp, and General Westmoreland, argued that it was important not to "kill the hostage" by attacking within Hanoi's protective ring. At the meeting on April 20 in Honolulu, McNamara's memorandum was discussed, and the group considered the proposal to alter the main purpose of ROLLING THUNDER to harassing the LOC, supply lines, and infiltration points until such time as the DRV was willing to begin negotiations.

The first sign of internal dissent in the air war came from Director of Central Intelligence John McCone, who submitted a letter and memorandum to President Johnson expressing his concern about the limited scale of the air war over North Vietnam.[4] McCone did not think the restrictive air war would cause the DRV to seek a peaceful resolution to the conflict because the North Vietnamese were easily absorbing the bombing sorties. He argued that the limited air war signaled to the DRV that the United States was more concerned about widening the war in Southeast Asia than forcing the DRV out of South Vietnam. His calls for broadening the air war received stiff opposition from the politicos in the White House and Congress. McCone's letter came after the Honolulu Conference, where the participants all agreed that the air campaign would take at least six months to show results even after extending the target list north (but excluding Hanoi). McNamara argued that ROLLING THUNDER pressure was right on target and that any increase in pressure would be satisfied through repetition and continuation.[5] Johnson chose to follow McNamara's strategy as significant targets around Hanoi remained restricted from air strikes.

The largest ROLLING THUNDER strike since the operation commenced took place on April 23, 1965. The U.S. and VNAF sorties targeted seven strategic bridges and, with 285 tons of bombs, destroyed spans on each. The targets of opportunity for this phase focused on transportation operations and LOC hubs. Fixed targets included the power plants at Thanh Hoa and Ben Thuy, the sea facilities at Ben Thuy and Phuc Loi, the supply and ammunition depots at Vinh, Thien Linh Dong, and Phu Van, the Mu Gia pass, and the citadel and barracks at Dong Hoi. CINCPAC then wanted to focus on targets north of the 20th parallel outside of Hanoi and Haiphong. Air Vice Marshal Nguyen Cao Ky pressed the Americans to include all NVA headquarters and barracks south of the 20th parallel to demoralize the DRV. Ky also called for a psychological operations program to explain to the people between the 17th and 20th parallels why they were being bombed and what the DRV needed to do to stop the bombing. Ky also wanted the northerners to understand that the VNAF was involved. As long as the bombing stayed below the 20th parallel, Ky believed that the Chinese would not join in the conflict and North Vietnam would not attempt an all-out invasion of South Vietnam.

Bombs were not the only load delivered from U.S. and VNAF aircraft during ROLLING THUNDER as the military engaged in less-than-successful psychological warfare over North Vietnam. Operation FACT SHEET was designed to drop leaflets explaining why the United States was conducting the air campaign and how the North Vietnamese could end the bombings

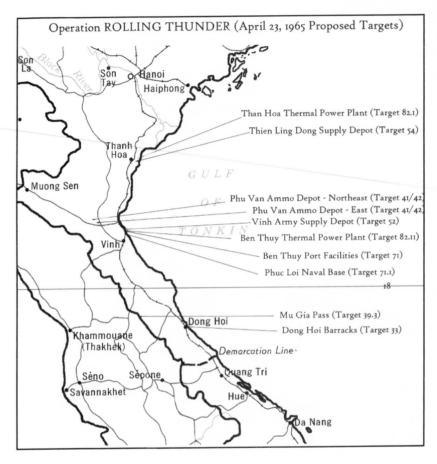

Operation ROLLING THUNDER (April 23, 1965 Proposed Targets)

by turning against their government. The leaflets also warned the North Vietnamese to stay away from military facilities and to consider the benefits of living in South Vietnam. On April 14 the VNAF, with A-1s, dropped over one million leaflets on Dong Hoi, Ha Tinh, Vinh, and Thanh Hoa. The USAF, in F-105s, flew the second mission and released 1.2 million leaflets on Bai Thung, Ha Trung, Thanh Hoa, Phu Qui, Phu Dien Chau, Vinh, and Ha Tinh. Additional million-plus distributions occurred on April 28, May 20, May 22, and May 23. Despite few positive results, almost five million more leaflets were dropped in June and nearly ten million in July. While the leaflets did not cause the DRV to change its strategy and tactics against the air war, the operation did cause some civilians to move away from military facilities. The disruption did not lessen the DRV's ability to conduct the war in the South.

The United States struck within 75 miles of Hanoi at the Thien Linh Dong supply depot on April 30 but continued to intensify the raids over Vinh, in an effort to isolate that city, and south of the 20th parallel through the beginning of May. The U.S. military sent special reconnaissance missions over the DRV in mid-May to make a bombing damage assessment. From the intelligence gathered during these flights, a picture emerged of a North Vietnam that seemed willing to absorb the ROLLING THUNDER damage and continue to intensify its support for the insurgency in the South on a twenty-four-hour basis. It was during this time that the United States discovered that the DRV was moving to a schedule of night-time transportation and daytime repair. A similar schedule was being adapted along the transportation lines in Laos. In response to this new tactic, PACAF recommended additional and continual armed reconnaissance on the choke points of routes 1, 7, 8, 12, and 15 to target the transportation points, truck parks, and all river traffic. After fourteen weeks of ROLLING THUNDER, the United States had managed to change transportation patterns and logistical support in North Vietnam. The Viet Cong, however, were not completely dependent upon North Vietnamese supplies for their survival or for maintaining their attack against the South Vietnamese government. Despite considerable destruction of barracks, roads and railways, bridges, and supply depots, the war in South Vietnam continued to intensify and the challenge to the RVN was a threat without an increased American presence. The United States had reduced the flow of supplies south, but it had not convinced the DRV that its direct involvement in the war would mean their destruction, nor did it persuade the DRV that it was willing to stay the course in Southeast Asia until the war was over.

On May 11, 1965, the Johnson administration called for a bombing pause to begin on May 13, based upon indications that the DRV might be interested in discussing a peaceful resolution to the growing conflict. The United States continued to conduct reconnaissance missions over North Vietnam while this first of many pauses in the air campaign over the North was allowed to run its course. The pause did not last long. It was clear that Hanoi officials were not interested in discussions leading to a peaceful resolution unless it was on their own terms—terms with which the United States could not agree. ROLLING THUNDER recommenced on May 18.[6] McNamara had stated that the purpose of ROLLING THUNDER was to destroy targets necessary for the infiltration of personnel and supplies into Laos and the RVN, and to convince the DRV that it must cease its aggressive conduct. When it was revealed that the DRV might have come around to this point, the Johnson administration authorized the first pause. In his carrot-and-stick approach, the president and his top advisers believed that it was only a matter of time before the DRV had to submit. This pause was the first of many frustrating American attempts to resolve the conflict with varying levels of force. The irony was not lost on the DRV, who used Johnson's carrot-and-stick approach to redouble their air defenses in the North and repair transportation facilities that would lead to greater infiltration into the South.

After the first bombing pause, CINCPAC forwarded to the JCS a ROLLING THUNDER plan that included at least one target above the 20th parallel in addition to the 400 sorties per week that would target the DRV's ability to sustain any war south of the 17th parallel. Bombing north of the 20th parallel meant an increase in the MiG threat. By the end of May another threat loomed on the horizon, as three SA-2 SAM sites around Hanoi appeared to be on the verge of operational status. Active SAM sites posed a grave threat to the high-flying U.S. aircraft that were conducting strikes and reconnaissance. A combination of SA-2 and AAA sites not only endangered the American aircraft overhead but also increased protection for MiG fighters and IL-28 bombers stationed at the Phuc Yen airfield. The inability to hit the MiGs on the ground meant that their threat in the air would remain. Each SAM site would become a primary target along with the MiG facilities in the coming months. Westmoreland argued that the SAM sites should be targeted and destroyed until they ceased to exist. Plans were developed to counter the SA-2, MiG, and IL-28 threat despite the very real danger that an attack so close to Hanoi might result in Soviet or Chinese intervention.

As June arrived, another concern regarding the air campaign tactics was the increasing loss of U.S. aircraft. Up to this time, ROLLING THUNDER air strikes had followed a common pattern based upon a six-target package per week. The DRV understood these tactics of a desired damage level and rearranged AAA sites around the targets most likely to be restruck in a given week. The DRV also took advantage of the American pattern of having bomb damage assessment and air reconnaissance immediately following the initial strikes, which allowed the DRV to concentrate its AAA fire against smaller follow-up U.S. strikes and reconnaissance sorties. This tactic resulted in the lessening of air strike effectiveness as second runs over a bombing area required bombers to either attack at a higher altitude or move faster over the target to avoid enemy fire. The ROLLING THUNDER missions had to be modified to preserve the pilots and aircraft. CINCPAC recommended an increase in the number of targets per week to stretch the

DRV's air defenses and to eliminate the policy of maximum feasible damage on a target to lessen concentrations of AAA over targets that had to be restruck more than once. CINCPAC also wanted to increase ROLLING THUNDER cycles to a two-week period and to use electronic counter measures (ECM) aircraft to disrupt radar-directed AAA fire. By the end of June, the U.S. military estimated that the DRV had accumulated over 3,000 AAA weapons concentrated around strategic sites with five SA-2 sites operational. It also estimated that the DRV had sixty-six MiG 15 and MiG 17 and eight IL-28 available at Phuc Yen.

On June 1, Secretary of State Rusk asked Ambassador Taylor a series of questions regarding the buildup in Vietnam and the possible approaches the United States might take to win the war in the South. Rusk outlined two air war strategies—one placing the air campaign in an ancillary role to the ground war, and the other putting more emphasis on the role of air power as the deciding factor. In the post-Honolulu Conference environment, the statement from the U.S. embassy in Saigon would carry some weight with the president and his political advisers as ROLLING THUNDER continued to come into focus.

Taylor's response is indicative of the problems with the growing war in Vietnam. From the perspective of the embassy in Saigon, Taylor called for a merging of the two approaches, as neither one alone would yield satisfactory results. Increasing air strikes with the sole purpose of raising South Vietnamese morale, decreasing North Vietnamese morale, and interdicting personnel and supplies carried past the 17th parallel would not win the war. It would also not pressure the DRV to seek a peaceful resolution unless the target list was expanded to inflict maximum damage and force the DRV to undergo the destruction of the air campaign. Taylor did not call for altering the bombing strategy to compensate for losses in the South; rather, he argued that an effective air campaign had to focus on both the NVA/Viet Cong troops in the South with the objective of denying them any hope of victory while bearing down on the DRV through the gradual intensity of ROLLING THUNDER cycles. Taylor was less concerned about provoking the Chinese with occasional, well-placed air strikes in and around Hanoi. Indeed, he promoted the idea as it would demonstrate to the DRV that it would have no sanctuary.

This concept was generally accepted in the new round of ROLLING THUNDER missions, although the effect on the North Vietnamese was less than expected or hoped for. The inability of political leaders in Washington to understand their counterparts in Hanoi continued to frustrate ROLLING THUNDER objectives through 1965, as the air campaign strengthened DRV resolve rather than weakened it. The combination of bombing pauses with peace overtures followed by the resumption of bombing encouraged Hanoi leaders to keep on with the war. They interpreted the direction of Operation ROLLING THUNDER as an air campaign that was dividing the political and military leaders in the United States. There was no question that ROLLING THUNDER was causing the North Vietnamese some concern, but it was not enough to significantly alter the southern war strategy. Intelligence gathered from Free World sources and postal intercepts identified a growing spirit of resistance to the air campaign despite some disruptions in the economy.

The eighteenth ROLLING THUNDER week, June 11–17, 1965, included a series of air strikes and armed reconnaissance above the 20th parallel. Because of the air threat, the strikes would consist of a smaller number of aircraft. Despite the move north, which would intensify over the next two weeks, the United States still kept the area around Hanoi and Haiphong off-limits because of political considerations. All air strike pilots had strict orders to avoid dense population centers even though the DRV had moved its strategic war-making facilities within these areas.

By the beginning of July, ROLLING THUNDER had achieved impressive results on paper, with sixty bridges destroyed and another 152 damaged. Twenty of the twenty-four bridges on the JCS list south of the 20th parallel had been damaged beyond use, while 1,151 buildings had been destroyed. By mid-July, ninety-one of the 117 targets established by the JCS south of the 20th parallel had been hit.[7] These air strikes had also hit all of the POL facilities and airfields in this region outside the restricted areas. The United States had struck only eighteen of the 132 JCS targets north of the 20th parallel by mid-July. Of great frustration to those who flew the missions, the Phuc Yen and Bat Bi airfields had not been targeted. The United States also had not struck the SA-2 sites and had paid no attention to the naval bases at Haiphong and Hon Gai, despite the fact that both were used to import war materials that found their way to the NVA/Viet Cong who were fighting in South Vietnam. Through July 22 the USAF, USN, and VNAF had conducted 6,861 sorties with sixty-three aircraft lost. Over 10,000 tons of bombs had been expended along with 3,940 rockets, 179 antipersonnel bombs, 449 air-to-ground missiles, and an assortment of other ordnance.[8]

While Washington pointed to some success in the air campaign, the JCS mounted growing complaints that ROLLING THUNDER was not producing real results that would eventually lead to the war's end. A presidential meeting was called on July 22 to discuss the air strategy. The majority of participants, including McNamara, Rusk, and the president, preferred to continue the restrictions around the Hanoi area because of an estimated one-in-five chance that the Soviets would respond with force. McNamara, in particular, continued to maintain that bombing the DRV was the right decision. He argued that the United States had to focus on the threat of future bombings to get the North Vietnamese to do what it wanted, rather than to intensify or expand the bombings. The key to a successful air campaign over the DRV was presenting a "credible threat of future destruction which can be avoided by agreeing to negotiate or agreeing to some settlement in negotiations."[9] McNamara further argued that ROLLING THUN-DER'S strategy should allow periods of time in which the DRV could enter into negotiations without causing a loss of credibility. Bombing pauses would provide this opportunity. The secretary of defense opposed bombing SAM sites or the airfields housing the MiGs and IL-28 bombers for fear that such a move would escalate the war and force the DRV to seek Soviet or Chinese assistance. He reasoned that the threat of the SA-2 and bombers on U.S. forces in South Vietnam was minimal while the risk of escalation was great. Johnson agreed with the assessment and likened the air campaign to a prize fight: the right hand was the bombing strikes and the left hand, the peace offerings. Working both together would result in a favorable result for the United States.

In July 1965 the USAF and USN flew nearly 1,200 sorties per week, and the VNAF accounted for about an additional 130. The United States continued to push north while the VNAF remained closer to the 18th parallel. With the Americans threatening the strategic areas north of the 20th parallel, the DRV sent its MiG force to intercept. By mid-July both the USN and USAF had had encounters with MiG fighters. Of greater importance was the increasing number of SAM sites discovered in the target areas. The United States employed the RB-66 (ELINT) system to intercept DRV radar signals, including the guidance system used by the SA-2. By July 23 the U.S. military had identified twenty-three SA-2 sites, and on the next day a F-4C was hit by a SA-2 that had originated near the Hanoi protective corridor.

The downed jet prompted the United States to launch a dedicated attack against two SAM sites suspected of launching the deadly SA-2. Six of the fifty-four aircraft that conducted the strike were shot down in what appeared to be a trap, as neither SAM site was occupied. The DRV had created a series of SAM sites in which they rotated their SA-2 missiles. The United States would later learn that the SA-2s were further protected with multiple bunker complexes and thoroughly camouflaged. A program called

IRON HAND was initiated to counter the emerging SAM threat. IRON HAND used ELINT and photographic reconnaissance—BLUE TREE missions—to identify SAM sites and immediately target them for destruction by napalm, cluster bomb units (CBU), and 750-pound bombs. IRON HAND proved unsuccessful during the first weeks of operation. In addition to the SA-2 sites, the DRV had constructed approximately 6,250 AAA sites for the estimated 4,200 air defense weapons in its arsenal.

North Vietnamese antiaircraft artillery unit, Thach Ha district, Ha Tinh province. *Douglas Pike Collection, The Vietnam Archive, Texas Tech University*

All intelligence from the reconnaissance flights conducting bomb damage assessment indicated that ROLLING THUNDER had seriously affected the DRV's transportation system even though supplies entered the country through China and the port at Haiphong. During August the United States concentrated on armed reconnaissance missions as the air strikes progressed northward with the objective of destroying the transportation infrastructure as well as the SA-2s. Included in the strikes was the Thanh Hoa bridge, which had proved stubborn. The bridge had been targeted in every ROLLING THUNDER cycle. The United States dropped 3,000-pound bombs on the bridge during cycles 24, 25, and 28 with more positive results. Still, the bridge was able to support walking traffic and remained a target during this period. By the end of

September the United States had struck eighty-five of the ninety-three JCS targets south of the 20th parallel and thirty of the 125 targets to the north of the 20th parallel.

ROLLING THUNDER cycles 34 and 35 started at the beginning of October 1965 with the added target of the supply routes between China and North Vietnam. The USAF focused on the Lang Met highway bridge and the Lang Het ammunition depot while the USN targeted the bridges at Xom Phuong and Vu Chua. The USAF and USN flew 1,300 sorties during the cycles with eight downed aircraft, but each succeeded in destroying their targets as well as a number of additional bridges that were important for the transportation and supply system during the wet season in North Vietnam. Cycles 36 and 37 continued to attack the bridges between China and the DRV and destroyed or damaged all targets. IRON HAND missions were also prevalent during the remainder of 1965 as more SA-2 launches were sighted during ROLLING THUNDER missions. As the United States continued to strike and down spans of strategic roadways between China and the DRV, the North Vietnamese MiG force intensified its coverage above the 20th parallel. Despite their increased presence, the MiGs posed little threat as the American aircraft were able to evade the jet fighters with little trouble.

In November the United States conducted more nighttime armed reconnaissance with the objective of disrupting the LOC and destroying military targets. Aircraft involved in BARREL ROLL and STEEL TIGER missions in Laos that were returning to airfields via North Vietnam were also authorized to conduct armed reconnaissance with any remaining ordnance after their primary strikes. Despite the intensity of the war, the USAF and USN were still restricted to within twenty-five miles of the Chinese border, thirty miles around Hanoi, and ten miles around Haiphong. The DRV continued to take advantage of the U.S. military's restraint by placing SAM sites as well as war-related industries within the protective circle. On November 27 the USAF destroyed 15 percent of the Dong Em SAM support facility with 55 tons of bombs. Even though weather cancelled many of the USN sorties, over 1,000 armed reconnaissance flights were launched. In mid-December the United States attacked the Uong Bi thermal power plant, which generated nearly 15 percent of the DRV's total capacity. After five days and twenty-eight strikes, the plant was hit seven times and the boiler house destroyed. A 91-sortie attack started ROLLING THUNDER 46 and 47 on December 24, but the cycle was short-lived as the United States announced that it would initiate its second bombing pause on that same day.

The second bombing pause lasted from December 24, 1965, to January 30, 1966, not only to observe the Christmas and Tet holidays but also to give the DRV another chance to reconsider its support of the insurgency in South Vietnam. Like the first bombing pause, the United States did not cancel reconnaissance flights over North Vietnam; and also like the first one, the DRV wasted no time in organizing repairs on damaged roads, railways, and bridges while increasing the air defense system around these strategic areas. From a U.S. perspective the bombing pause was considered a necessary part of the political process that would eventually allow the DRV to ask for a peaceful resolution to the war. What political leaders in Washington did not realize at the time was that their counterparts in Hanoi interpreted the pause as a division in U.S. strategy rather than a means to end the war. Thus, 1965 ended with no air strikes over North Vietnam and no end in sight to the war in South Vietnam. The Johnson administration had committed 180,000 troops to South Vietnam by the end of the year, and General Westmoreland had already asked for tens of thousands more to stem the tide. The air campaign over North Vietnam would be a critical part of the American strategy to end the war as 1966 drew near.

ROLLING THUNDER Statistics through 1965

	Total Sorties	Strike Sorties	Aircraft Lost	Aircraft Damaged
USAF	25,971	10,975	80	189
USN	28,168	11,656	83	250
VNAF	652	563	8	11
TOTAL	54,791	23,194	171	450

Source: CHECO Report, Wesley R. C. Melyan and Lee Bonetti, "ROLLING THUNDER—July–December 1965—Continuing Report" (July 15, 1967), 23.

While ROLLING THUNDER had achieved some success, it had not reached military and political expectations by the end of 1965. The DRV continued to support the insurgency and had infiltrated both personnel and supplies to match the American troop escalation. It appeared to the United States that the DRV was intent on a long struggle despite damage inflicted through the air campaign. However, the air campaign did force the North Vietnamese to divert a significant portion of their military resources to repair damage done during the air strikes and to augment their air defenses to counter the increase in sorties flown in ROLLING THUNDER. Although the flow of supplies had not been stopped, it had been slowed down. Moreover, the air campaign had affected North Vietnamese morale in the heavily bombed areas. The year 1966 would be a critical one for the United States in its war in Southeast Asia, and the air campaign would become a significant part of the war strategy. As more and more sorties were flown over North Vietnam, the coordination between USAF and USN aircraft became more significant. At the end of 1965, Admiral Sharp divided North Vietnam into a series of bomb areas called "route packages." The USAF had responsibility for the inland targets while the USN focused on the majority of coastal, or near water, targets.

ROLLING THUNDER Statistics through 1965 (Destroyed)

	Total Damaged	Total Destroyed
Transportation vehicles	477	740
Buildings	2,339	2,516
Bridges	246	656
Road cuts	0	847
Railway cuts	0	92
Ferry slips	15	76
Runways	0	13
AAA sites	60	55
SAM sites	5	6
Radar sites	10	41
POL areas	0	6
Power plants	3	2
Locks, dams	2	0

Source: CHECO Report, Wesley R. C. Melyan and Lee Bonetti, "ROLLING THUNDER—July–December 1965—Continuing Report" (July 15, 1967), Figure 9.

Operation ROLLING THUNDER underwent an evaluation at a conference in Honolulu on January 17–31, 1966. The participants, who included military and political leaders involved in guiding the United States in Vietnam, discussed the objectives of ROLLING THUNDER and the force requirements to meet those objectives. For 1966 the primary goal for the air campaign would remain the disruption of the DRV's ability to support the insurgency war in the South. Three tactics were identified to meet the objective:

- Reduce or eliminate the military support that the DRV received from other countries
- Destroy the DRV infrastructure that supported the war
- Interdict the movement of personnel and supplies used to maintain the war[10]

It was agreed that the United States had enough air assets in Southeast Asia to meet ROLLING THUNDER requirements and that a steady level of sorties on selected targets would accomplish the goal. Each objective shared common targets, although the conference participants acknowledged that stopping the flow of military supplies into the DRV and destroying the infrastructure would yield the most results for the United States.

To reduce or eliminate external assistance to the DRV required mining the harbor at Haiphong as well as destroying the bridges and railways between China and the DRV. These targets had been omitted from the bombing list because of the political implications involved in destroying them. In eliminating the infrastructure, the conferees identified nine major POL sites and six thermal power plants as the primary targets with an additional ten POL sites as secondary ones. Destroying these targets would severely limit the DRV's ability to produce war materials. The participants also recommended the continuance of armed reconnaissance despite the fact that these missions employed the majority of sorties with mixed results. Armed reconnaissance had a psychological effect on the DRV because no convoy or transportation hub would know when it might be struck. These missions also hampered crews whose sole purpose was to repair bridges and other transportation facilities necessary for the war effort. The ability to disrupt the LOC would help further the main objective of the U.S. air campaign over North Vietnam.

President Johnson ended the 27-day bombing pause on January 31, 1966, after failed diplomatic attempts at a peaceful resolution to the war. The first targets for this next phase in ROLLING THUNDER were moving objects such as trucks and trains, while truck parks, transportation hubs, bridges, and supply depots filled out the secondary targets. The new bombing phase did not have an auspicious beginning; poor weather and the failure to initiate any surprise attacks limited the number and quality of the sorties. A notable feature of the new phase was the introduction of radar-guided bombs. These weapons used a B-66 pathfinder aircraft to guide the crews to their targets, in all weather conditions, and increased the accuracy of the strikes. As the weather over North Vietnam was usually poor during the spring months, the deployment of the B-66 meant that fewer missions were cancelled and more territory would fall into the potential bombing area. The United States also established greater radar coverage over North Vietnam and more sophisticated bomb damage assessment and photographic reconnaissance. It introduced to Southeast Asia the B-57 bomber, which could also serve as a pathfinder aircraft. Thus, missions with B-57 bombers had more flexibility with secondary targets if the primary target was not accessible.

Starting on March 1, 1966, additional restrictions were placed upon air strikes over North Vietnam. Several locks and dams that had been authorized as targets were now restricted, while coastal reconnaissance missions were modified to allow engagement of DRV naval vessels if fired upon first, except within twenty-five nautical miles of China or within ten nautical miles of Haiphong. The JCS authorized 8,100 sorties per month—5,100 in North Vietnam and 3,000 in Laos. Sorties could not be carried over from month to month if the total number was less than the number allocated. Armed reconnaissance continued to avoid populated areas and did not receive authorization to attack airfields from which MiGs operated. The DRV had few weapons with which to counter the air strikes over North Vietnam. The resources available were used to their maximum capability, and, while the military threat to the U.S. aircraft was never serious, for a period of time the DRV played to American political weaknesses. The weapons used by the North Vietnamese were the SAM, radar-controlled AAA, individual AW fire, and aircraft interceptors.

The SAM missile appeared in the DRV early in the war with the introduction of the Soviet-built V-75 missile (designated the SA-2 by the United States). The SA-2 had the advantage of being a mobile weapon with easy-to-understand guidance and firing systems. Its main weapon was a Mach-3 300-pound warhead that exploded on contact. The SA-2 was principally employed on high-elevation targets and used an electronic guidance system to hone in on its target. The first U.S. aircraft lost to the SA-2 was a USAF F-4C, shot down on July 26, 1965. The Soviet Union continued to export the SA-2 to North Vietnam so that by the end of 1965 there were fifteen SA-2 battalions in the DRV. The North Vietnamese adopted the Soviet deployment of the SA-2 with a configuration of six launchers and support equipment in a star pattern. As the war progressed and the air war intensified, the DRV sometimes reduced the number of launchers to three or four when necessary to provide more coverage of the ROLLING THUNDER targets.

The initial SA-2 battalions were concentrated around Hanoi and Haiphong within the U.S.-created safe corridor. As more battalions arrived in the DRV in early 1966, SA-2 sites were discovered near Thanh Hoa and the Mu Gia pass. The United States had identified 135 SAM sites by June 1966, although not every site was occupied with SA-2 missiles. When it began targeting the POL storage facilities in June, the majority of SA-2 battalions moved back to the North. Because of this redeployment, the U.S. military had to decrease the number of B-52 sorties in route package 5 and 6 as well as around the few SA-2 sites remaining at the Mu Gia pass and Vinh. The SAM threat also caused the United States to reevaluate its mission priority and to increase the number of IRON HAND missions to target and eliminate the SA-2 threat. An increase in EB-66 ECM aircraft was also employed with some success to help counter the SA-2 and radar-guided air defenses.

By November 1966 the United States had identified thirty SA-2 units in North Vietnam with a concentration of battalions around Hanoi, Haiphong, and in the Red River Delta. The North Vietnamese took advantage of the self-imposed American restrictions on firing within thirty nautical miles of Hanoi and ten miles of Haiphong and had moved almost all of their SA-2 battalions within this area. The North Vietnamese fired 908 SA-2 missiles at U.S. aircraft during 1966, but this weapon accounted for only 5 percent of the USAF and USN aircraft losses. While the percentage is low, the numbers do not account for the ability of the SA-2 to alter American aircraft flight paths to a lower altitude and therefore make them more susceptible to AAA and AW fire. The SA-2 was not the most sophisticated weapon in the Soviet air defense arsenal, but it was the only SAM missile exported that could target high-altitude fighters and bombers. It performed poorly in humid and hot conditions, as was the case in North Vietnam, and was vulnerable to American ECM.

China was the first to provide jet fighters to the DRV. The Soviet-built Mikoyan-Gurevich (MiG) fighter was designed by Artyem Mikoyan and Mikhail Gurevich and exported to Communist-bloc and other countries in conflict with the Western powers. In August 1964, immediately following Operation PIERCE ARROW—the U.S. reprisal attack for the Gulf of Tonkin incident—the DRV received about three dozen MiG-15 and MiG-17 aircraft. This initial force was supplemented with additional MiGs from the Soviet Union in the summer of 1965. When Operation ROLLING THUNDER commenced, the DRV had a force of nearly 100 MiG-15 and MiG-17 and another eight IL-28 bombers. The MiG-21 was introduced to the air war in December 1965, when eleven MiG-21 were discovered at Phuc Yen.

In 1966 the DRV established a series of protective air rings around strategic North Vietnamese centers that included radar-guided AAA, SA-2 battalions, and MiG interceptors. In the beginning of the war the DRV had only a few serviceable airfields from which it could launch and recover its MiGs; the two most visible were at Phuc Yen and Kep. As the air war entered its second year, the DRV constructed several airfields around the country capable of accommodating the MiG. It was important to disperse the MiG fighters throughout the country to avoid U.S. air strikes against the fighters in stationary and vulnerable positions.

The Johnson administration did not consider the MiG threat to be significant through the middle of 1966. During the early part of the U.S. air campaign over North Vietnam, the MiG fighters were used primarily against high-altitude unarmed reconnaissance in the northern part of the DRV. The DRV's tactic was to conduct surprise attacks against this type of aircraft and then retreat to the protective SAM rings around Hanoi and Haiphong before the Americans could respond. The DRV learned early in the air campaign that U.S. aircraft would jettison their ordnance to increase their speed and maneuverability if confronted with MiG fighters. In many cases the MiG needed only to make an aggressive pass at the strike force before it released its bombs and evaded. While this tactic did result in the loss of several MiGs to F-4C MiG Combat Air Patrol, it achieved some modicum of success for the undermanned and overpowered North Vietnamese Air Force.

When MiG fighters engaged U.S. aircraft in the early part of 1966, the tactics were predictable. Unarmed reconnaissance aircraft were the primary targets, and air-to-air combat occurred at over 10,000 feet. The MiG, preferring to attack from behind, always attempted to surprise its target. In May the DRV stood down its MiG activities to retrain and to analyze American tactics. When the MiGs returned to the air on June 12 the DRV tactics had adapted to those of the United States. MiGs attacked all types of U.S. aircraft over North Vietnam and focused on the strike forces between 1,500 and 3,000 feet. For a period of six weeks the new MiG tactics helped to disrupt the American air campaign over North Vietnam. The DRV underwent another standdown from late July to September for further training with the MiG-21. In September, seventy-one MiG fighters encountered U.S. strikes over Vietnam. These engagements continued through the end of the year with the largest number of MiG-U.S. contacts in December. The DRV had forced almost 100 American aircraft to jettison their ordnance before completing their sorties, but this success cost the MiG force twenty fighters. The stepped-up activity at the end of 1966 forced the United States to reevaluate the MiG threat. However, the MiG fighters experienced the same difficulties in environment as did the American aircraft. The monsoon season limited the number of interceptors, and so did the numerous days of low-level clouds and the number of serviceable aircraft and parts availability.

Democratic Republic of Vietnam (DRV) Air Defense Systems, 1967–1968

Date	SAM Firings	SAM U.S. Aircraft Losses	MiG Engagement	MiG Aircraft Losses	U.S. Aircraft Losses	AAW/AW Positions	AAW/AW Positions (Occupied)	AAW/AW U.S. Aircraft Losses
Jan 67	271	3	16	9	0	28,826	7,126	17
Feb 67	132	2	2	0	0	29,507	4,037	5
Mar 67	158	3	6	2	0	31,479	4,094	21
Apr 67	246	5	50	29	7	32,479	7,179	17
May 67	431	9	72	26	2	32,695	7,227	29
Jun 67	205	2	25	5	1	33,899	8,335	24
Jul 67	298	6	12	3	0	34,632	8,511	31
Aug 67	441	8	16	4	2	34,964	8,796	29
Sep 67	169	2	16	0	1	35,140	8,964	13
Oct 67	582	8	29	8	3	34,572	8,479	28
Nov 67	349	11	27	3	6	35,708	7,966	18
Dec 67	246	2	34	4	3	36,266	7,930	11
Jan 68	140	4	29	4	6	36,303	7,830	8
Feb 68	170	4	18	5	4	37,242	7,641	2
Mar 68	216	0	5	0	0	37,630	7,443	6
Apr 68	8	0	0	0	0	38,163	7,278	8
May 68	33	0	2	0	1	38,985	8,000	13
Jun 68	16	1	7	0	1	41,492	7,686	6
Jul 68	11	0	3	1	0	43,275	8,188	13
Aug 68	19	1	3	3	0	43,635	8,018	8
Sep 68	16	1	3	1	0	44,397	7,891	12
Oct 68	17	1	0	0	0	37,647	5,232	12

Source: CHECO Report, James B. Overton, "ROLLING THUNDER—January 1967–November 1968—Continuing Report" (October 1, 1969), Figure 6 for 1967 statistics and Figure 16 for 1968 statistics.

The third option in the DRV air defense network was antiaircraft artillery. When the air war started over North Vietnam in 1964, the DRV possessed a moderate number of .50-caliber machine guns modified as AAA weapons and acquired from the Chinese. At the beginning of 1966 there were an estimated 5,000 AAA weapons. The number had increased 50 percent by the end of 1967. The individual weapon was not very effective against fast-moving U.S. fighters and bombers, but when grouped together and upgraded with a radar guidance system, it posed a measurable threat to low-flying U.S. aircraft.

The DRV also upgraded its AAA weaponry with 100mm. guns in the latter months of 1966. The greatest concentration of AAA sites was in U.S. route packages 1, 5, and 6. In route package 1 the DRV placed AAA guns with SA-2s around the major lines of communication and the coastal cities of Dong Hoi, Ron, and Quang Khe. Hanoi and Haiphong also had concentrated pockets of AAA weaponry. When working in co-ordination with the SAM sites and MiG interceptors, the AAA weapon proved difficult for U.S. aircraft. To avoid the SA-2 missiles, American pilots flew at a lower altitude, which put them within range of the AAA guns. If they flew at a higher altitude, the aircraft were more susceptible to SA-2 missiles. Through 1966 the majority of U.S. aircraft destruction or damage was the result of flying at an altitude below 4,500 feet and was caused by AAA fire.

The influx of Soviet and Chinese technology and technical expertise helped to develop, by the end of 1966, one of the most sophisticated air defense systems in the world. The three air defense weapons were enhanced with a growing complex of radar installations that provided earlier warning and guidance for the fire systems. The DRV took advantage of the political climate in Washington by housing most of their expensive air defense systems within areas that the United States would not bomb because of the concentration of civilians.

MiG activity was minimal through most of 1965 and early 1966. The MiG threat grew in 1966 with the introduction of the more sophisticated MiG-21 jet fighters and the large inventory of MiG-15 and MiG-17 already in the DRV. This force was protected by a growing ring of SA-2 SAMs and radar-guided AAA weaponry. The DRV began constructing additional airfields capable of handling the MiG throughout the country, and the new runways dispersed the aircraft and made it harder to locate and destroy them. To counter the MiG threat, the United States developed a two-prong strategy of nighttime raids over suspected MiG facilities—a break from the previous restrictions that did not allow attacks on the airfields—with immediate daytime follow-up attacks to destroy any remaining aircraft and target likely dispersal points after the nighttime raids.

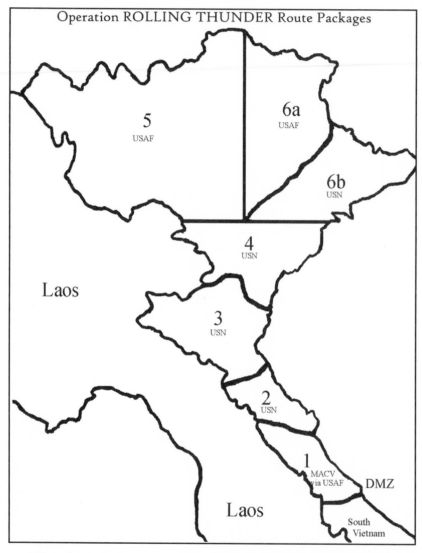

When the MiG-21 came into service over Vietnam, the DRV increased its air interdiction over 10,000 feet and lost five MiG-17 and one MiG-21. The DRV stood down its MiG flights for a month as it continued to train pilots, assess American tactics, and develop its own counter tactics. When the MiG force re-entered the air in June 1966, it engaged all types of U.S.

aircraft at all altitudes. It again stood down in July but returned in September, when it forced fifty-six U.S. aircraft to jettison their ordnance prematurely. This tactic continued through the end of the year, culminating in 118 sorties. The MiG threat was real by the end of 1966, but the United States found itself in a difficult position. Its aircraft loss due to MiG interceptors had not reached a significant level, although it was expected that attacks upon MiG airfields would result in considerable losses. If the United States was successful in attacking and destroying the MiG force, it might result in a more dangerous military and political situation. The DRV could request the assistance of Soviet or Chinese pilots, a greater and/or newer MiG fighter force, or it could station its MiG force within China, thus compelling the United States to either ignore it completely or expand the war beyond the borders of Vietnam.

Earlier, on March 22, 1965, General Westmoreland had offered a plan to Admiral Sharp to restructure the southern part of Operation ROLLING THUNDER along the same lines as Operation TIGER HOUND in Laos. Westmoreland reasoned that route package 1 and 2 were critical to the ground war below the 17th parallel and therefore required greater coordination with MACV. He had already assumed command of Operation TIGER HOUND, which was an area carved out of Operation STEEL TIGER.[11] Westmoreland wanted to draw together the bombing area for TIGER HOUND, route package 1, and the air campaign over South Vietnam. This consolidation under MACV, and specifically under Westmoreland, would enable him to divert sorties within these three areas as needed or desired. Sharp concurred and assigned route package 1 to the 7th Air Force and route package 2 to the naval commander of Task Force 77. The 7th Air Force and Task Force 77 also created a Joint Reconnaissance Coordinating Committee to facilitate the exchange of photography, intelligence, and bomb damage assessment. While route package 1 was under the 7th Air Force, Westmoreland retained full control over the air operations and provided day-to-day guidance on targets and resource allocation. He also received authorization to use the VNAF in route package 1 for ROLLING THUNDER missions.

The JCS reissued instructions for ROLLING THUNDER operations in April 1966, which included many of the restrictions already in place, and added some specifics for the more intense air campaign:

1. Attacks would avoid populated areas. Utmost caution would be exercised in the attacks to keep collateral damage to the minimum consistent with the desired objective.

2. Certain types of targets would not be attacked. These included hydropower plants, locks and dams, fishing boats, sampans or houseboats in populated areas that appeared to be water homes, the Yen Phu barracks, and the Vinh barracks. Attacks could be made on these targets only when specifically designated by a CINCPAC directive.

3. Certain areas were designated as restricted areas. No attacks of any type were authorized in those areas, except as approved on a case-by-case basis or specifically cited in the execution message. Specific CINCPAC direction would be required for entry of BLUE TREE resources into these restricted areas. The areas restricted specified:
   - No closer than thirty nautical miles from the center of Hanoi
   - No closer than ten nautical miles from the center of Haiphong
   - A zone along the Chinese border thirty nautical miles wide from the Laotian border east to 106° latitude and twenty-five nautical miles wide from there to the Gulf of Tonkin

4. The Chinese border would be avoided. Flight paths to and from target areas had to be planned so that they would not come any closer than twenty nautical miles to the Chinese border. Armed reconnaissance attacks had to be within the approved armed reconnaissance area.

5. IRON HAND missions were restricted to the authorized ROLLING THUNDER armed reconnaissance. This restriction remained unless CINCPAC directed otherwise.

6. Aircraft could enter into the restricted areas when engaged in immediate pursuit. However, during such pursuit, these aircraft were prohibited from getting any closer to the Chinese border than twelve nautical miles. While in pursuit these aircraft could not attack SAM sites that were located within thirty nautical miles of Hanoi. Moreover, they could not strike the North Vietnamese bases from which the attacking aircraft were operating.

7. Care would be taken in the employment of ECM. Employment on a carefully planned basis was considered essential to minimize degradation of U.S. capability by overexposure. It was believed that the enemy forces could reap major benefits through the indiscriminate use of ECM. Moreover, indiscriminate use could degrade Single Integrated Operational Plan (SIOP) capability.

8. Caution would be used at all times to avoid any inadvertent

release of weapons in the De-Militarized Zone (DMZ). When flown during the night or when under conditions of limited visibility, any strike within twenty nautical miles of the DMZ would be conducted only with AC or radar confirmation of position. Command signals would be dual flagged as appropriate. This could be done since the ROLLING THUNDER, BLUE TREE, and IRON HAND programs were closely related and mutually supportive.[12]

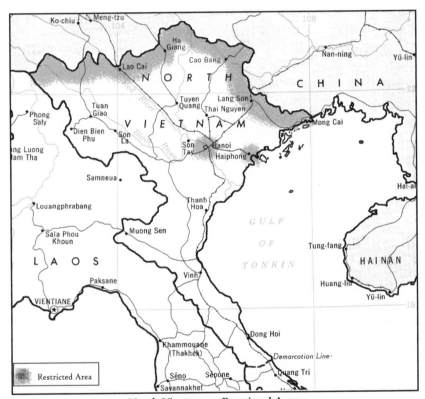

North Vietnamese Restricted Areas

The restrictions continued to hamper the air campaign as the American aircraft found it increasingly difficult to strike at a mobile force that did not rely on conventional methods of travel and used the restrictions to its advantage. There were too many targets of opportunity that escaped attack because of the restrictions, while MiG, SAM, and other air defense measures as well as a significant percentage of the DRV's war industry remained protected within the restricted areas.

Another concern for the spring of 1966 was the NVA/Viet Cong buildup to counter the increasing number of American troops. These troops fought to stem the tide in South Vietnam while air power was expected to halt the flow of soldiers from North Vietnam. The NVA/Viet Cong buildup was one of the reasons that Westmoreland was able to gain control of route package 1 and TIGER HOUND. The air campaign for this region focused on the city of Vinh. To the north of Vinh the air campaign concentrated on interdiction sorties against specified choke points while armed reconnaissance dominated the sorties in the southern region. From this two-part strategy a plan developed, named GATE GUARD, to stop the flow of supplies into Laos and via Laos into South Vietnam. GATE GUARD called for daytime sorties to focus on interdiction while night missions would involve armed reconnaissance. Rather than dividing route package 1 through Vinh, GATE GUARD covered the whole route. The plan began in May but was hampered by poor weather conditions. Through June and July, GATE GUARD forced the North Vietnamese to devote a considerable amount of resources to keeping the LOC open. Intelligence reports indicated that the number of NVA infiltrating below the 17th parallel had been cut nearly in half.[13]

Infiltration was the main concern at the DMZ, but an increase in third-country, or neutral, shipping in the waterways near Haiphong troubled Admiral Sharp. Early April was witness to a large number of transports offloading materials to lighters for delivery into Haiphong. The United States could not attack the third-country ships without serious political repercussions, nor could it allow the unfettered stream of war materials into the DRV. Sharp wanted to attack the North Vietnamese vessels as they made the transit between the neutral ships and Haiphong or, even better, to conduct air strikes against the concentration of shipping at Haiphong. The U.S. military had conducted operations at the minor port area of Cam Pha and had dissuaded the neutral ships from continuing with their debarkation plans. The use of Haiphong as a sanctuary for the importation of foreign materials into the DRV continued to be a problem for the Johnson administration. It would not be until 1972, during the Nixon administration, that the United States struck at Haiphong for effect and damaged a number of transports offloading. The failure to block the Haiphong choke until 1972 remains a controversial part of the air war over Vietnam.

The U.S. military was very familiar with Haiphong and the waterways leading from that port to the sea. Haiphong and the Do Son peninsula had played a significant and strategic role in the USN operation in 1954–55, when over 100 ships participated in Operation PASSAGE TO FREEDOM, which evacuated over 310,000 Vietnamese and French civilian and military personnel as well as over 410,000 long tons of materials. The strategic value of Haiphong was evident as was the intelligence gained in 1954 when the USN surveyed the waterways. The sinking of a few well-placed ships could have effectively blocked the entrance to Haiphong and stopped the flow of supplies into the DRV by sea. Coupled with an effective air campaign to interdict the land routes between China and the DRV, it would have isolated North Vietnam. The same political considerations that limited bombing around Hanoi and the Chinese border applied to attacking ships around Haiphong and the Do Son peninsula. The United States was not willing to risk an international incident that might precipitate overt Soviet or Chinese involvement in the war.

The worry of provoking the DRV's supporters did not apply to interdiction of choke points outside the zones of restriction. On April 11, 1966, the B-52 bomber made its first sorties over North Vietnam to strike against the Mu Gia pass. Thirty B-52s dropped over 585 tons of bombs on the pass. The effects were devastating but shortlived. A BLUE TREE mission the next day revealed that the craters from the 750- and 1,000-pound bombs had been filled in by the North Vietnamese, and trucks had already begun to run on the bombed roads.

On April 23–24 the Viet Cong launched a series of attacks on South Vietnamese industries and successfully hit cement roofing and textile factories. The attacks prompted Westmoreland to call for a retaliatory strike against similar industries in the DRV and specifically to target the Thai Nguyen Iron and Steel Works (target 76 on the JCS list). For Westmoreland, the retaliation would demonstrate to the North Vietnamese and Viet Cong that attacks against RVN industries would cost them more than the benefits of trying to disrupt the South Vietnamese economy. Destruction of the Thai Nguyen complex would significantly decrease the country's iron and steel output and hamper the production and repair of transportation equipment. Admiral Sharp did not disagree with Westmoreland's assessment but argued that the Viet Cong strike was further justification for a strike against the previously off-limits POL fields. Wiping out these resources would considerably slow down the war capacity of the DRV as well as its ability to continue to infiltrate the South. Sharp went to the JCS with a plan to use cycle 50 to target and destroy several of the key POL facilities, airfields, power plants, and the Defense Ministry in Hanoi. It was important to strike at concentrated resources as reconnaissance photography showed the beginning of dispersal and underground storage construction to protect strategic materials. Sharp called for a relaxation of the restriction imposed on ROLLING THUNDER before it was too late to make a significant air strike against the target.

Air strikes within thirty miles of Hanoi and ten miles of Haiphong had been prohibited until this point because of the large number of expected civilian casualties, international condemnation, and possible retaliation against South Vietnam. It was clear that ROLLING THUNDER had not achieved its intended results despite some periods of success. By June 1966, Westmoreland and Sharp concurred that South Vietnam was strong enough to absorb any retaliation while all targets south of the 17th parallel held resources that were redundant throughout the country. Any attack in South Vietnam would pale in comparison to the destruction of the Hanoi or Haiphong POL sites. Sharp again recommended strikes against POL sites on June 6, with the added argument that foreign imports were not enough to fulfill the DRV's wartime needs if the POL fields were destroyed. Destruction of the POL sites would throw off the summer offensive season and allow the United States to continue to gain the upper hand below the DMZ.

KC-135 Stratotanker, refueling A-4 airplanes. *Wise Collection, The Vietnam Archive, Texas Tech University*

The JCS finally authorized strikes against the facilities on June 16, although it initially kept the safe zone for Hanoi and Haiphong. On June 22 the JCS revised the restrictions and approved as targets the POL storage facilities at Hanoi, Haiphong, Nguyen Khe, Bac Giang, Do Son, Viet Tri, and Duong Nam for the next ROLLING THUNDER cycle. The JCS authorized the

ROLLING THUNDER 50-Alpha targets, as they were designated, to begin with strikes on the Hanoi and Haiphong POL sites on June 24 if the weather permitted. The JCS also wanted guarantees that there would be a minimum of civilian casualties and that the destruction would be notable. ROLLING THUNDER 50-Alpha would use the most experienced pilots, who would be briefed in detail on the need to keep casualties low in acceptable weather conditions. When the planning stage of the cycle was complete, the weather did not accommodate the time schedule and the air strikes were delayed.

On June 28 the JCS sent a message to Admiral Sharp stating that both targets did not have to be hit simultaneously. On June 29 the USAF and USN attacked the Hanoi POL site with twenty-four F-105s and a support force of eight F-105s in an IRON HAND role, twenty-four F-4Cs and two F-104s flying escorts, and four EB-66 ECM aircraft to disrupt the radar of AAA and SAM weaponry. The United States lost one F-105 in the attack and scored one MiG-17 shot down as it dropped 70 tons of bombs on the target. Reconnaissance bomb damage assessment flights after the attack showed twenty-eight of the thirty-two POL tanks damaged or destroyed. These assessment flights also confirmed that civilian structures received minimal damage. The United States was also able to hit the Haiphong POL, resulting in an estimated reduction of the DRV's total storage capability by two-thirds.

On July 1, Secretary McNamara joined a conference with Admiral Sharp to evaluate the air campaign for 1966 based upon the criteria formulated at the Honolulu Conference earlier in the year. The U.S. strategy on the ground, at this point, was to fight a war of attrition. One of the main objectives for the air war was to assist in the attrition strategy. It was estimated that the air campaign in route package 1 and TIGER HOUND accounted for monthly manpower losses for the North Vietnamese of approximately 6,100 while the infiltration rate was at 6,900.[14] It was clear that the air campaign attrition strategy had not been successful. McNamara questioned the infiltration rate, although he did agree that it was probably higher than the attrition rate, and suggested that the additional wounded be included in the statistics to balance the difference. This combination of statistics gave a false sense of success in the war of attrition, as not all wounded soldiers ceased their movement south nor did the United States have any factual data to back up its estimates.

The other primary target was the POL facilities. The United States had just begun a systematic program to destroy the storage tanks as well as the transportation system necessary to ship the POL. The June air strikes had dissuaded neutral ships from coming too close to the North Vietnamese coastline, and it was expected that additional strikes at Hon Gai and Cam Pha would achieve the same results. The U.S. military also kept a close eye on the railway to the north of Hanoi for evidence of POL shipments. It was estimated that the DRV had 90,000 metric tons of storage capability left after the June strikes. The North Vietnamese had made it a priority to empty the large storage tanks into 55-gallon drums and 5-gallon cans on trucks. A new mission for the USAF and USN would become armed reconnaissance with the specific target of this mobile POL storage as well as identified temporary storage sites and water transport. Despite the dispersal of POL resources, the United States estimated that it had destroyed at least two-thirds of the available POL and storage facilities in North Vietnam.

On July 18, 1966, General Westmoreland introduced a new bombing campaign in the DMZ that would attempt to locate and eliminate new supply routes to the NVA/Viet Cong in the South. Operations TIGER HOUND and MARKET TIME, the interdiction of the sea routes used for resupply, had forced the DRV to find alternative ways of refitting its troops. This new operation, TALLY HO, used the same concepts as TIGER HOUND to locate and eliminate the NVA's 324B Division that was organizing these new routes and threatening an offensive. The TALLY HO area of operation was from the northern section of the DMZ to 17° 30' north. As with other air campaigns in route package 1, TALLY HO came under the operational control of the 7th Air Force and utilized aircraft from the USAF, USN, USMC, and United States Army. When lucrative targets were located, sorties from TIGER HOUND could also be diverted for maximum effect. TALLY HO continued until the monsoon rains turned the DMZ into a large lake in October and November. While TALLY HO did not stop the flow of personnel and materials into South Vietnam, it denied the DRV free passage and made it much more difficult for supplies to reach the 324B Division, thus forestalling the offensive.

As the second half of the 1966 air campaign gathered momentum, the United States found itself without enough aircraft to conduct all of the sorties required in the various operations in Southeast Asia. The deficit was due in part to aircraft losses over North Vietnam as well as to the increased sortie rate needed to sustain the offensive capability expected during the year. The U.S. military had called for a 10,000-sortie rate per month in Vietnam and Laos. There was no problem in July and August because of unusually poor weather conditions in route packages 5 and 6. Four out of five sorties were cancelled because of weather during these two months, which usually were considered the best for flying. The September air strikes were focused on armed reconnaissance from the JCS target list as the DRV program to disperse the POL had reduced the number of lucrative targets. The DRV also increased its air defenses around the existing POL sites.

The weather continued to hamper air operations in the northern part of the DRV for the months of October and November. This period was marked with some internal controversy in the USAF as it attempted to counter complaints that it was performing below expected levels in attacking POL sites. One of the problems emerging from these POL missions and DRV dispersal of storage facilities was the influx of intelligence and other data regarding possible POL sites. A lack of coordination of the information from BLUE TREE and other intelligence missions caused an increase in possible targets. The USAF had a limited amount of resources with which to attack the targets on this growing list, and it was hampered by the fact that many of the possible POL sites were discovered to contain an insignificant POL cache. Admiral Sharp directed those providing the targets to ignore secondary sites attached to truck parks or supply depots as POL sites and to discriminate between a legitimate POL target and a suspected one. He also called for better bomb damage assessment, which had been citing possible POL sites by fire and smoke without confirming the source.

At the Honolulu Conference in October, the USAF identified twenty targets within its area of responsibility, but because of the weather, it had not been able to attack any of them by mid-December. The monsoon season in the North did allow for more sorties in route packages 1 and 2 as well as in TIGER HOUND areas. The redirection of air strikes had some positive results, as the concentration of NVA troops north of the 17th parallel had not been able to move in force into South Vietnam to begin its fall offensive. Despite the large buildup of American troops in Combat Tactical Zones (CTZ) 1 and 2 in the northern part of South Vietnam, NVA/Viet Cong combat troops still outnumbered the United States in the field. Air power continued to play a significant role in maintaining the balance of power. Even with the redirection of sorties, Sharp still worried that U.S. air power over Southeast Asia—specifically North Vietnam—had decreased in intensity when it should have increased.

To make better use of the U.S. air assets in Southeast Asia, Sharp recommended broadening the available targets over North Vietnam so that there would never be any regularity in the scope of the ROLLING THUNDER missions. If the United States kept the North Vietnamese off balance, there would be less likelihood of concentrated air defenses and American aircraft losses. The psychological advantage of the new tactics would demonstrate to the North Vietnamese that no target was safe from bombs. Sharp believed that if the United States did not adopt this more aggressive tactic, the DRV would continue to expand its support for the insurgency and infiltrate troops to counter the American buildup. A less aggressive air campaign would also have negative effects on U.S. allies involved in the war, on which the Johnson administration had begun to place more pressure to assist in the defense of South Vietnam. General Westmoreland concurred with Sharp's assessment and maintained that after the POL storage tanks were destroyed, the United States needed to concentrate on logistic and maintenance centers, SA-2 sites near Hanoi, the Haiphong port, the twelve thermal power plants, and the MiG airfields. As the political leaders discussed the possibility of another bombing pause, Westmoreland urged strikes against these targets before any such action was considered. During cycle 52 of ROLLING THUNDER, weather again played a role as only four of the thirteen strikes set for mid-November occurred. It was also during November that the JCS proposed a new set of strikes, named COMBAT BEAVER, designed to intensify the air war over North Vietnam in all areas and focused on the logistical centers. COMBAT BEAVER was essentially the same as ROLLING THUNDER. Sharp argued against the concept as it would disrupt the flow of the ROLLING THUNDER cycles.

The JCS also proposed reinstituting a successful operation used during the Korean War to encourage MiG pilots to defect with their aircraft. In the Korean War, Operation NOLAH had offered $50,000 to any MiG pilot who surrendered and delivered his aircraft to United Nations forces in South Korea, with another $50,000 for the first pilot to do so. The announcement of the reward halted MiG flights for over one week and resulted in fewer intercepts as all MiG pilots were reviewed by the DRV for their loyalty and reliability. (For the Vietnam War, Operation FAST BUCK would provide the same incentive to DRV pilots.) The JCS believed that the operation would result in the following:

- Capturing MiG jet fighters, including the MiG-21 and other aircraft
- Securing additional intelligence on DRV air and air defense tactics from pilots who defected
- Raising the level of suspicion within the North Vietnam Air Force
- Reducing the number of MiG sorties and limiting the jet's area of operation

- Improving South Vietnamese and international opinion for the U.S. defense of the country by showing a higher level of defection[15]

Operation NOLAH was approved with the suggestion that it include all types of aircraft to limit Soviet political propaganda, even though it might result in a number of lesser aircraft coming across the 17th parallel. Sharp recommended a $100,000 payment for aircraft, with a $50,000 bonus for the first and a $25,000 bonus for the second. Another reward system of $25,000 for DRV pilots who jettisoned into the sea and were rescued by American forces was intended to add to the total number of pilots who crossed over. While it was possible that the operation could backfire and reinforce a negative image of the United States or result in harsher treatment for prisoners of war (POWs) held in the North, the rewards outweighed the risks.

In December the United States struck two targets within the Hanoi safe radius. On December 4 the USAF dropped 36 tons of bombs on the Ven Dien vehicle depot and hit it again on December 13 and 14 with another 75 tons; bomb damage assessment flights showed massive destruction. The USN had also struck the depot earlier in December. Yen Vien was also hit within the safe zone. The press within the DRV and Communist-bloc countries immediately began to report that the Americans had struck civilian areas with over 100 killed. Newspapers in the United States picked up the story. It was only a matter of time before the air strikes over North Vietnam would kill a large number of civilians. The DRV had reorganized its strategic resources around civilian centers and had deliberately placed much of its population in harm's way.

The difference between the Americans and the North Vietnamese was the degree to which each side was fighting. For the DRV it was total war, and all members of the population were expected to contribute to the war effort and assume some risks. The United States had not declared war and had as its stated objective the defense of South Vietnam. As press reports about bomb damage emerged and the North Vietnamese continued to influence the outcome of the conflict, it was more and more difficult for the Johnson administration to justify its strategy to the American people and the international community. Hanoi and Washington agreed to a two-day truce during the Christmas holiday, thus ending the air war over North Vietnam for 1966.

As 1966 ended, the United States assessed its success in Operation ROLLING THUNDER and determined what the priorities for 1967 would be, given the military and political situation in Southeast Asia and the United

States. The Americans had conducted over 44,500 sorties over North Vietnam in 1966 and had dropped over 70,000 tons of bombs, rockets, and
other explosives during the year at a cost of 339 aircraft lost: 217 for the
USAF and 122 for the USN. The majority of these losses occurred over
North Vietnam.

ROLLING THUNDER Statistics through 1966 (Destroyed)

	Total Damaged	Total Destroyed
Transportation vehicles	2,654	2,762
Buildings	7,101	6,548
Bridges	1,454	2,999
Road cuts	0	8,114
Railway cuts	0	887
Ferry slips	34	195
Runways	0	21
AAA sites	825	385
SAM sites	70	35
Radar sites	32	131
Rivercraft	3,930	6,397
Aircraft	24	5

Source: CHECO Report, Wesley R. C. Melyan and Lee Bonetti, "ROLLING THUNDER,
July 1965–December 1966—Continuing Report" (June 15, 1967), Figure 20.

In assessing whether the air campaign in the North was a success, one
category was the infiltration rate of the North Vietnamese into South Vietnam. The attacks in route package 1 were designed to destroy the LOC
and transportation hubs with the effect of eliminating, or at least slowing
down, troop and supply movements. This goal was a significant part of
Westmoreland's attrition strategy as the United States continued its
buildup and fought for the initiative. The U.S. military determined that
40,000 North Vietnamese troops entered South Vietnam in 1966, with another 40,000 probable or possible during the same period. It was estimated
that the North Vietnamese would be able to continue sending 7,000 to
9,000 soldiers across the DMZ per month. This number suggested that the
United States was winning the attrition war as battlefield NVA/Viet Cong
killed-in-action (KIA) and wounded-in-action (WIA) statistics were much
higher. In 1966, despite some sources within Vietnam that questioned the
attrition rates, Westmoreland used these numbers to continue his military
tactics and pressed the USAF and USN to commit aircraft resources to
TIGER HOUND and route package 1 to interdict personnel and supplies
from entering South Vietnam. If the United States was able to cut off the

flow of personnel and supplies from the North, then it would be better able to handle the war in the South.

The air war over North Vietnam was critical to the success of this strategy, but all of the air campaigns combined could not eliminate the fact that the NVA/Viet Cong forces in South Vietnam received the majority of their food from sources south of the 17th parallel and were able to control the intensity of the war based upon the supplies that made it to the South. When the air campaign was particularly successful in a given month, the NVA/Viet Cong offensive slackened; it intensified when more supplies made it through the supply lines. While the ability to lessen the supplies through the air war was an achievement, it would never bring a successful end to the conflict. There is no question that the U.S. air campaign over North Vietnam had altered DRV strategy and forced the North Vietnamese to divert more resources to air defense and repairing war damage. It is a reasonable assumption that the intensity of ROLLING THUNDER helped to limit NVA/Viet Cong offenses south of the 17th parallel.

Through 1966 the United States had used its air assets to try to force the DRV to the peace table while the North Vietnamese viewed this threat as one more obstacle to the overall strategy of eliminating foreign interference in Vietnam and the end of the RVN. The United States had learned several lessons through 1966. The air campaign had not had the psychological effect on the DRV that it had hoped for through the gradual intensity of the bombing. Especially relevant to this outcome was the fact that targets within the Hanoi and Haiphong protective circle remained unscathed. The air campaign strategy for 1967 needed to change to achieve better results. The commander in chief of the Pacific Air Force, General John D. Ryan, recommended a more aggressive strategy for 1967 that concentrated on targets that would cripple the DRV's ability to wage war. These targets included port facilities, power plants, and maintenance and repair shops. General Ryan wanted to maximize the USAF sorties to truly demonstrate to the DRV that the United States was serious in its goal of maintaining a sovereign RVN and would tolerate no interference from North Vietnam. Only by selecting targets based upon military significance without any concern for political repercussions would the United States be able to make evident to the DRV that the only alternative to defeat was a peaceful resolution to war.

With 1967 came a new initiative for ROLLING THUNDER as more targets were approved for air strikes. The new targets represented, in part, the understanding that the only way to hurt the DRV was to strike at its real warmaking potential, including targets that had previously been denied. The United States also introduced more aircraft into the operation in 1967 by employing new technology in ordnance. Just as Westmoreland had planned to make 1967 a turning point in the ground war, the air war was also at a crossroads as the United States finally had enough air assets available to make a significant difference. In the first three months of 1967 weather again was a factor as the northern monsoon left most of route packages 5 and 6 in low-level clouds. A few sorties made it through but not in the volume anticipated or needed to impede the DRV in its support of the southern insurgency. While the monsoon season did hamper ROLLING THUNDER operations, it did not stop another operation from taking place that hurt the DRV's air defense system.

The MiG threat to the bomber force employed in ROLLING THUNDER continued to grow as the U.S. attacks moved closer to Hanoi and Haiphong. The growing sense of frustration in not being allowed to target the airfields housing the MiG force resulted in a plan of deception that would bring the MiGs to the USAF—a target of opportunity that the DRV could not resist. MiG fighters were hesitant to engage F-4Cs in air-to-air combat even though the newer MiG-21 had some advantages. The North Vietnamese pilots were more willing to attack the slower-moving and more vulnerable F-105 bombers. General William Momyer, commander of the 7th Air Force, and his staff developed Operation BOLO to trick the DRV into believing that it was intercepting a group of F-105. Instead, these potential targets would be a group of F-4C with ordnance designed for air-to-air combat. If the United States could not directly attack the MiG airfields, then it could at least damage the MiG fleet by direct assault in the air. On January 2, 1967, Colonel Robin Olds led a sortie of disguised F-4Cs in a much-used flight route toward Hanoi. The North Vietnamese MiG pilots believed the F-4Cs, which were flown in bomber sortie formation, to be F-105s and intercepted the flight. It took less than fifteen minutes for the American pilots to shoot down seven MiG fighters with no losses. This stunning air victory damaged the DRV's MiG force. Four days later two more MiGs were shot down and the MiG force stood down until May 1967.

Even with the MiG threat suppressed for the first part of 1967, the weather continued to play a major role in the number of sorties flown over the northern part of the DRV. The bulk of the sorties in ROLLING THUNDER occurred closer to the DMZ and involved armed reconnaissance. The United States had been able to strike at some of the targets in the northern area and had scored hits against the Viet Tri and Thai Nguyen thermal power plants, shutting down both of them for several months. It was not until April 17 that the monsoon lessened and targets in route packages 5 and 6 were truly accessible for daily air strikes. One of the first targets struck was the Thai Nguyen Iron and Steel Works. Unlike previous attacks on the complex, the April 23 attack and subsequent restrikes resulted in its destruction. Through April and May the United States tried to make up for lost time by striking all of the targets approved in the ROLLING THUNDER cycle, while in June the air strike concentrated on the railways between China and the DRV. With good weather the attacks against the railways severed the lines as well as the major rail artery between Hanoi and Thai Nguyen and the Kep airfield. Additional air strikes against the major power plants also reduced electrical capacity by 85 percent.

The summer air campaign continued to restrike DRV repairs of the railways and refocused on the storage depots and other transportation facilities in North Vietnam until the weather worsened in August. The 1967 ROLLING THUNDER cycles had an effect on the war-making resources in the DRV and forced the North Vietnamese to devote a tremendous amount of resources toward repair and air defense. Estimates ranged from 500,000 to 600,000 civilians tasked for these jobs. While the U.S. air strikes did increase the pressure on the DRV as the United States continued its support of the war in the South, this did not alter the North Vietnamese position toward the conflict nor did it result in a resumption of concrete peace negotiations.

A primary target in the summer, in addition to the railways, was the strategic port of Haiphong. Its harbor had served as the entryway for international imports, and it was a significant lifeline to the outside world's support of North Vietnam. While the United States continued to maintain a tight restrictive ring of nearly three miles around the city that precluded air strikes, it also began to target the four major bridges between Haiphong and the rest of the DRV. The air strikes succeeded in destroying parts of the Kien An highway bridge and the various Haiphong highway and railway bridges. The strategy was to isolate Haiphong and limit the ability of the North Vietnamese to distribute war materials that arrived in the city to points outside the restrictive zone. However, the North Vietnamese had committed a significant amount of resources to repair these damaged arteries and keep the flow of supplies moving out of Haiphong. Even when the bridges were down, the North Vietnamese diverted the materials to smaller water vessels and moved them out under cover of darkness. As with other objectives in the air campaign, the United States achieved partial success in isolating Haiphong only to face additional challenges as the North Vietnamese formulated alternative tactics to counter the air strikes. It was impossible to interdict all of the small watercraft, and once they were beyond the city of Haiphong, much of the war materials reached the NVA/Viet Cong fighting in South Vietnam.

In September 1967 many of the sorties committed to the air campaign against North Vietnam were diverted south of the 17th parallel as the United States flew a number of missions in support of the USMC under siege around the city of Con Thien, about three miles south of the DMZ. Under Operation NEUTRALIZE, the USAF, USN, and USMC flew artillery-suppression missions to eliminate the constant artillery bombardment of Con Thien and employed their superior firepower to dissuade a North Vietnamese invasion across the 17th parallel. While the siege was not lifted until October 31, the air campaign over North Vietnam resumed a higher sortie rate in October with better weather conditions and a diminished threat to Con Thien. Just as the sortie rate was reaching its springtime high, poor weather conditions again covered North Vietnam over route packages 5 and 6, and the sortie rate fell to a low of 164 in December.

ROLLING THUNDER Statistics through 1967

	Total Damaged or Destroyed
Transportation vehicles (motor)	5,576
Transportation vehicles (rail)	2,507
Buildings	3,516
POL areas	130
LOC sites	6,485
Railway yards	179
Ports	84
Power plants	30
AAA, AW sites	1,923
SAM sites	227
Communication sites	140
Rivercraft	11,698
Staging, supply areas	1,568

Source: CHECO Report, James B. Overton, "ROLLING THUNDER—January 1967–November 1968—Continuing Report" (October 1, 1969), Figure 5.

Despite poor weather conditions for a number of months during 1967, the air strikes achieved some success against North Vietnam. Reconnaissance bomb damage assessment flights showed that a significant portion of North Vietnam's war-making potential had been destroyed. Although the studies admitted that the DRV had been able to replace much of the lost war goods through additional imports, it had had to divert a significant amount of its civilian resources toward this goal at the expense of the domestic economy.

It is interesting to note that General Westmoreland credited ROLLING THUNDER with forcing the North Vietnamese to commit to total mobilization of its population for the war effort. He maintained that the long-term effects of this war mobilization would test the limits of the DRV's economy and the population's commitment. He argued that the air war would eventually bring down the Hanoi government because it would no longer be able to feed its people or provide an economy that would sustain the population. In planning for the 1968 air campaign, he continued to assert that these problems, coupled with a war in the South that brought no major victories for the DRV and the loss of a significant number of North Vietnamese youth, would eventually result in a move toward a peaceful resolution of the war. However, one might argue that previous air campaigns against populations had the opposite result: in World War II the British rallied to the flag during the German blitz in 1940, and the German people continued to produce at an amazing rate in 1944 and 1945 despite day-and-night bombardment of their industries by U.S. and Allied aircraft.

The year 1968 was a turning point for the United States in Vietnam both militarily and politically. On the ground the U.S. military would face its toughest challenge during the Tet Offensive as the NVA/Viet Cong launched a coordinated attack throughout the country. While the United States emerged from the attack in a much better military position than the NVA/Viet Cong, the administration in Washington suffered a severe defeat as war weariness dominated the domestic landscape. The war claimed a political casualty in Lyndon Baines Johnson, who on March 31, 1968, stated in a nationally televised broadcast that he would neither seek nor accept the Democratic Party's nomination for the presidency. For the air campaign over North Vietnam, the year 1968 marked the end of ROLLING THUNDER and the beginning of a period of relative quiet over the DRV. Before Tet and Johnson's announcement to curtail operations, 1968 promised to be the most active year to date.

The primary missions for ROLLING THUNDER in 1968 remained consistent with earlier objectives:

- Reduce or deny economic, material, and war-supporting assistance to North Vietnam from external sources
- Disrupt and destroy in depth those resources that contributed to the support of the North Vietnam effort
- Harass, disrupt, and impede movement of men and materials to Laos and South Vietnam.[16]

The weather over North Vietnam for the first quarter of 1968 was the worst experienced since the beginning of ROLLING THUNDER, with only four days of good flying conditions. This problem did not stop regular sorties that employed radar to guide the bombs, but it did limit bomb damage assessment. In fact, the number of sorties increased, although almost one-half were flown over route package 1 in an effort to limit DRV resupply for the forces involved in the Tet Offensive. Weather conditions in February and the requirement to support U.S. and allied forces in South Vietnam engaged in countering the Tet Offensive dropped the number of sorties to about 3,350, with 72 percent flown over route package 1.

The trend would continue through November 1968 as the United States used its air power to destroy exposed NVA/Viet Cong forces reeling from their defeat during Tet. While the weather also influenced the number of sorties to the North of route package 1, the fact that there were fewer lucrative targets in the DRV also played a role. By the end of March, eighty-five of the original ninety-four targets in cycle 57 of ROLLING THUNDER had been attacked and neutralized. The DRV was efficient in repairing targets, but the damage was still extensive. In the first quarter of 1968, air strikes had resulted in significant destruction:

- *Power*: North Vietnam's electrical power capacity had been disrupted extensively. Fourteen of the twenty-four power plant targets had been struck and six were shut down completely.
- *Industry*: Twenty-two percent of the industrial targets had been destroyed, including the Thai Nguyen Iron and Steel Works.
- *Transportation*: Forty-seven percent of the targeted transportation systems were destroyed or abandoned, although most major LOC hubs had traffic moving through them.
- *Military*: 117 of the 144 targeted military facilities had been attacked, and 106 were destroyed or no longer in service.

- *Petroleum, Oil, and Lubricants*: About 65 percent of the DRV's POL storage capacity had been destroyed, with the remainder scattered throughout the country.
- *Air Defense*: The airfields at Kep, Kien An, Hoa Lac, Cat Bi, and Phuc Yen had been attacked with some minor damage. Many of the MiG fighters had been moved to the Gia Lam airfield or were stationed outside the DRV.[17]

Despite these statistics the NVA/Viet Cong were still able to launch the Tet Offensive and threaten the entire country. Not only had ROLLING THUNDER failed to dissuade the North Vietnamese from pursuing the war in the South, but it had also failed to stop the largest and most coordinated attacks against South Vietnamese and U.S. forces in the war to that point. The air campaign also did not stop the influx of foreign goods into Haiphong as an estimated 118 ships arrived during the first three months of 1968 with 450,000 metric tons of POL, food, and other materials. Despite the American air strikes around the area, there was a long line of ships waiting to offload materials to the DRV, including thirty ships from Free World countries.[18] For USAF and USN military leaders, the first quarter of 1968 was a frustrating time that culminated in a shift of tactics announced by President Johnson in his dramatic address on March 31.

When Johnson revealed that he would not seek the presidency for a second term, he also announced that he would de-escalate the air campaign over North Vietnam as a show of good faith toward the resumption of peace negotiations. Beginning on April 1, Johnson ended all ROLLING THUNDER air strikes north of the 20th parallel, where the majority of the DRV population was situated. On April 3 he ordered the cessation of air strikes north of the 19th parallel. For the United States this move was significant for the peace process as the vast majority of worthwhile targets were above the 19th parallel. For the remainder of 1968 the elimination of one-half of route package 3 and all of route packages 4, 5, and 6 did not decrease the number of American sorties against North Vietnam. In fact, the number increased with a concentration of force against route package 1. In the second quarter of 1968 the United States flew 27,406 sorties over North Vietnam, nearly doubling the number from the first three months of the year.

The bombing pause north of the 19th parallel allowed the DRV to repair and improve the LOC and transportation system supporting the war in the South. The increased number of sorties over route packages 1 and 2 helped to compensate for the improved DRV supply lines.

Sortie Rate over North Vietnam, 1968

	Jan.	Feb.	Mar.	Apr.	May	June	July	Aug.	Sept.
USAF	2,930	1,840	2,835	2,850	3,164	4,090	6,512	6,366	5,216
USN	2,648	699	1,624	3,399	5,823	5,432	5,948	5,193	4,468
USMC	779	689	580	1,010	752	853	1,879	1,381	909
TOTAL	6,357	3,228	5,039	7,259	9,739	10,375	14,339	12,940	10,593

Source: CHECO Report, James B. Overton, "ROLLING THUNDER—January 1967–
November 1968—Continuing Report" (October 1, 1969), Figure 12.

While the United States might have been successful in interdicting personnel and supplies through route package 1 and TIGER HOUND, the bombing pause allowed for a greater concentration of reinforcements and supplies above the 19th parallel. Intelligence reports indicated that imports by
sea routes were at their highest rate in the war, with food and POL supplies entering North Vietnam at double the 1967 monthly rate. Similar intelligence-gathering sources showed a decline in truck transportation of between 30 and 40 percent from the 1967 rate. The statistics are impressive,
but the quantification of this aspect of the war was misleading. The DRV
could continue to determine the intensity of the war in the South by the
amount of supplies that made it through route package 1. ROLLING THUN-
DER, with its current status, would not put any additional pressure on the
DRV to peacefully resolve the conflict.

A-6 Intruder. *Admiral Elmo R. Zumwalt Jr. Collection, The Vietnam Archive, Texas
Tech University*

Summer sortie rates continued to increase in route package 1 as
did the DRV's AAA and AW air defenses. Despite greater numbers of
both, American aircraft losses did not increase in proportion. This result was due, in part, to a large percentage of sorties flown at night and to

Air Force Captain Eben D. Jones, a forward air controller with the 37th Tactical Fighter Wing's unique Commando F-100 FAC unit, celebrates after becoming the first pilot to complete 100 missions over North Vietnam. *Douglas Pike Collection, The Vietnam Archive, Texas Tech University*

increased technological advances in radar-jamming and early-warning equipment. IRON HAND missions south of the 19th parallel effectively eliminated the SAM threat with no reported aircraft lost to the SA-2 from March to September 1968.

The last quarter of 1968 would also be the last quarter for ROLLING THUNDER, although, as when it began, the status of the three-and-one-half-year air campaign was still in question. In October the aircraft involved in ROLLING THUNDER conducted over 1,200 more sorties than in the previous month despite poor weather. The United States had developed technology to overcome this problem. The F-105F, F-4D, A-6, and F-111 used internal radar and a bombing computer in poor weather conditions to maneuver to their targets, where the ordnance was automatically released. This technology, named Commando Nail, resulted in more precision bombing sorties and greater flexibility in operating in North Vietnam's unstable atmospheric conditions. The United States also used ground-based radar sites, named Combat Skyspot, to identify a target and direct the aircraft over it. These technologies allowed the United States to strike areas that seldom had been hit during the monsoon seasons because of the low cloud cover. In route package 1 the six major choke points were targeted eight times daily during mid-October, with over 10 tons of ordnance released. Assessments showed extensive damage to the hubs and transportation equipment caught in the bombed area.

From July 14 to the end of October, ROLLING THUNDER missions under the 7th Air Force concentrated on an air-interdiction campaign. In route package 1 the roads leading to the Mu Gia and Ban Karai passes were primary targets, with the result that DRV trucks and supplies were severely damaged. In October the closure of the Ban Laboy ford stopped the flow of supplies into southern Laos. American military intelligence reports indicated that this interdiction program had caused the withdrawal of eighteen NVA regiments from South Vietnam due to food, medicine, and ammunition shortages. While the USAF attacked the inland areas of route package 1, the USN concentrated on the shoreline and targeted water-based vessels used for transportation.

On November 1, Johnson issued a proclamation ending ROLLING THUNDER—a political move to help Hubert Humphrey's chances against Richard Nixon in the 1968 presidential election, but the end of the air campaign was symbolically linked with the end of the Johnson presidency. Was Operation ROLLING THUNDER successful, or did it fail to achieve its objective? The air campaign was not designed to win the war in South Vietnam; rather, its main objective was to make it impossible for the DRV to continue supporting the war in the South and to force it to seek a peaceful resolution. As stated at the outset of the campaign, this would be achieved by:

- Reducing or eliminating the military aid the DRV received from other countries
- Destroying the DRV infrastructure used to support the war
- Interdicting the movement of personnel and supplies used to support the war

There is no question that ROLLING THUNDER caused the DRV to alter its strategy south of the 17th parallel. The effectiveness of the interdiction program throughout the three and one-half years forced the NVA/Viet Cong to regulate the intensity of their involvement in the conflict based upon U.S. sorties against the northern supply line. The air campaign did not induce the North Vietnamese to end their support of the war in the South, nor did it eliminate the influx of NVA troops and materials south to support and prolong the war. It did cause the DRV to devote more resources than desired to the logistical system above the 17th parallel to keep the supply lines open.

In ROLLING THUNDER assessments by USAF officials, the argument that the air campaign denied North Vietnam sanctuary to export war materials is also questionable, even though the operation's statistics show impressive results. ROLLING THUNDER sorties destroyed or damaged building, bridge, depot, and transportation targets that had backed the war effort, but the DRV was remarkably adaptable in finding alternative means to keep the supply lines open. There is no defense against a repair crew that fills in craters on a major road almost immediately after the bombing takes place, unless there is continual bombardment of that area. The United States did not have the resources to drop ordnance everywhere all of the time, nor would the DRV allow such sortie rates without inflicting damage on U.S. aircraft.

The political constraints placed upon ROLLING THUNDER cycles offered protection to some of the most important DRV war-making infrastructure. When restrictions were eased or lifted, the U.S. military was not always successful in its overall strategy even though individual targets were destroyed or damaged beyond use. For example, when the POL storage facilities in the DRV were reduced to less than 15 percent of pre-bombing capacity, the flow of personnel and materials to the South did not stop, nor did the NVA/Viet Cong troops ease their pressure on the

RVN government. While the NVA/Viet Cong war fought between 1965 and 1968 needed support from the North, it was not completely dependent upon that support for survival. Because of this situation, it was almost impossible for ROLLING THUNDER to achieve the objectives stated in 1965.

NOTES

1. Memorandum from the JCS to Secretary of Defense McNamara, February 11, 1965, *Foreign Relations of the United States* (hereafter cited as *FRUS*), *January–June 1965* (Washington, DC: Government Printing Office, 1996), document 109. See also Secretary of State Dean Rusk Paper, February 23, 1965, *FRUS, January–June 1965*, document 157.

2. CHECO Report, SEA CHECO Team, "ROLLING THUNDER— March–June 1965—Continuing Report" (March 28, 1966), 1–13.

3. For Gromyko's reaction, see *American Foreign Policy: Current Documents, 1965* (Washington, DC: Government Printing Office), 841–42. For U.S. reaction to the lack of international protest, see Memorandum from the President's Special Assistant for National Security Affairs, McGeorge Bundy, to President Johnson, *FRUS, January–June 1965*, document 183.

4. Memorandum from Secretary of Defense McNamara to President Johnson, April 21, 1965, document 265, and McCone to Johnson, April 28, 1965, document 234, *FRUS, January–June 1965*.

5. Diary entry by Ambassador Maxwell Taylor, April 20, 1965, *FRUS, January–June 1965*, document 264, and Memorandum from Secretary of Defense McNamara to President Johnson, April 21, 1965, document 265, *FRUS, January–June 1965*.

6. For a discussion on the decision to recommence the air campaign, see *FRUS, January–June 1965*, document 304.

7. CHECO Report, SEA CHECO Team, "ROLLING THUNDER," 65.

8. Ibid., 67.

9. McNamara memorandum to Johnson, July 30, 1965, *FRUS, July–December 1965* (Washington, DC: Government Printing Office, 1996), document 100.

10. CHECO Report, Wesley R. C. Melyan and Lee Bonetti, "ROLLING THUNDER—July–December 1966—Continuing Report" (July 15, 1967).

11. For more information on Operations STEEL TIGER and TIGER HOUND, see chapter 4.

12. Sharp message to Westmoreland, April 1966, reprinted in CHECO Report, Wesley R. C. Melyan and Lee Bonetti, 45–47.

13. Ibid., 51.

14. Ibid., 72.

15. Ibid., 96.

16. CHECO Report, James B. Overton, "ROLLING THUNDER—January 1967–November 1968—Continuing Report" (October 1, 1969).

17. Ibid., 22.

18. Ibid., 24.

CHAPTER **Three**

IN COMMAND AND CONTROL
THE SOUTH VIETNAM AIR CAMPAIGNS, 1965–1968

THE WAR IN SOUTH VIETNAM OFFERED SEVERAL UNIQUE CHALLENGES for the United States and its allies in the 1960s. The air campaign over South Vietnam included all types of missions flown during the conflict:

- *Ground Support*: One of the principal objectives of ground support, or close air support, was to cause as many enemy casualties as possible while keeping American and allied casualties to a minimum. This use of air power gave the allied forces an overwhelming advantage in firepower. Included in this category was the use of the B-52 Stratofortress, which conducted Arc Light missions;
- *Airmobility*: Using helicopters and light fixed-wing aircraft, the concept of airmobility acted as a troop multiplier by allowing the United States and its allies to move quickly, and in large numbers, throughout South Vietnam to attack the NVA/Viet Cong;
- *Interdiction*: The air campaigns that emphasized interdiction limited the number of personnel and quantity of supplies that filtered into South Vietnam. The fewer NVA/Viet Cong that made their way into South Vietnam, the better the chances for U.S. and ARVN forces to control the countryside;

- *Defoliation*: The United States, through Operation RANCH HAND, conducted missions over South Vietnam to kill vegetation with herbicides in order to expose the enemy base areas, decrease potential areas of ambush, and deny food sources to the NVA/Viet Cong;
- *Reconnaissance*: Because Southeast Asia was a relatively unknown region for Americans, and the United States and its allies were fighting an elusive adversary, reconnaissance took on an important role in gathering intelligence and locating the NVA/Viet Cong;
- *Search-and-Rescue*: It was important to ensure that the highly trained crews who manned the sorties had every chance to survive if they were shot down. SAR sorties offered this opportunity, usually at grave risk to those SAR personnel who conducted the missions;
- *Tactical Airlift*: The long distance between the United States and Southeast Asia as well as the poor infrastructure in South Vietnam required one of the largest tactical airlifts ever conducted by the Americans. Tactical airlift moved an army to Southeast Asia and assisted in operations to move that army around South Vietnam to confront the NVA/Viet Cong.

Each of these types of sorties provided the United States and its allies with the maximum opportunities for air power during the war and gave the Americans an unmatched military advantage over the NVA/Viet Cong.

GROUND SUPPORT

Ground support for American troops remained constant throughout the war. When operations against the NVA/Viet Cong began, air power furnished a unique service to, and advantage for, the ground troops. Operations in 1965 typically lasted for only a few days and targeted known or suspected concentrations of NVA/Viet Cong soldiers. By 1966, as more of its combat troops were available, the United States began to strike against NVA/Viet Cong positions for longer periods. Air power not only provided reconnaissance and airlift, but it also added a tremendous amount of firepower to the men on the ground. The NVA/Viet Cong did not have the exclusive advantage of fighting on the ground and the timing of its choice, as had been the case in the past. The United States was able to deliver a significant amount of ordnance on the NVA/Viet Cong located by ground or visual reconnaissance. Air power resulted in an immediate response to contact and allowed the U.S. military to use fewer troops in operations because its firepower and quick reaction time served as a multiplier to the troops in the field. In providing ground support, the use of aircraft allowed the United States to modify its strategy and tactics to better accomplish its goals. However, air power did not alleviate all of the problems associated with ground operations during the war. It remained difficult to locate and identify NVA/Viet Cong forces, and the terrain and climate of Vietnam added to the challenges. Aircraft made it possible for the United States to fight a more efficient war in Vietnam, but it did not guarantee success.

In January 1966 top-ranking American military and political leaders met in Honolulu to discuss the strategy for Vietnam. From the discussions the air war was assigned four objectives:

- Continue to make it difficult and expensive for the DRV to support the Viet Cong
- Add to the South Vietnamese government's control of territory and people by driving the NVA/Viet Cong from their base of operations
- Assist in the elimination of the NVA/Viet Cong south of the 17th parallel
- Deter intervention by the PRC or eliminate Chinese troops if the PRC decided to overtly enter the war[1]

In order to satisfy these objectives, air power concentrated on destroying known NVA/Viet Cong bases and working with ground forces to open these areas for the South Vietnamese. In the Johnson administration's strategy of attrition—killing more of the enemy than could be replaced on the battlefield—aircraft provided an extra level of firepower for the United States and its allies in destroying the NVA/Viet Cong and driving their forces north. The use of air power in 1966 demonstrated its worth as the United States began to strike at the NVA/Viet Cong bases previously left untouched. Air strikes allowed the U.S. military to continue its buildup into 1967.

The large-scale introduction of American air assets into Vietnam also resulted in an increase in the efficiency of the VNAF. In 1966, VNAF forces flew 12,938 sorties with over 19,300 hours of flying time.[2] The VNAF had undergone a rapid increase up to 1965, but training did not match its expansion. When, in 1965, U.S. aircraft and pilots had entered the war in strength, they had taken over the majority of the critical sorties, which left the VNAF more time to train in more modern aircraft. Created as a counterinsurgency weapon, the VNAF was not designed to sustain a strategic bombing campaign. Throughout the war, it concentrated on ground support, medical evacuation, resupply, reconnaissance, and psychological warfare sorties. As the VNAF matured during the conflict, and with the decreased availability of the A-1 Skyraider, the United States introduced jet fighters into the VNAF. The F-5 and A-37 eventually replaced, or supplemented, the A-1.

The goals for the air war over South Vietnam in 1967 remained similar to those in 1966. The objective of air power was to take the war to the NVA/Viet Cong by continuous air strikes while ground operations expanded efforts to seek-and-destroy NVA/Viet Cong personnel and bases. The combination of these objectives aided the South Vietnamese in expanding their area of control, thus denying valuable resources to the NVA/Viet Cong. Military leaders believed that the United States had staved off defeat, and they called for a continuation of these strategies and tactics. For air power over South Vietnam, this meant an increase in both combat and noncombat sorties. Air assets were involved in all of the major ground operations and provided the necessary support to take the war to the NVA/Viet Cong. In all military accounts, the United States at this time was winning the war in South Vietnam. On February 22 the United States took part in Operation JUNCTION CITY, the first airborne assault since the Korean War, when 700 paratroopers from the 173rd Airborne Brigade jumped into War Zone C north of Saigon. The mission also dropped 189 tons of heavy equipment and twenty-four tons of supplies. Airborne assaults were not as practical in Vietnam as they had been in Korea. American tactical airlift capabilities negated the necessity of paratroopers.

Nineteen sixty-eight was a year of decision for the United States as it fought, and won, a major battle against the NVA/Viet Cong during the Tet Offensive. The year also marked the end of the Johnson presidency as well as a redirection of the air war over Vietnam. At the beginning of the year, all eyes were turned toward Khe Sanh, a remote village along the Laotian border near the DMZ, near which the USMC had established a firebase. The Khe Sanh firebase was located in a strategic area of Vietnam, near one of the exits of the Ho Chi Minh Trail. The battle around Khe Sanh began in the fall of 1967 but intensified in January 1968, when NVA/Viet Cong forces probed and surrounded the firebase in an attempt not only to assess its strength but also to draw attention away from its activities around the country.

Khe Sanh became the focus of the military and the media as the pivotal battle in Vietnam. By the third week of January, Khe Sanh was under siege. During this period, U.S. air power took part in a search-locate-annihilate-monitor operation called NIAGARA. Air assets were responsible for interdicting NVA/Viet Cong personnel and supplies flowing into the area as well as for Combat Air Support for USMC troops engaged with 35,000 NVA/Viet Cong troops. During the second week of the siege, on January 31, 1968, the NVA/Viet Cong launched its Tet Offensive, which struck at every large city and a majority of the provincial capitals. Its purpose was to bring about a popular uprising of the people against the Saigon government, thus causing its downfall and forcing the United States out of the country during the American election year.

C-123 Provider, touching down at Khe Sanh beyond the leveled ammunition dump. *Brigadier General Edwin H. Simmons Collection, The Vietnam Archive, Texas Tech University*

The Tet Offensive did not last more than a few days except in isolated spots and in Hue, where the NVA/Viet Cong captured parts of the ancient citadel and had to be extracted building by building. The siege of Khe Sanh was lifted on April 12, 1968, after 23,831 tactical strike sorties, 1,124 airlifts for reinforcements, and 1,453 reconnaissance flights to gather intelligence on the disposition of the NVA/Viet Cong. Air power dropped over 96,000 tons of ordnance around Khe Sanh compared to 3,600 tons delivered by artillery. Captured documents examined after the offensive showed the psychological and physical power of U.S. air assets, especially the B-52 ARC LIGHT strikes. It was air power that enabled the USMC to control the battlefield and maintain the firebase. The NVA/Viet Cong launched a second offensive in May, which differed from the first in that the strategy was to inflict casualties and not trigger a national uprising against the Saigon government. The NVA/Viet Cong targeted Saigon and its suburb of Cholon but failed to make any headway. Air sorties increased during this period to include strikes against NVA/Viet Cong positions in the Saigon area. While there was destruction, the city held against the attack.

American and ARVN forces, with USAF, USN, and USMC air power, were able to stabilize the battle in May just as they had in January. A by-product of President Johnson's bombing halt north of the 19th parallel was a large number of aircraft left without a target. A number of sorties were diverted to Laos, but the majority were concentrated below the 19th parallel in route package 1 for a new interdiction campaign. The 30-day campaign lasted from July 14 to August 16, 1968, and was designed to preempt the expected third phase of the Tet Offensive set for August. The initial phase was extended until Johnson ordered a bombing halt for all of North Vietnam on November 1, just days before the presidential election. A final push in August targeted Da Nang (I CTZ) and Tay Ninh (III CTZ). The third Tet Offensive against these two areas failed to gain any momentum as U.S. air power targeted the concentration of NVA/Viet Cong troops and either destroyed or dispersed them before they could act. Aircraft were critical in the defense against these attacks as well as in the airlift of troops and supplies to fight the NVA/Viet Cong.

The United States used a combination of aircraft and gunships to target and destroy the exposed NVA/Viet Cong troops, who did not generate the uprising they had expected. In-country sorties during the first phase of the offensive numbered 20,000 in February and 21,000 in March. The NVA/Viet Cong lost an estimated 30,000 men during the offensive, including the exposure and disintegration of the Viet Cong leadership, labeled the Viet Cong Infrastructure. After Tet, the American air assets started a program of interdiction in the vicinity of the South Vietnam-Laotian border in a coordinated effort with increased sorties over route package 1 and Laos. A number of specified strike zones were created around Special Forces camps that had been sited to deny the NVA/Viet Cong entry into South Vietnam. The Johnson administration surmised that the weakened Viet Cong infrastructure and a closed border would bring about ideal conditions for the pacification of South Vietnam. American aircraft played a

Sorties Flown over South Vietnam, 1969

	1968 Average	Jan	Feb	Mar	Apr	May	Jun	Jul	Aug	Sep	Oct	Nov	Dec
USAF	11,302	9,471	8,555	9,726	9,351	9,460	9,227	8,318	8,614	6,468	5,633	6,158	5,669
USMC/USN	5,861	5,307	4,882	5,809	6,517	6,419	6,222	5,818	5,883	3,853	2,825	2,647	2,599
RAAF*	237	221	217	246	241	239	234	240	241	180	242	241	240
VNAF	2,223	2,069	2,026	2,429	2,349	2,912	2,773	3,092	3,593	3,022	3,491	3,523	3,576
TOTAL	19,623	17,068	15,680	18,210	18,458	19,030	18,456	17,468	18,331	13,523	12,191	12,569	12,084

Source: CHECO Report, Kenneth Sams et al., "The Air War in Vietnam—1968–1969" (April 1, 1970), Figure 15.
*Royal Australian Air Force

Total Combat and Support Aircraft in Southeast Asia, 1968–1969

	January 1968	January 1969	December 1969
USAF	1,702	1,759	1,765
USMC	585	536	367
USN	399	307	311
U.S. Army	3,004	3,645	4,089
VNAF	366	361	420
RAAF*	8	8	8
TOTAL	6,064	6,616	6,960

Source: CHECO Report, Kenneth Sams et al., "The Air War in Vietnam—1968–1969" (April 1, 1970), 16.
*Royal Australian Air Force

vital role in the interdiction of NVA/Viet Cong forces as well as supplying airlift and tactical air support to beleaguered Special Forces camps targeted by the NVA/Viet Cong for elimination.

Shortly after the Tet Offensive and, in part, in response to the large number of sorties flown against NVA/Viet Cong troops in January and February, the USAF created the single management system that integrated planning, coordination, and control of all air assets within South Vietnam. This system allowed for effective use of the large number of aircraft and sortie rates flown over South Vietnam in 1968 and 1969.

After the Tet Offensive, the U.S. military instituted the Accelerated Pacification Campaign (APC), which called for American and ARVN forces to place continuous pressure on the remaining Viet Cong Infrastructure in the South Vietnamese countryside, depriving them of the populated areas and the food supplies. Thus began an intense program of training Vietnamese forces to defend their own villages and providing weapons. The APC achieved some success, but its late start, November 1, resulted in a number of the Viet Cong Infrastructure escaping to Cambodia and Laos.

The goals for the air war over South Vietnam in 1969 were to:

• Organize, equip, modernize, and employ the VNAF to achieve a maximum state of combat effectiveness
• Inflict more losses on the enemy than they could replace
• Assist in increasing the percentage of the population and territory under RVN control through an expanded pacification effort
• Reduce the ability of the enemy to conduct ground attacks or attacks by fire against population centers, economic areas, and bases
• Deny the maximum number of base area sanctuaries in RVN to the enemy by destruction or continual neutralization
• Assist in restoring and serving to the greatest extent possible the road, railroad, and waterway LOC
• Assist in neutralizing the enemy infrastructure in all pacification priority areas
• Coordinate intelligence collection and counterintelligence activities to the maximum extent possible[3]

The NVA/Viet Cong conducted limited operations during 1969, although U.S. intelligence showed activity in Cambodia and Laos. Tet 1969 was not a repeat of 1968 as sporadic NVA/Viet Cong attacks were nothing more than hit-and-run attempts to inflict casualties. With the limited success of APC and decreased NVA/Viet Cong activity, newly elected president

Richard Nixon announced a policy of gradual withdrawal of American troops from Vietnam under a program of so-called Vietnamization—turning the war over to ARVN while still providing training and equipment. The first U.S. troops departed from Vietnam in June 1969, while the air component felt the effects of the program in August 1969 with an ordered cutback of daily in-country sorties from 583 to 500 per day. ARC LIGHT sorties also decreased from 1,600 to 1,400 per month. The reduction in quantity did not reflect a reduction in quality as U.S. aircraft continued to interdict the NVA/Viet Cong and support American and ARVN troops. The USAF also intensified its training of the VNAF and began its part of Vietnamization by turning over aircraft and equipment to build up the VNAF.

In IV CTZ, which included the Mekong Delta, the tactical air power consisted of ground support, medical evacuation (medevac), airlift, and reconnaissance. The VNAF used the 74th Tactical Wing for many of the missions and had the only squadron of tactical fighters in the area, the 520th Fighter Squadron, made up of A-1H aircraft. The USN and Army flew the majority of the remainder of the sorties in the Delta. Interdiction was the primary mission as the United States sought to eliminate sea infiltration from North Vietnam and the land route through Cambodia on which the NVA/Viet Cong relied to convey the majority of their war materials. In IV CTZ, there were few major American and allied bases; rather, ARVN set up a series of smaller outposts defended by South Vietnamese soldiers or militia. The NVA/Viet Cong targeted these outposts, usually at night, because they were the most likely to be overrun. The VNAF used the AC-47 gunship to augment the firepower and provide illumination during the night attacks to even the odds. Tactical air power had some remarkable results in IV CTZ. When the American 9th Infantry Division began operations in the area in January 1967, aircraft accounted for many of the NVA/Viet Cong killed in action. The war in the Delta relied on air power to provide mobility and destructive force to make it possible for the American and ARVN soldiers to fight the VNA/Viet Cong in the diverse and rugged terrain.

During the April and May 1970 siege and assault against the Civilian Irregular Defense Group (CIDG) camp at Dak Seang, it was air power that prevented the NVA/Viet Cong from overrunning the defenders. After the battle, U.S. military officials estimated that the Dak Seang camp would have fallen within seventy-two hours. While the defenders and artillery accounted for many of the NVA/Viet Cong killed and wounded, air power secured the camp's survival. Dak Seang also served to expose the weaknesses of ARVN command and control. As air power underwent Vietnamization, the need to instruct officers in conducting air operations became more apparent. The United States had taken over the air war in the early 1960s, and, as it planned its departure in 1970, ARVN and the VNAF did not have the expertise in personnel to take over the entire responsibility.

In providing ground support to the American and allied troops, one of the most formidable weapons was the B-52 Stratofortress bomber. Under the SAC 3rd Air Division, B-52 aircraft conducted ARC LIGHT bombing missions that delivered a tremendous amount of munitions in a short time. In 1964, SAC issued OPLAN 52-65 in which it outlined the framework for the ARC LIGHT missions using conventional weapons against predetermined targets in Southeast Asia. The objective for ARC LIGHT remained constant throughout the war. General Westmoreland, who had selected initial targets for approval in 1968, stated that the purpose of the missions was "to assist in the defeat of the enemy through maximum destruction, disruption, and harassment of major control centers, supply storage facilities, logistic systems, enemy troops, and lines of communication in selected target areas."[4] Through ARC LIGHT the USAF used the B-52 in a very different role from that for which it was intended. Traditionally, air support for ground troops had been reserved for the tactical fighter while the B-52 was designed to carry nuclear weapons against the Soviet Union. For the military leaders conducting the war and the ground troops, the B-52 and the ARC LIGHT mission became an indispensable part of the strategy to keep American troops out of harm's way and inflict the maximum number of casualties on the NVA/Viet Cong.

The first ARC LIGHT mission took place on June 18, 1965, when B-52s from the 2nd and 320th Bombardment Wings stationed at Andersen Air Force Base (AFB) on Guam launched an attack on a Viet Cong base in Binh Duong province to the north of Saigon. The B-52s saturated the target area and took no AAA or AW fire from the ground. The mission would have been textbook had it not been for a tragic accident during aerial refueling, when two of the B-52s collided killing eight of the twelve crewmen aboard the two bombers. Despite this ominous start to ARC LIGHT, the USAF was undeterred. Sortie rates continued to increase through the year. The monthly average for the B-52 bomber in 1965 ranged from 200 to 300 sorties but reached the 1,800 mark during the later part of the 1968 Tet Offensive. ARC LIGHT missions lasted from June 1965 to August 1973.

From the beginning, issues of command, control, and coordination were central to ARC LIGHT missions. The commander in each of the four CTZs nominated ARC LIGHT targets to MACV. The Special Targets Section, J-2 evaluated the target line to establish a priority and reviewed it with the director of the Combat Operations Center and the headquarters staff, MACV. Once per day a priorities list was presented to Westmoreland, who reviewed and approved the ARC LIGHT missions. The 3rd Air Division then made sure that all operational aspects of ARC LIGHT were in accordance with the target. As the war progressed and more American and allied ground troops populated Vietnam, it became necessary to adjust the ARC LIGHT mission in progress to meet critical situations on the battlefield.

B-52 Stratofortress, the primary heavy bomber over Southeast Asia. *Douglas Pike Collection, The Vietnam Archive, Texas Tech University*

The rules governing an ARC LIGHT mission followed these criteria:

- Missions would avoid noncombatant casualties.
- A distance of one kilometer should separate the target from monuments, temples, and other historic landmarks if the destruction of that site would cause political repercussions.

- Emergency release of bombs would not threaten noncombatant areas.
- Any strike in Laos would have the concurrence of the U.S. embassy in Vientiane.
- ECM/ELINT and anti-SAM aircraft would accompany any mission within a known SAM location.
- A target must be at least 3,000 feet away from known U.S., RVN, and Free World force positions.[5]

Because Andersen AFB was located on Guam, it took B-52s almost six hours to reach their targets in Southeast Asia—a turnaround time of twenty-four hours from when the target was nominated to when it was struck. One response to this problem was the Quick Reaction Force (QRF), which placed B-52s and aerial refueling KC-135 aircraft on standby alert. This status cut the turnaround time to an average of nine hours. Another solution was the Ground Diverted Force concept, which called for the diversion of a preplanned strike to another target opportunity before it was launched. Finally, the USAF established two additional airfields capable of handling the B-52. The Kadena Air Base at Okinawa, Japan, and the U-Tapao Royal Thai Air Force Base in Thailand handled over two-thirds of the B-52 sorties at the height of ARC LIGHT.

The sortie rate for the B-52 bomber increased significantly over the course of the war. The goal was to achieve 1,800 sorties per month, which was finally reached in March 1968. When SAC planned to use B-52s in Southeast Asia, there were only twelve operational bombers at Andersen AFB. After OPLAN 52-65, SAC rotated thirty-three B-52Fs into the Southeast Asian theater, capable of carrying fifty-one 750-pound bombs per aircraft. Grouped in threes, the B-52F provided significant firepower in support of the ground troops in Vietnam.

The use of B-52s in ARC LIGHT missions was a highly appealing weapon for the United States. The NVA/Viet Cong had no defense against the bomber when it was flown over South Vietnam and rarely had any warning of an attack until after it had commenced. Given the element of surprise, it is understandable that commanders on the ground wanted to maximize the B-52 in ARC LIGHT missions. No one involved in the war disagreed that 1,800 sorties per month were effective, but signs of stress with the high rate did begin to show in mid-1968. SAC recommended reducing the sortie rate to 1,200 in order to maintain its nuclear readiness in Western Europe as well as to save some $155 million over a six-month period in munitions. USAF commanders argued that B-52 redeployment to raise the rate back up to 1,800 sorties per month would take only a week, and they maintained that the United States had enough air assets in the Southeast Asian theater to handle any threat or mission. The ground commanders countered that the B-52 threat was so significant that it altered the NVA/Viet Cong strategy. To reduce the number of sorties would deny the United States a formidable weapon and eliminate its ability to rescue ground troops caught in critical situations. The B-52 was indeed a formidable weapon for the United States in Vietnam. While critics maintained that its use was overkill and that it was too indiscriminate in dropping bombs, the B-52 was one of the most feared aircraft flown during the war.

3rd Air Division B-52 Sortie Rate, 1965–1968

July–September 1965	218	December 1967	815
October–December 1965	309	January 1968	926
January–March 1966	378	February 1968	1,475
April–June 1966	411	March 1968	1,877
July–September 1966	445	April 1968	1,804
October–December 1966	542	May 1968	1,879
January–March 1967	761	June 1968	1,777
April–June 1967	831	July 1968	1,836
July 1967	855	August 1968	1,866
August 1967	837	September 1968	1,812
September 1967	845	October 1968	1,878
October 1967	863	November 1968	1,812
November 1967	821	December 1968	1,871

Source: CHECO Report, Warren A. Trest, "USAF SAC Operations in Support of SEAsia—Special Report" (December 17, 1969), Figure 4.

AIRMOBILITY

Army aviation began during World War II with the assignment of ten light fixed-wing aircraft to each Army division. The aircraft assisted artillery in locating and targeting opposing forces. During the Kennedy administration, the United States developed its first airmobile unit spurred in part by Secretary of Defense Robert McNamara. Under the command of the Army, airmobile units employed helicopters for troop lift, aerial fire support, reconnaissance, and resupply. Army aviation also included SAR and medical evacuation into the airmobile concept, starting with the Korean War. An Army Aviation unit was designed to move fast and engage its opponent with an element of surprise. The tactic was put to the test in

Vietnam in December 1961 when twenty-one CH-21 helicopters were introduced into South Vietnam to provide transportation for ARVN troops. Army helicopters served in a transportation role until the beginning of U.S. ground troop escalation in 1965. Although ARVN did not achieve the desired results, the concept of airmobility was confirmed as a viable option to engage the NVA/Viet Cong in and around South Vietnam and became a part of the American tactics for fighting the Vietnam War.

Heavily laden South Vietnamese (ARVN) infantrymen of the 1st Battalion, 1st Regiment, 1st Division offload from a helicopter to a mountaintop landing zone overlooking Ba Long valley, Quang Tri province. *Douglas Pike Collection, The Vietnam Archive, Texas Tech University*

There were three categories of Army aviation units during the war. The first was the two airmobile divisions—1st Cavalry and 101st Airborne—that relied on airmobility in fighting the NVA/Viet Cong. The second category consisted of aviation units assigned through the table of organization to Army units without an airmobile configuration. Each division had an aviation battalion and air cavalry troop assigned to it while brigades and other units had smaller, though comparable, attachments. The third category included aviation units that supported the four Corps Tactical

Zones. Three of the CTZ had an aviation group that was responsible for supporting the military units in the Corps depending upon assignment by Corps Headquarters G-3 (Operations) or Army commanders on the ground who were directly engaged with the NVA/Viet Cong. The fourth, in I CTZ, had an Aviation Battalion that backed up the Marines. In all cases, the helicopter was used as another asset in the U.S. military arsenal for which operations with a heavy concentration in airmobility were easier to conceive and conduct. The helicopter was not without its disadvantages. It was loud. Moreover, after the initial shock of its appearance over the battlefield wore off, the element of surprise was lost. The helicopter was also vulnerable on the ground and during approach and takeoff from a landing zone. While tactics were developed to cope with this vulnerability, the NVA/Viet Cong still took advantage of it.

UH-1 Iroquois and light observation helicopter. *Curtis Knapp Collection, The Vietnam Archive, Texas Tech University*

Several different types of aviation units were involved in operations during the war. The main aviation unit was the Assault Helicopter Company (AHC). These companies, usually two per division or ten per CTZ, had a number of responsibilities in their areas of operation. The highest priority mission was conducting air assaults in support of ground troops. The AHC also flew sorties in response to NVA/Viet Cong military action and on the basis of intelligence gathered by other units. The AHC had a lower priority of obtaining intelligence through surveillance and reconnaissance and of conducting airlift operations between U.S. bases. The AHC used UH-1B and UH-1C Iroquois helicopters, nicknamed Huey, and the AH-1G Cobra. The AHC could also carry an armed platoon as a reaction force to be committed to battle if necessary. Helicopters, when not carrying troops, were used in groups of two (light-fire team) or three (heavy-fire team) to support each other with gunfire or report the situation if one helicopter was struck by enemy fire and forced down.

Aviation units were also involved in "white" team operations, in which a light observation helicopter was flown for visual reconnaissance, and in hunter-killer teams, which involved a propeller-driven aircraft or light observation helicopter to draw NVA/Viet Cong fire and an AH-1G to attack once the enemy had exposed their position. A typical AHC averaged 2,800 hours of flying time per month, which was about 75 percent of its capability before taking into account the loss of helicopter and crew in combat and routine maintenance. Aviators were not allowed to exceed 140 hours of flying time in a 30-day period, with no more than ten hours in a 24-hour period or fifteen hours in a 48-hour period. These restrictions were not enforced when there was an emergency that required a pilot to exceed the maximum. A second type of aviation unit was the Assault Support Helicopter Company, which was primarily responsible for providing medium- and heavy-lift capability for moving troops and carrying ammunition and supplies to American fire support bases or camps away from the main roads or to areas inaccessible except by helicopter or fixed-wing aircraft.

The third type of aviation unit was the Air Cavalry. These units, separate from the 1st Air Cavalry, were assigned to army divisions or CTZ to provide the airmobility needed for the topography of Vietnam. An Air Cavalry regiment had three air cavalry troops (A, B, and C) and one troop (D) that was similar to regular ground forces. The final aviation units consisted of special types of support for the Army. These units supplied the administrative aircraft for the commanders to move throughout Vietnam and utility aircraft to transport passengers and cargo. There were also units dedicated to surveillance and reconnaissance. Surveillance missions were designed to cover a large terrain in response to intelligence already gathered. These missions were continuously flown over the target area and used sophisticated equipment to verify intelligence and determine the next military step. The reconnaissance mission was directed toward a single target, often in a single sortie, to gather intelligence about enemy positions or strength.

CH-54 Skycrane, lifting a UC-123 Provider aircraft. *Ranch Hand Association Vietnam Collection, The Vietnam Archive, Texas Tech University*

Airmobility remained a prevalent tactic throughout the war, with the major advantage of moving a large number of troops over rugged terrain in a limited time period. This capability allowed the ground forces to approach an area of operation from any direction and arrive on the battlefield without fatigue. Quick movement by helicopter often caught the NVA/Viet Cong forces by surprise. The Army used the UH-1D and UH-1H model helicopters, nicknamed the Slick, to move six or seven fully equipped soldiers to a landing zone. Airmobility also allowed ground troops to operate in areas where resupply overland was prohibitive. Helicopters could fly in food, ammunition, reinforcements, and other materials necessary for the operation while carrying killed and wounded soldiers back to the base areas. The helicopter opened up all of South Vietnam to the United States and allied soldiers and left no location completely safe from the possible insertion of troops.

Because the helicopter was vulnerable on the ground or during its approach and takeoff from a landing zone, the AHC would prepare the area first and remain overhead in case of contact. One of the difficulties with airmobility was the often rugged terrain in which the helicopters had to land to disembark troops. Landing zones often had to be carved out of dense jungle or underbrush. Early efforts at creating these zones were not very successful. Until 1970, forward air controllers (FAC) would guide bombing sorties over an area until it was cleared and suitable for helicopter landings. This strategy often eliminated the element of surprise.

On December 9, 1967, the USAF tested its first "big" bomb for landing zone clearings. The 3,000-pound M-118 tested near Dak To leveled an area 150 feet wide and cleared away pre-positioned booby traps designed to ascertain its effectiveness. Testing continued over the next year in the United States as well as in a December 1968 series of ten tests near Saigon of the 10,000-pound M-121 by the 834th Air Division at Tan Son Nhut Air Base, under the code name Combat Trap. The concept of a heavy bomb used to clear an area for five helicopters evolved into a program called COMMANDO VAULT. The United States continued to use the M-121 until its inventory of the weapon was gone and until its transition to a 15,000-pound BLU-82/B, which was easier to produce and just as effective as the M-121. By October 1970 the 834th Air Division had expended 323 bombs to create landing zones and assist in the construction of firebases.[6]

A routine mission took six days to plan and obtain the appropriate approval, although emergency missions were organized within twenty-four hours. The "big" bombs were dropped from a C-130 and exploded near ground level after gliding down on a parachute. The M-121 had a blast diameter of 60 meters (2,800 square meters) while the BLU-82B had a larger blast diameter of 80 meters (4,800 square meters). COMMANDO VAULT solved some of the problems of ambush by the NVA/Viet Cong against the helicopters as they approached an operational area. The blast pressure of both weapons debilitated the NVA/Viet Cong soldiers within 500 meters of Ground Zero and produced a detonation strong enough to expose or destroy booby traps designed to harm American and allied ground troops. COMMANDO VAULT was a successful way to create landing zones, and although it came late in the war, it demonstrated how air power worked well with ground troops in difficult terrain that demanded flexibility in approach and procedure.

INTERDICTION

Air power was also responsible for the interdiction of NVA/Viet Cong personnel and supplies that made their way into South Vietnam. The NVA/Viet Cong had established a series of trails, waterways, and roads along what had become the end of the Ho Chi Minh Trail, leading from Laos and Cambodia to their base areas within South Vietnam. To take control of the battlefield, the United States needed to interdict the DRV personnel and supplies. Air power served as the primary means. One such operation was TRUSCOTT WHITE, an April 1968 joint Army-Air Force effort to close the roads in the area where South Vietnam, Cambodia, and Laos meet. The army deployed long-range reconnaissance patrols and O-1 aircraft with side-look airborne radar and infrared viewers to locate the NVA/Viet Cong while USAF FACs patrolled over the area to direct tactical air sorties. The first phase of TRUSCOTT WHITE included eighteen B-52 ARC LIGHT strikes at the north end of the area of operations. The USAF would coordinate with the B-52s to suppress AAA positions and drop XM-41 gravel mines and CS-1 gas along the major roads. The CS-1 gas was found to be very effective in keeping repair crews away from damaged roads and bridges. Phase II included heavy artillery and air power against known targets while B-52 aircraft returned to join phase III to attack additional targets found through visual and photographic reconnaissance, infrared, side-look airborne radar, and long-range reconnaissance patrol activity.

O-1E Bird Dog forward air controller. *Douglas Pike Collection, The Vietnam Archive, Texas Tech University*

Between April 7 and June 29, 1968, the United States flew 1,420 sorties in TRUSCOTT WHITE. The interdiction campaign was successful in stopping the flow of trucks down route 613 while other roads showed little or no signs of use. The result did not preclude large numbers of NVA/Viet Cong in the TRUSCOTT WHITE area. TRUSCOTT WHITE ended with the monsoon season as air power was diverted to other operations. By the next dry season, the NVA/Viet Cong had set up bypasses around the previously cut roads in TRUSCOTT WHITE and continued to supply their forces in South Vietnam.

There were several other interdiction campaigns in South Vietnam during the war. In the Mekong Delta, the USAF coordinated with the USN in their efforts to halt supplies coming into South Vietnam from Cambodia. The USAF also participated in Operation KEEP OUT, when it dropped antipersonnel CBU-42B trip mines along known NVA/Viet Cong land routes and MK-36 mines in contested waterways along the border. Interdiction efforts in South Vietnam had mixed results. In many cases, the USAF was able to coordinate with the USN, USMC, and Army to conduct effective interdiction operations. It was more difficult to coordinate in-country (Vietnam) and out-country (Laos) interdiction campaigns because of different command and control governing the air assets. The coordination was even more difficult as the air war in Laos was classified and required separation from the air campaigns in Vietnam. The USAF attempted to bring the interdiction campaigns together in 1968 but were never able to merge the air wars in Laos and Vietnam under one command and control. The interdiction campaign in South Vietnam also suffered throughout the war because the 7th Air Force did not have facilities appropriate for evaluating and exploiting intelligence reports and bomb damage assessment. This lack resulted in poor weather forecasting, incomplete reconnaissance reports, and inaccurate bomb damage assessment follow-ups.

Prior to the Tet Offensive, the interdiction campaign over Vietnam was considered a moderate success. The Tet Offensive changed this thinking and spurred the debate between two ways of conducting the campaign. Interdiction had two main components—destroying transportation and supply before materials reached South Vietnam, and bottlenecking supply routes to make it as hard as possible for the enemy to move supplies south. The U.S. air war had combined these two objectives, and each had champions within the USAF, USN, and MACV. The 30-day campaign would concentrate on choke points to limit the quantity of supplies reaching the NVA/Viet Cong in South Vietnam.

This method had been attempted in the air war previous to 1968, as seen in the 1966 GATE GUARD operation that had tried to establish choke points in route package 1. The 1968 campaign had one advantage that was not a factor in 1966—an almost unlimited number of sorties to concentrate on interdiction. Added to the USAF aircraft available, the USN concentrated on the three passes—Nape, Mu Gia, and Ban Karai—that led from North Vietnam to Laos, and then seeded the waterways with 500-

pound MK-36 magnetic water mines in addition to targeting ferries, bridges, and routes 102 and 103 that led into the DMZ. By June 1968 the USN had dropped more than 20,000 MK-36 with plans for an additional 13,000 per month. The Navy's success helped the USAF to simplify its 30-day campaign, allowing for a more focused attack in a concentrated area.

The 30-day campaign called for the USAF to create two interdiction points—routes 15 and 137—and four river transportation points. These points would be targeted day and night for maximum harassment. The USAF chose the Song Giang-Song Troc river complex as it allowed for better targets of opportunity. The 30-day campaign was divided into six parts with a planned 270–300 sorties per day:

- 24 sorties of F-4 and F-105 for air defense suppression
- 24 sorties of B-52 ARC LIGHT against known enemy bases and assembly points
- 66 sorties of tactical air interdiction against road and river choke points
- 122 sorties of armed reconnaissance, focused primarily along the coast
- 34 sorties of tactical reconnaissance to gather intelligence and provide bomb damage assessment
- 24 sorties of ARC LIGHT protection to include four EB-66 that provided ECM, eight F-4 fighters for MiG Combat Air Patrol, four F-102 escorts, and eight F-105 IRON HAND aircraft to destroy radar-guided air defense weapons[7]

After discussions between PACAF and SAC, the B-52 ARC LIGHT sorties were limited to below the 17°10' parallel. While the 30-day campaign could have used the B-52s above this line, it did free up additional tactical air sorties as less ARC LIGHT protection was required below the 17°10'.

Route 15 was an unsurfaced two-lane road that traversed through many fords and over a number of small bridges. As it went through the Mu Gia pass, it turned into a one-lane road with a series of switchbacks through the mountainous region in Laos. Route 137 was a new road built in rugged terrain that led to Laos. Both routes had prime interdiction points that, if closed, would choke the movement of supplies and personnel. The 30-day campaign achieved enough success to have it continue beyond the August 16 deadline. Interdiction in route package 1 lasted until November 1, 1968. Portions of routes 15 and 137 were closed for periods of time, and the campaign was credited for the lackluster attempt of the third phase of the Tet Offensive. Critics of this interdiction campaign pointed to the adverse weather conditions—two tropical waves moved through route package 1 during the campaign—as the reason fewer trucks were seen rolling through the area. While weather might have played a small role in intensifying the efforts of the 30-day campaign, the NVA had previously been successful in overcoming weather as it sent supplies south.

The intensity of the air strikes and coordination between the USAF and USN air assets made a serious impact on the NVA's ability to supply its forces in South Vietnam. When President Johnson ordered the bombing halt in November, the campaign ended, and any long-lasting gains brought about by the interdiction campaign in route package 1 were quickly reversed by the NVA. Interdiction never proved to be as satisfactory as hoped by the United States. The American campaign was designed to attack conventional supply lines and a modern logistics system. The DRV was not conventional nor were the road, sea, and pathways that comprised the logistics system. The United States achieved some moderate success throughout the war, but the DRV was always able to overcome any obstacles with patience and an ample labor pool.

DEFOLIATION

The use of herbicides in Vietnam became one of the great controversies of the postwar period. Herbicide operations had two primary objectives: to clear jungle and vegetation in areas held by the NVA/Viet Cong and to destroy the enemy's food sources. The strategic concept behind the herbicide operations was valid. The NVA/Viet Cong used the terrain to their advantage during the war. Their base camps were often sited under the double- and triple-canopy forest, which made reconnaissance almost impossible. They also set up ambushes within the vegetation along highways and waterways. If the United States destroyed the vegetation, it was thought, then the NVA/Viet Cong could no longer take advantage of it. Herbicide operations also cleared the vegetation around Special Forces camps and firebases where a clear and long field of fire was essential in thwarting surprise assaults. Because the NVA/Viet Cong lived off the land or depended on the villagers in their area of operation, the destruction of food crops became a high priority for herbicide operations. By eliminating food sources, the NVA/Viet Cong would be forced to move from their fortified base camps to new locations. Not only would they be more vulnerable in the new locations, but they would also be susceptible to aerial reconnaissance during the move. Herbicide operations had value in Vietnam during the war, even though its postwar legacy has become clouded in legal and medical controversy.

In July 1961 the Kennedy administration considered the use of herbicides to decrease the number and intensity of Viet Cong ambushes along the major South Vietnamese highways and to target the main Viet Cong bases in the Mekong Delta. The Chemical Department Test Center was formed to research the practicality of employing herbicides for defoliation and crop destruction. The first test took place in August along route 13 in Chon Thanh with promising results. On November 28, six C-123 aircraft with specially installed 1,000-gallon MC-1 spray tanks and modified to remove all unnecessary equipment began the journey to Vietnam. Along with the six C-123 aircraft (later designated the UC-123), sixty-nine personnel arrived at Tan Son Nhut Air Base on January 7, 1962. The VNAF also had a C-47 and several H-34 helicopters that would join the herbicide operations. On January 12 the first RANCH HAND mission, as the herbicide operations would become known, was launched along route 15 to the northwest of Saigon.

The early sorties were primarily designed to test whether defoliation could provide strategic gains and how the best mixture of herbicides would work on the vegetation in South Vietnam. The results of the early tests were extremely promising, as 90 to 95 percent of the vegetation had been cleared from the sprayed area. RANCH HAND continued during the rest of 1962 with the priority of ridding the major highways, waterways, and communication routes in South Vietnam of vegetation. Most of the RANCH HAND missions were flown in the morning hours because environmental conditions for optimum spraying required cooler temperatures and little or no wind. Night missions were rejected because the flares required to illuminate the spray area also lit up the UC-123 and made SAR operations more difficult. During the monsoon season, weather prohibited the spraying of herbicides. During this time, RANCH HAND aircraft were diverted to logistics, testing navigational aid equipment, and flying radar targeting missions. After the first monsoon season ended in June 1963, herbicide operations started again with the defoliation of the Ca Mau peninsula, a stronghold for the Viet Cong, while VNAF H-34 conducted an operation along the power lines from Saigon to Dalat. The H-34 helicopters were preferred over UC-123 aircraft in the mountainous interior of South Vietnam when specific targets were identified. RANCH HAND aircraft also sprayed insecticides. In August 1963 the UC-123 sprayed insecticide in Thailand to combat a horde of locusts. Throughout the war, UC-123 aircraft were used to control the mosquito population and the spread of malaria.

Through the end of the Kennedy administration, RANCH HAND sorties had covered almost 100 square kilometers and destroyed 950 acres of crops. Under the command of the 315th Air Commando Wing, the missions increased during the Johnson administration, especially after the March 1965 insertion of U.S. Marines at Da Nang and the beginning of American ground troop escalation in Vietnam. In December 1965, RANCH HAND was extended to the South Vietnamese border with Cambodia and Laos to improve visual reconnaissance and surveillance of the Ho Chi Minh Trail. RANCH HAND sorties started to spray sections of the 5,600-square-mile trail complex to better interdict the increasing quantity of supplies flowing down the trail and into South Vietnam.

The United States used several different types of herbicides during the war. The three most prevalent were Agents Orange, Blue, and White, so named after the colored bands on the 55-gallon drums in which they were transported. Each herbicide had special advantages. Agent Orange was the most common, accounting for almost 60 percent of the herbicides sprayed, or over twelve million gallons. A mixture of 2,4-D (2,4 dichlorophenoxyacetic acid) and 2,4,5-T (2,4,5 trichlorophenoxyacetic acid), Agent Orange worked well on broad-leaf vegetation as did Agent White, also a mixture of 2,4-D and 2,4,5-T, although it had a low volatility. Agent Blue consisted of sodium cacodylate and dimethylarsinic acid and was very effective on grass. It was a water-based desiccant that killed by drying. Between 1962 and 1971 the RANCH HAND operation sprayed over nineteen million gallons of herbicides. Although most areas required multiple applications, results were striking. In the postwar years, Agent Orange grew in controversy as it was believed to have caused medical complications for those exposed and deformities in their offspring. The effects of Agent Orange continue to be debated by veterans, scholars, scientists, and the government with compelling evidence on both sides of the argument.

The use of herbicides in combating the NVA/Viet Cong was pursued in many different ways. In addition to defoliation and crop destruction, the United States experimented with herbicides on bombing missions to burn out NVA/Viet Cong strongholds. The first such attempt was Project Sherwood Forest in December 1964. The USAF targeted a 48-square-mile section of the Boi Loi woods to the north-northwest of Saigon near the Cambodian border. The NVA/Viet Cong had constructed a sophisticated series

UC-123 aircraft in Operation RANCH HAND. *Ranch Hand Association Vietnam Collection, The Vietnam Archive, Texas Tech University*

of tunnels, bunkers, and trenches under a thick jungle canopy to elude reconnaissance and ground patrols. RANCH HAND sorties, under the 12th Air Commando Squadron, sprayed 78,800 gallons of defoliant in the target area between January 22 and February 18, 1965. By March, much of the vegetation had been affected by the herbicides and was ready for the second phase of the project. With A-1 and B-57 aircraft the USAF dropped Incendijel and incendiary munitions over the target area to create a firestorm and burn it out. The area was immediately engulfed in flames, and secondary explosions indicated that NVA/Viet Cong structures and supply depots were being destroyed. The intense heat and debris from the fires helped to seed an already moist sky, and a major rain cloud formed over the target area. Heavy rain put out all of the fires by the next day. While parts of the Boi Loi woods were burned out, the project was rated a failure. These less-than-perfect results did not end this type of operation. Projects Hot Tip I and II on the Chu Pong mountains and Project Pink Rose in war zones C and D to the north of Saigon also experimented with herbicides and jungle burning with mixed results.

As RANCH HAND operations became more prevalent and the effects of the herbicides exposed the NVA/Viet Cong bases, destroyed their food crops, and limited the surprise factor in ambushes, the C-123 aircraft became priority targets. RANCH HAND required slow-moving aircraft during the spraying phase of the sortie, which made the C-123 vulnerable to ground fire. At first the U.S. military sent fast-moving jets to prestrike the RANCH HAND area with the hope that this action would push the NVA/Viet Cong underground or away from their air defense weapons. This tactic was less than effective as, after a few missions, the bombing sorties signaled the imminent arrival of the C-123 aircraft. The C-123 was designed to take a lot of damage and did not suffer significant losses, although it was clear that new procedures were needed to protect the RANCH HAND operations. Therefore, the A-1 was introduced into RANCH HAND. The A-1, a propeller-driven aircraft, was capable of maintaining the slow cruising speed of the C-123 during spraying. It carried a large amount of ordnance and had an adequate time-over-target to complement the C-123. The A-1 had more than enough firepower to dissuade the NVA/Viet Cong from exposing themselves as the C-123 aircraft flew overhead.

The United States continued RANCH HAND operations until 1971, with the peak in 1967 when over 1.5 million acres were sprayed with herbicides. In addition to South Vietnam, Laos and North Vietnam were sprayed in areas where the NVA/Viet Cong and Pathet Lao (the Laotian Communists) hid their military activities under jungle cover. It is impossible to determine how many tons of NVA/Viet Cong food crops were destroyed or how many American and ARVN lives were saved because vegetation along roads suitable for ambush was eliminated. Herbicides played a strategic role in the Vietnam War and a significant part in the air campaign over South Vietnam.

RECONNAISSANCE

Just as not all American soldiers who served in Vietnam were involved in combat, not all aircraft participated in combat sorties. During the war, U.S. air power conducted a number of different missions. Three common types were reconnaissance, SAR, and tactical airlift. While these missions were not combat oriented, they often involved contact with the NVA/Viet Cong and were indispensable to the air war over Southeast Asia.

The U.S. air war would never have had a chance at success in Southeast Asia had it not been for the reconnaissance aircraft that gathered the intelligence from which missions were planned. When the United States entered the ground war in Vietnam, it did not possess detailed information on where and how many troops the DRV had in South Vietnam, nor did it have intelligence to detail the extent to which the DRV could sustain a war against the South. Because of the geography of Southeast Asia, the U.S. military relied on aerial photography to gather information on the DRV as well as on the terrain where American forces would engage the NVA/Viet Cong. These reconnaissance sorties provided valuable topographical information for the United States and its South Vietnamese allies. As reconnaissance developed during the Vietnam War, it introduced a variety of new technologies. Over North Vietnam the 7th Air Force flew reconnaissance sorties over route package 1 while the USN had responsibility for route packages 2 and 3 to the 19th parallel. SAC conducted reconnaissance flights above the 19th parallel. In South Vietnam, U.S. and South Vietnamese reconnaissance flights were divided by area of operation while the USAF conducted the majority of flights in Laos and Cambodia. These reconnaissance flights, carried out by the USAF, USN, and USMC, had different objectives based upon the needs of the day. These objectives included:

- Identifying and photographing fixed targets such as strategic structures, DRV air defense installations, storage facilities, and NVA/Viet Cong bases
- Identifying and photographing moving targets such as convoys, NVA/Viet Cong troops, and shipping
- Providing bombing damage assessment of completed missions to determine their accuracy, the extent of damage, and whether retargeting was required
- Gathering intelligence and taking topographical photographs in order to better understand the terrain on which the United States and its allies would engage the Communist forces in Vietnam, Laos, and Cambodia

The first reconnaissance aircraft introduced to Southeast Asia was a SC-47, a modified version of the C-47 transport, which arrived in Vientiane, Laos, in January 1961. It flew reconnaissance missions over northern Laos in support of Major General Vang Pao's Hmong forces, who were engaged with the Pathet Lao. The SC-47, dubbed the Gooney Bird, flew thirty-eight missions before it was shot down on March 24 on the Plaines des Jars.

In October 1961 the RVN organized an air show in Saigon to showcase the VNAF and invited the United States to participate. It sent four RF-101 (a modified version of the F-101) aircraft with camera equipment that enabled them to photograph from as high as 50,000 feet. Because the

RF-101 was a jet, it was less vulnerable to AAA than the slower-moving propeller-driven aircraft. The RVN cancelled the air show but asked the U.S. military to keep the RF-101 in Vietnam. Under the guise of providing SAR assistance in the flooding Mekong Delta, the United States used the RF-101 to conduct reconnaissance over the southern part of South Vietnam and, under Project Pipe Stem, photographed examples of Soviet aid to the Pathet Lao forces in northern Laos. The Americans introduced a technical team and equipment that included photograph developing and analysis capability to complement the reconnaissance flights. The RF-101 remained in Vietnam until November 21, but upon its departure from South Vietnam, the photography team and equipment stayed in Saigon.

Shortly after the RF-101 aircraft left Vietnam, the United States sent a task force, code-named Able Mabel, to the Don Muang Royal Thai Air Force Base to provide reconnaissance over Laos. In December this task force redeployed to Tan Son Nhut Air Base in Saigon to offer intelligence-gathering assistance to ARVN and the American advisers. Able Mabel remained in Vietnam and eventually became part of the 460th Tactical Reconnaissance Wing that operated in South Vietnam after the introduction of U.S. ground troops. The United States deployed a variety of aircraft for reconnaissance during the war, from modified World War II B-26s to the modern SR-71s that could fly at extremely high altitudes.

After the Gulf of Tonkin incident and the initiation of the air campaigns over North Vietnam, the U.S. military committed to aerial reconnaissance to determine effectiveness and targets of opportunity. The RF-101 was the lead aircraft in reconnaissance flights over North Vietnam in the early years of the war, as most of the bombing was south of the 19th parallel. As the war moved northward, the United States introduced the SR-71 to limit combat casualties as well as other technologies designed to maximize photography and minimize danger to personnel. In April 1965 a U-2 aircraft photographed a SAM site, which signaled a change in air operations over North Vietnam. The SA-2 posed a greater threat to U.S. aircraft than did traditional AAA batteries and AW fire, even though it accounted for fewer downed aircraft.

Reconnaissance sorties south of the 17th parallel experienced very different conditions from those over North Vietnam. Most of the sorties relied on visual reconnaissance or infrared and side-look airborne radar to gather intelligence. In South Vietnam the targets were often moving, so rapid reaction was important. Armed sorties dominated thereconnaissance mission, as did intelligence gathering for ARC LIGHT missions that targeted predefined areas. The United States was very sensitive about protecting cultural and religious sites during the war. Detailed reconnaissance was often a prerequisite before targeting an area unless NVA/Viet Cong forces were spotted or had engaged American and allied troops. In Cambodia and Laos the same rules applied. Reconnaissance flights identified and plotted civilian villages, historic monuments, and religious sites in order to avoid these areas when supporting Cambodian and Laotian troops engaged with the NVA or regional Communist forces. Reconnaissance is often the first mission in a war, and Vietnam was no different. From the 1967 siege at Con Thien, when reconnaissance flights determined exact NVA artillery placement coordinates to the nationwide intelligence effort to locate remnants of NVA/Viet Cong units after the failed 1968 Tet Offensive, U.S. reconnaissance played an important role.

An F-101 Voodoo from the 460th Tactical Reconnaissance Wing lands at Tan Son Nhut Air Base. *Douglas Pike Collection, The Vietnam Archive, Texas Tech University*

One of the more significant, if not the most frustrating, reconnaissance missions was providing intelligence on the movement of personnel and supplies down the Ho Chi Minh Trail from North Vietnam through Laos and Cambodia and into South Vietnam. Intense DRV air defenses and a jungle canopy that camouflaged roads and trails made it very difficult for the United States to obtain reconnaissance photographs. It experimented with several different methods to gather intelligence. One of the more successful was the use of sensors to detect movement and relay this information back to a clearinghouse for further exploitation. The Igloo White program, as it would be named, yielded valuable intelligence where visual reconnaissance was not effective.

As early as 1964 the USAF flew an unmanned drone over North Vietnam. Bumble Bug missions had the advantage of taking high risks without the possibility of human losses. Drones were programmed for prearranged flights and then a return south of the 17th parallel for recovery. With improving photographic technology, the drone proved to be a useful tool in the reconnaissance war. Despite limitations such as poor weather, early drones located SAM sites and DRV FANSONG radar used to control SAM and AAA firing. During the monsoon season in Vietnam and Laos, drones were often the only reconnaissance available because of the low cloud ceiling. The USAF drones were based on the 1951 model created by the Ryan Aeronautical Company. Operation of drone reconnaissance aircraft fell under the command of SAC because it was considered a function of national reconnaissance. Under the 100th Strategic Reconnaissance Wing at U-Tapao RTAFB, drones were launched over Laos and North Vietnam after receiving mission directives based on 7th Air Force and MACV requirements from the SAC Reconnaissance Center at Offutt AFB in Nebraska.

There were two types of drones employed over North Vietnam, a low- and a high-altitude model. Both were equipped with cameras that produced reasonably high-quality imagery of selected targets. Modified DC-130 aircraft launched the drones and monitored their progress after release. Internal navigation allowed them to fly a preplanned path, which included several passes over the assigned target. Low-level drones, usually between 200 and 2,000 feet, would glide to their assigned altitude before beginning the reconnaissance flight, while high-level drones gained an altitude of at least 50,000 feet before reaching the reconnaissance area. Low-level drones, known as Buffalo Hunter missions, provided better imagery while sacrificing total surface area covered. These low, fast drones had a high survival rate. The high-level drones were able to cover greater areas but supplied lesser-quality reconnaissance data. After completion of the mission, all drones were programmed to go to the recovery area off Da Nang. Each drone had a parachute, which was released as its engine shut down and was caught by a USN CH-3 in a midair recovery. This recovery procedure was very effective during the war, although there were some water and surface recoveries throughout the period of drone operation. The USN also developed a drone program in Vietnam, named Belfry Express, that was active for a time in 1969 and 1970. The main role of the USN was to recover all drones, which were programmed to return to a position offshore of Da Nang.

Once drone photography or manned reconnaissance flights returned home, the film needed to be developed and analyzed. From the analysis, the U.S. military could make better decisions on whether to target, or re-target, an area for a bombing mission. An early problem with this procedure was the lag time associated with the development and analysis of the intelligence gathered and its transit to Washington, DC. Because many of the targets over North Vietnam required the approval of the president, the secretary of defense, or the JCS, moving targets of opportunity vanished before authorization was received to develop missions to eliminate them.

Different types of reconnaissance flights were devised to take care of this problem. One method was to create areas in which armed reconnaissance sorties provided their own firepower. Often these sorties would operate in hunter-killer teams, where one aircraft would act as an observer (usually an OV-1 or OV-10) while another with more firepower waited for ground fire or a positive identification of a target. These missions were very successful throughout Southeast Asia during the war. In July 1967 the courier time it took for images to reach Washington, DC, decreased significantly with the introduction of the COMASS LINK Satellite Transmission System. With three 40-foot vans located at Tan Son Nhut Air Base, Hawaii, and Washington, DC, the USAF started to transmit 4.5 x 4.5-inch photographs using a laser light source. Light passed over the reconnaissance images in the Tan Son Nhut van, with this data translated by a photo multiplier tube into an electronic signal and sent to the van in Hawaii by satellite. At this station the signal was strengthened and resent to Washington via another satellite. In Washington the image was reproduced with up to sixteen shades of gray and thirty lines per millimeter. The first computer scanners in Vietnam transmitted images in minutes rather than the hours it had taken couriers to hand deliver them.

By 1969 a majority of the reconnaissance sorties were flown by the RF-4C and the EC-47. These aircraft were supplemented with the RB-57, RF-101, EB-66, EC-121, and EC-130. The E-types flew electronic surveillance or ECM sorties to disrupt DRV radar and electronic-guiding firing control. Reconnaissance strength reached its peak in 1970, after which it began a process of Vietnamization. As the VNAF assumed more responsibility for aerial reconnaissance, U.S. elements withdrew from the country. As with other examples of Vietnamization,

reconnaissance did have its problems. There were not enough skilled technicians with enough command of the English language to complete the training course. The result was a low level of equipment and aircraft maintenance. Photograph development and analysis also suffered from a slower
turnaround time, resulting in missed targets of opportunity. Despite these
early setbacks, the Vietnamese managed to take over most of the reconnaissance effort as the U.S. ground forces left Vietnam. A majority of the reconnaissance effort was within South Vietnam with limited sorties above the
17th parallel. Unfortunately, reconnaissance was useful only if the Air Force
and ground troops were able to react effectively to the intelligence gathered.

F-4B Phantom aircraft. *Wise Collection, The Vietnam Archive, Texas Tech
University*

SEARCH-AND-RESCUE

*It is my duty, as a member of the Aerospace Rescue and Recov-
ery Service, to save life and to aid the injured.*

*I will be prepared at all times to perform my assigned duties
quickly and efficiently, placing these duties before personal
desires and comforts.*

These things I do that others may live.[8]
                                      —*From the Service Code*

SAR played a major role in the air war over Southeast Asia. The knowl-
edge that help was on the way to those pilots who were shot down was

a significant morale booster as each mission brought with it an unknown outcome. While the air war did not begin in earnest until 1965, U.S. air assets were involved in the training of VNAF until 1961. The FARM GATE and JUNGLE JIM operations brought USAF personnel into combat as they flew with and trained VNAF pilots. With the real possibility of downed American airmen came the recognition that a SAR program was required in South Vietnam.

The Pacific Air Rescue Center was designated and assigned to Hickam AFB, Hawaii, on October 8, 1961, and from there Detachment 3 was organized at Tan Son Nhut Air Base in Saigon on April 1, 1962. Its role was to coordinate and control SAR operations through the Search-and-Rescue Coordinating Center at Tan Son Nhut, even though it had no aircraft. SAR missions relied on ARVN troops to search a crash site and on U.S. Army or Marine helicopters for transportation. While the system was fraught with obstacles, only two of 240 air crashes in Vietnam between January 1962 and June 1964 were not located. ARVN's support was less than satisfactory during this time as it often refused to send less than regimental-size forces to a crash area and its SAR helicopters did not always arrive on the scene in a timely manner.

The shortcomings of ARVN and the growing U.S. commitment spurred the approval of a USAF SAR force in May 1964. SAR operations grew during the remainder of 1964, from one detachment to the 3rd Aerospace Rescue and Recovery Group (ARRG) with two squadrons and two detachments. While the USAF had determined South Vietnam to be the primary area of activity, YANKEE TEAM operations in Laos required the first rescue helicopter to be placed at Nakhon Phanom in Thailand to support the reconnaissance flights.

While the USAF continued its buildup in Southeast Asia, SAR received a boost from Air America, Civil Air Transport, Continental Air Service, and Bird & Son. These private organizations were funded by the Central Intelligence Agency to conduct air operations in support of the Royal Laotian Air Force (RLAF) and to assist U.S. forces when politically feasible. Air America was credited with twenty-one successful pilot recoveries in Laos between June 1964 and June 1965, compared to four recoveries by USAF helicopters. The SAR work of Air America remained classified during the war. As USAF SAR resources increased the need for Air America, SAR's missions decreased, although it continued to provide this service for the RLAF and any pilot in need.

CH-53 Sea Stallion. *Admiral Elmo R. Zumwalt Jr. Collection, The Vietnam Archive, Texas Tech University*

SAR sortie crews, depending upon the aircraft, were made up of the following:

- *Rescue Crew Commander*: The rescue crew commander was responsible for coordinating the SAR mission and keeping updated on intelligence information and known North Vietnamese air defense locations.
- *Rescue Crew Copilot*: The copilot was in charge of navigation and assisting the commander in his duties.
- *Flight Engineer*: The flight engineer arranged for the preflight of the helicopter and supervised the loading and stowing of any rescue equipment needed for the mission. He also manned the gun position on the right side of the aircraft and acted as an observer for any North Vietnamese aircraft. During a recovery operation, the flight engineer operated the hoist and coordinated with the pilot in positioning the aircraft over the downed pilot.
- *Pararescueman*: The pararescueman loaded any special recovery equipment, first aid equipment, and survival gear and was responsible for the left side and rear of the helicopter over hostile territory. The pararescueman also backed up the flight engineer in operating the hoist and was lowered in the hoist to aid the downed aircrew. He was trained as a medical technician, qualified in scuba and jump, and versed in survival and mountain skills.

There were no typical SAR missions during the war, but the USAF was able to devise a system to deal with the diversity of these missions in Southeast Asia. Over Laos and North Vietnam a basic SAR task force consisted of two HH-3 helicopters, four A-1 aircraft escorts, and one HC-130 as the rescue control aircraft. When notification of a downed pilot reached the task force, two A-1 and the HC-130 would go directly to the suspected crash site to assess the situation and locate the aircrew. The remaining A-1 and HH-3 aircraft would follow and begin extraction once the area was secure. The A-1 would provide suppression fire for the HH-3 with rockets, guns, CBUs, and CS gas around the downed aircrew.[9] In the early stages of the air war, the tactic worked reasonably well.

Total Search-and-Rescue (SAR) Saves, 1964–1969

	Combat Saves	Noncombat Saves
1964–65	127	39
1966	403	73
1967	407	239
1968	572	344
1969	333	145
TOTAL	1,842	840

Source: CHECO Report, James B. Overton, "USAF Search and Rescue (SAR) in SEA—November 1967–June 1969—Continuing Report" (July 30, 1969), 66.

By the end of 1971, SAR missions had accomplished 2,348 combat rescues and 1,133 noncombat rescues. There were still areas off-limits to the SAR task force because of intense air defense or MiG fighters, and the northern part of North Vietnam along the Chinese border remained closed to SAR missions. Despite the problems of the growing SAR operations, such as unfamiliarity with the terrain, maintenance of aircraft, and political constraints imposed by the U.S. government, SAR coverage was respectable.

SAR missions over South Vietnam were very different from those conducted in the North or over Laos. NVA/Viet Cong forces in South Vietnam posed less of a threat while reaction time to crash sites was often less than fifteen minutes. In North Vietnam, pilots had to evade and escape in a hostile countryside, but downed pilots in South Vietnam were never too far from a U.S. or ARVN base. There, too, the NVA/Viet Cong were less likely to commit forces to an aircrew capture at the risk of facing a concentration of American forces and air power.

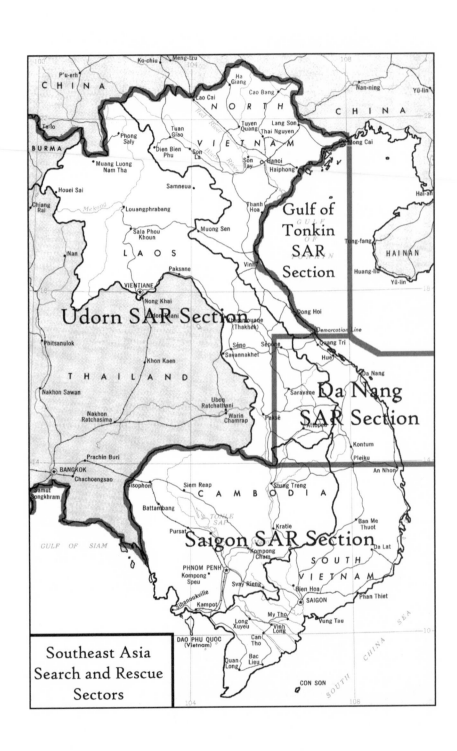

Southeast Asia
Search and Rescue
Sectors

By 1966, SAR operations had become more regulated. The 3rd ARRG, under the commander of the 7th Air Force, controlled four Aerospace Rescue and Recovery Squadrons (ARRS):

- 37th ARRS (Da Nang, RVN) flew HH-3 and HH-53 helicopters. On a typical day the 37th had two aircraft on alert and two available at its forward base at Quang Tri.
- 38th ARRS (Tan Son Nhut, RVN) flew HH-43B and HH-43F. The 38th flew one aircraft from each of its detachments on a 24-hours-per-day, 7-day alert from each of its fourteen bases in South Vietnam and Thailand. The 38th was inactivated on June 30, 1971.
- 39th ARRS (Tuy Hoa Air Base, RVN) flew HC-130. The 39th flew morning and afternoon Laos orbits: one aircraft on ground alert at Udorn, Thailand; an overwater morning orbit and afternoon in-country orbit; and a final aircraft on ground alert at Tuy Hoa. The 39th was inactivated on March 31, 1972.
- 40th ARRS (Udorn, Thailand) flew HH-3, HH-53B, and HH-53C. The 40th kept two aircraft on ground alert at Nakhon Phanom, Thailand, and two aircraft at Lima Site 98 in northern Laos, alternating between ground alert and airborne orbits. Its detachment at Nakhon Phanom also kept two aircraft on ground alert for possible missions in northern or southern Laos and two in central Laos.

The SAR units in Southeast Asia distinguished themselves in their day-to-day actions. SAR personnel earned one Medal of Honor, eighteen Air Force Cross medals, 260 Silver Stars, seven Legion of Merits, and 1,269 Distinguished Flying Crosses among their over 9,131 medals and awards. By the end of the war in Southeast Asia, SAR crews had conducted over 2,800 successful rescues while suffering seventy-one casualties and forty-five aircraft destroyed.

TACTICAL AIRLIFT

The countryside of Vietnam and Laos was rugged with few major roads and several areas that were inaccessible during the monsoon season. For the United States and ARVN, who depended upon mobility to surprise the NVA/Viet Cong, the terrain and climate presented a formidable challenge. Tactical airlift represented the best opportunity to achieve the results desired by the U.S. military and ARVN. The principal tactics employed by the United States during the war were cordon-and-search and search-and-destroy. These operations involved moving large numbers of troops to a specific area to search for the NVA/Viet Cong or attack a known enemy military base. For operations that did not require the element of surprise, transport aircraft moved personnel and materials. Airlifts supplied the troops in the field when road accessibility was minimal or dangerous due to threats of ambush. Reconnaissance and SAR missions increased the effectiveness of the air campaigns and reassured those pilots who risked their lives that they would be taken care of if fortune failed them.

Tactical airlift began in 1953 when American aircraft from the 315th Air Division moved French personnel and supplies to assist in France's struggle against the Viet Minh. Under Operation IRON AGE the United States moved almost 13,714 personnel and 21,422 tons of material between December 5, 1953, and August 1, 1954.[10] In Operation WOUNDED WARRIOR, the 6481st Medical Air Evacuation Group worked with the 315th to transport 502 wounded French soldiers home, and airmen from the 315th provided maintenance and training to French personnel operating U.S. C-119 transports. The American airlift duties in Indochina were neither easy nor safe. The facilities in Indochina were not equipped to handle heavy cargo until the United States provided it, which forced many of the early aircraft to return to their points of origin without delivering their loads. American personnel were not immune either, when, on June 14, 1954, five crewmen from the 483rd Tactical Combat Wing and 8081st Aerial Resupply Unit were taken prisoner during a swimming party near Tourane (later renamed Da Nang).

American tactical airlift responsibility remained consistent through the 1950s and included personnel and cargo movement, resupply, evacuation of civilians and wounded, air control, air terminal operations, and other special missions such as psychological warfare. During the 1950s and early 1960s the United States used C-54, C-124, and C-150 aircraft while Air America, which contracted with the USAF for additional airlift capability, employed C-46 and DC-4 transports. When, on December 7, 1961, South Vietnamese president Ngo Dinh Diem requested an additional U.S. commitment, the 315th Air Division sent C-123 aircraft to assist in military operations. The first C-123 transports arrived in Vietnam on January 2, 1962, as part of Project Mule Train under Operation FARM GATE. ARVN used these aircraft for combat airlift and logistical support. The C-123 aircraft from Mule Train, C-47 aircraft from the VNAF, and United States Army CV-2 established a quick-reaction force under Project Fire Brigade. This force was capable of moving 500 airborne troops in thirty minutes at any time during the day and reinforced besieged ARVN troops or small outposts during NVA/Viet Cong attacks. President Kennedy also authorized Project Barn Door, which airlifted a Tactical Air Control System to Vietnam to coordinate and support air assets involved in operations.

Tan Son Nhut Air Base, one of the busiest in the world by 1967. *Douglas Pike Collection, The Vietnam Archive, Texas Tech University*

On July 3, 1963, the United States created the 315th Troop Carrier Group (Assault), with three squadrons and fifty-one C-123B aircraft to match the increase in NVA/Viet Cong activity in South Vietnam. As the war escalated, so did the role of the 315th Air Division and its tactical airlift responsibilities. Its duties included the air transportation of personnel and equipment, illumination missions in support of ground and air operations, defoliation, and medical evacuation. This mission did not change much throughout the war. In 1964 the U.S. military began a buildup to include Third Country forces from Australia and the Republic of Korea that relied on American tactical airlift. Flooding in the Mekong Delta also put a strain on airlift in 1964 as the percentage of supplies moved by roadway decreased from 70 to 20 percent. The increase in number of American troops from 28,324 in January 1965 to 198,421 in December 1965 required a dramatic increase in airlift operations.[11] To handle the rising demands of supply and resupply, the United States augmented its transportation fleet and formed three Aerial Port Squadrons to offload supplies and distribute them throughout the four CTZs. These squadrons, under the 2nd Aerial Port Group, were responsible for loading and offloading materials and for processing personnel who entered and left Vietnam. In the first year of the ground war (July 1965–June 1966), the Tan Son Nhut squadron took care of more passengers than did O'Hare in Chicago, the busiest airport in the United States.[12]

Tactical airlift units were involved in growing numbers of military operations in which the aircraft provided transportation during the initial assault and were available to reposition troops as the operation warranted. These aircraft also took part in the evacuation of 1,682 American dependents immediately after the start of Operation FLAMING DART and in the introduction of U.S. combat troops in Vietnam. By 1966 the U.S. presence in Vietnam had outstripped the 315th Air Division's capability. In October 1966 the 834th Air Division was established and, in the late 1960s, became the largest air division in the world.

Tactical Airlift in South Vietnam, 1968–1971

	Passengers	*Cargo (in Tons)*
1961	172,778	25,983
1962	—	—
1963	222,631	46,180
1964	203,882	51,483
1965	718,900	207,702
1966	—	—
1967	—	—
1968	3,897,857	928,118
1969	4,644,367	911,419
1970	4,125,893	719,598
1971	3,175,102	397,323

Sources: CHECO Report, Robert Leo Vining, "Air Operations in the Delta—1962–1967—Special Report—Volume 1" (December 8, 1967); and CHECO Report, Ronald D. Merrell, "Tactical Airlift in Southeast Asia, 1969–November 1971—Continuing Report" (February 15, 1972).

After 1965 the United States utilized three different aircraft for the majority of the airlift responsibilities during the war: the C-7, C-123, and C-130. The C-7 and C-123 were better suited to the countryside because they could operate from shorter runways. The C-7 was more versatile and was used in rapid response to tactical emergencies or in airlifting supplies to smaller bases. The C-123 carried the bulk of the airlift while the C-130 had a greater range and load capacity but required longer runways. During the war the United States established four logistic points in Vietnam:

Qui Nhon, Da Nang, Cam Ranh Bay, and Saigon. From these bases, American aircraft could send personnel and supplies anywhere in South Vietnam. With these aircraft, the 834th Air Division could conduct a variety of missions, including the airlift of materials and personnel, the medical evacuation of seriously wounded but stable soldiers to more permanent hospitals outside of Vietnam, and the training of VNAF pilots and crews in tactical airlift operations. The 834th Air Division was also involved in herbicide and insecticide spraying as well as landing-zone establishment.

C-130 Hercules. *Admiral Elmo R. Zumwalt Jr. Collection, The Vietnam Archive, Texas Tech University*

The 834th Air Division was also responsible for the rotation of Thai and Korean troops who fought in Vietnam and the relocation of Vietnamese civilians whose lives were affected by the war. The United States also relied on air assets for psychological warfare. Aircraft would fly over NVA/Viet Cong-held territory to drop flyers and pamphlets to encourage defection. Helicopters with mounted loudspeakers broadcast messages to warn villagers of impending air strikes or to bring the NVA/Viet Cong to the South Vietnamese side. In 1966 the United States flew 12,903 psychological warfare sorties with 7,537 hours of loudspeaker time over South Vietnam. The effort resulted in over 20,000 people rallying to the South Vietnamese government.[13]

In some places in Vietnam, tactical airlift was the only feasible way to connect bases and outposts with major cities. In IV CTZ, where the

Mekong Delta dominated the terrain, it was estimated that 95 percent of the resupply was accomplished by air.[14] The 536th Troop Carrier Squadron flew C-7A aircraft from Vung Tau into the Delta on a daily basis while C-123 and C-130 aircraft flew similar missions from Tan Son Nhut. Until 1967 the units in the Delta also relied on helicopters because of the limited airfields and difficult terrain. By 1967 there were enough airfields that could handle the transport aircraft to relieve some of the helicopter demand.

Medical evacuations were also the responsibility of the 315th Air Division and 834th Air Division. Helicopters, known as Dustoffs, carried wounded soldiers to one of the medivac hospitals where they were treated or stabilized. Seriously wounded personnel who were stable enough for transport, or who had exceeded the 120-day limit for in-theater medical care, were shuttled by C-134 or C-141 out of Vietnam to facilities in Guam, the Philippines, or Japan for further treatment and release. Because wounded soldiers received almost immediate care on the battlefield and tactical air transport made it possible to move patients in quick, efficient ways, the vast majority of soldiers with life-threatening injuries survived.

Even though the sortie type for the air war over South Vietnam shared many similarities with the air campaign over North Vietnam, it was a very different war. U.S. aircraft did not have to make contingencies for the DRV Air Force as it did not threaten American assets below the 17th parallel. This allowed the United States to expand the role of air power in Southeast Asia as it became a critical component in fighting the war. In an assessment of the role of air power in South Vietnam, the noncombat sortie must be included. Because of Vietnam's rugged terrain for infantry operation, tactical airlift provided the means for U.S. and allied forces to traverse the countryside and take the fight to the NVA/Viet Cong. Defoliation missions gave the extra advantage when the topography of South Vietnam challenged the air campaigns. Interdiction from the air yielded the only real positive results in stopping the flow of personnel and supplies down the land routes through Laos and Cambodia into South Vietnam, and SAR by air allowed the United States and its allies the opportunity to preserve one of its greatest assets—those who manned the aircraft.

Most important, for those who fought the war from the ground, air power proved to be a powerful and reassuring ally when engaged with the NVA/Viet Cong. There were no estimates on the number of lives saved as a result of combat support missions, although the figure is considerable. The role of air power in South Vietnam did not win the war, but that was not its design. These air campaigns were intended to give the United States and its allies an advantage in an inhospitable terrain against an elusive adversary that fought an unconventional war. While the United States was unable to achieve the results it desired in the 1960s, it was not for lack of support from the air assets employed in South Vietnam.

NOTES

1. CHECO Report, Wesley R. C. Melyan, "The War in Vietnam—1965—Semi-Annual Report" (January 25, 1967), 5.
2. CHECO Report, Lee Bonetti, "The War in Vietnam—January–June 1967—Semi-Annual Report" (April 29, 1968), 67–68.
3. CHECO Report, Kenneth Sams et al., "The Air War in Vietnam—1968–1969" (April 1, 1970), 12–13.
4. CHECO Report, Warren A. Trest, "USAF SAC Operations in Support of SEAsia—Special Report" (December 17, 1969), 3.
5. Ibid., 25.
6. CHECO Report, Melvin F. Porter, "COMMANDO VAULT—12 October 1970" (October 12, 1970), 1–18.
7. CHECO Report, C. William Thorndale, "Interdiction in SEA—November 1966–October 1968—Continuing Report" (June 30, 1969), 22–26.
8. Code of the Aerospace Rescue and Recovery Service Man, CHECO Report, James B. Overton, "USAF Search and Rescue (SAR) in SEA—November 1967–June 1969—Continuing Report" (July 30, 1969), 69.
9. Ibid., 65–66.
10. Information on U.S. Tactical Airlift is cited from CHECO Report, Bernell A. Whitaker and L. E. Paterson, "Assault Airlift Operations—January 1961–June 1966—Continuing Report" (February 23, 1967), 3–7.
11. Ibid., Figure 6.
12. CHECO Report, Lee Bonetti, 147.
13. CHECO Report, Ronald D. Merrell, "Tactical Airlift in Southeast Asia, 1969–November 1971—Continuing Report" (February 15, 1972), 158–59.
14. CHECO Report, Robert Leo Vining, "Air Operations in the Delta—1962–1967—Special Report—Volume 1" (December 8, 1967), 25.

CHAPTER Four

THE SECRET WAR
THE AIR WAR IN LAOS, 1964–1975

L AOS PRESENTED A CONSTANT PROBLEM FOR THE UNITED STATES IN ITS
war in Vietnam. Through Laos, the North Vietnamese Army was
able to move personnel and materials in support of its operations in
South Vietnam as well as to support the Pathet Lao, the Communist insurgents who were determined to overthrow the U.S.-backed Royal Laotian
Government (RLG.) The RLG sought to defeat the Pathet Lao and maintain its regime in Vientiane. The NVA and Viet Cong also used Laos as a
sanctuary from which to attack South Vietnam with impunity. In response
to these threats, the United States initiated a series of air campaigns designed to interdict the Ho Chi Minh Trail complex and assist the Royal
Laotian Army (RLA) and the smaller, semi-independent Laotian armies
based on ethnic and regional identities, the largest of which was the
Hmong people.

The United States had the added problem of the convoluted political
situation in Laos. In 1962 the Kennedy administration had upheld the
Geneva Agreements, which sought to end the hostilities and establish neutrality in Laos. The agreements also prohibited the introduction of foreign
troops into the country. Both the United States and DRV were obligated
to respect the international agreement, but neither side could stand by as
the other worked from within the country to achieve its political and military goals. While the focus stayed on Vietnam, the United States fought an

undeclared and "secret" war in Laos against the Pathet Lao and NVA/Viet Cong forces that threatened the RLG and maintained the Ho Chi Minh Trail complex. The USAF flew over 500,000 sorties and dropped two million tons of bombs on Laos but suffered casualties of 380 planes and 200 American pilots. Because of the covert nature of the war, officials in Washington were never able to publicly acknowledge the air war or the losses and sacrifices of those who served in the air campaign.

The air war in Laos was given secondary priority to the war in Vietnam despite the fact that the two were interlinked; success in one theater depended on success in the other. The Laotian air campaign suffered from this lower priority when it came to the allocation of American air assets and other resources. It was used as an example of how to fight a war against Communist insurgents without introducing a massive number of U.S. combat troops, as was the case in Vietnam. It also showcased how U.S. air power, even when limited, had the ability to decide the battlefield. Air strikes during the dry season provided the RLA with enough firepower to resist the numerically superior NVA/Pathet Lao while the Americans put forth the firepower and airlift support that allowed the RLA to go on the offensive. Ultimately, the air campaign failed in Laos because it was not able to overcome the difficulties of training the Royal Laotian Air Force. When the United States left the region, the RLA and RLAF were not able to compensate for the loss of American air power and collapsed from the combined pressure of the NVA and Pathet Lao.

In Laos the air war was divided into two distinct parts based on the terrain of the country in relation to Vietnam and on the requirements for U.S. air assets in specific operations. In the northern part of Laos, specifically in Military Region (MR) II, the majority of USAF sorties were flown in support of the RLA, and Major General Vang Pao's guerrilla forces engaged in their struggle against the NVA/Pathet Lao. In MR III and MR IV the U.S. sorties were designed to interdict NVA personnel and materials flowing through Laos on the Ho Chi Minh Trail. Five major air campaigns were conducted against the NVA/Viet Cong/Pathet Lao in Laos:

- STEEL TIGER (1965–1968): Interdiction of NVA personnel and supplies moving from North Vietnam to South Vietnam through Laos via the Ho Chi Minh Trail
- TIGER HOUND (1965–1973): A portion of STEEL TIGER taken by General William Westmoreland, Commander, MACV to better coordinate the ground war in Vietnam with the air war in Laos

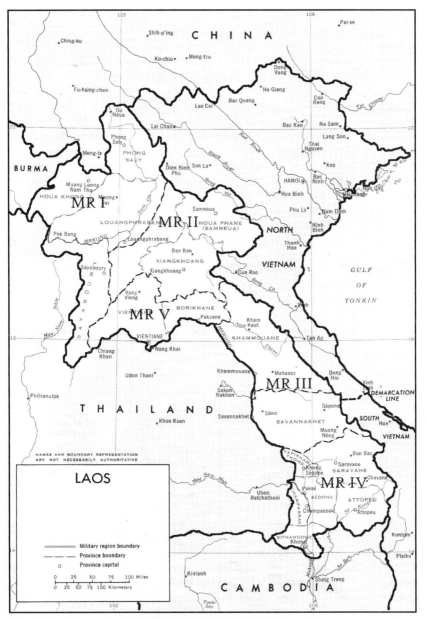

Military Regions I–V in Laos

- BARREL ROLL (1964–1973): The first air campaign that eventually focused on the defense of Northern Laos against NVA and Pathet Lao forces
- COMMANDO HUNT (1968–1972): The combination of air campaigns in Laos into one coordinated operation to maximize the limited resources available
- Lam Son 719 (1971): The 1971 South Vietnamese ground and air operation to cut the Ho Chi Minh Trail and destroy the buildup of NVA personnel and supplies near the strategic city of Tchepone

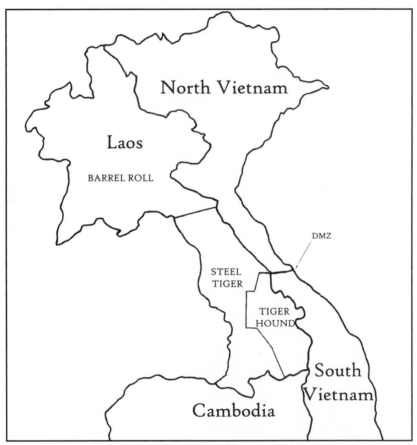

Operations BARREL ROLL, STEEL TIGER, and TIGER HOUND

In the course of these major operations, the role of the USAF in Laos was divided into four separate functions, each designed to aid the RLG and the Hmong in their struggle against the NVA/Viet Cong/Pathet Lao:

- *Air Strikes*: The USAF conducted thousands of air strike sorties against NVA/Pathet Lao positions in Laos. During the wet season, air strikes furthered RLA and military objectives throughout the country. Dry season air strikes supported the outnumbered RLA and irregular forces, made up of the ethnic minority called the Hmong, in their sometimes desperate battle to fend off NVA/ Pathet Lao attacks.
- *Helicopter Support*: The United States provided a number of helicopters in support of the RLA and irregular forces in Laos. Helicopters were instrumental in moving troops into position for the wet season offensives as well as in resupplying men on the move or positioned in defensive strongholds such as the numerous Lima Sites around the country.
- *Training and Maintenance*: The USAF was responsible for training the RLAF pilots and crew under the Waterpump program. It was through this program that the RLAF came of age by the 1970s and was able to take over many of the sorties previously flown by the USAF. Also under Waterpump, the USAF sent mechanics and weapons specialists to train RLAF personnel to service their own equipment.
- *Intelligence*: The USAF, under projects such as 404 and Palace Dog, helped to provide intelligence reports to the U.S. ambassador to Laos, William Sullivan. It also assisted in the maintenance of communication and administrative support among the five Military Regions in Laos.

The United States developed a number of techniques during the air war to improve interdiction of the NVA/Viet Cong. One such technique, used in Laos, was Search-Locate-Annihilate-Monitor, which had four basic steps:

- ARC LIGHT strikes
- Three-to-five-day tactical air strikes
- PRAIRIE FIRE ground teams (on ground reconnaissance)
- Psychological warfare leaflet drops[1]

The technique was designed to inundate an area with air power and small reconnaissance platoons to locate and destroy all NVA/Viet Cong personnel. There were six operations between 1966 and 1967 with a few very positive results.

The U.S. military was not alone in providing these services to the RLA and irregular forces. Operated by the Central Intelligence Agency, Air America and Continental Air Service offered the same type of support and often were present over the battlefield when the USAF was not available. As nonmilitary organizations, the personnel assigned to Air America and Continental Air Service had more freedom to move around the country and assist where needed.

The air war in Laos was further complicated by the command structure used to determine sortie rates and targets. Because the 1962 Geneva Agreements prohibited the introduction of foreign troops into Laos, the United States had to limit the amount and type of military force it could designate there. When the air war over Vietnam began in earnest in 1965, Ambassador Sullivan had control over all target selections in the country. This arrangement was important to maintain positive U.S.-Laotian relations as the ambassador had direct access to the RLG. The USAF assigned an air attaché (AIRA) to the ambassador, who served as his senior military adviser. Both men worked with the deputy commander of the 7th Air Force and 13th Air Force in finalizing bombing sorties. The organizational lines of command were further muddled when the MACV commander, General William Westmoreland, requested and took control of the bombing campaign over Laos from its southern border to the 17th parallel to better coordinate the air war with the ground war in Vietnam. The ambassador retained control over the northern Laotian theater throughout the rest of the war.

This division often resulted in frustrating situations as the three organizations involved in the air war in southern Laos—the U.S. embassy, 7th Air Force, and 13th Air Force—had to coordinate among themselves and with SAC, which oversaw the B-52 missions and MACV. In 1971, Major General Andrew J. Evans Jr., deputy commander of the 7th and 13th, commented on this situation in his end-of-tour report: "As long as the United States Ambassador has overall responsibility for military actions in Laos there seems little likelihood that significant improvements can be made in existing working relationships between 7/13AF, combat air support, and AIRA—the three principal United States agencies coordinating military operations in Laos."[2] The involvement in the air war of civilian agencies such as Air America, Continental Air Service, and the Central Intelligence Agency further complicated the American effort during the "secret" war in Laos.

By 1964 there was enough evidence of North Vietnamese infiltration through Laos to justify some type of American response. In December

1964 the United States initiated Operation BARREL ROLL to harass and interdict the NVA/Pathet Lao in Laos. On December 24 the USAF flew the first sortie in support of Vang Pao's irregulars, who were loyal only to Vang Pao. These American-trained forces fought with guerrilla tactics and relied on U.S. air power to offset the numerically superior NVA/Pathet Lao. BARREL ROLL called for two bombing missions per week with no more than four F-105 per mission. They were not very successful in the early stages of the air campaign because of the series of restrictions placed upon the air strikes. The U.S. embassy in Vientiane selected the targets and based these decisions on diplomatic considerations rather than on military necessity. Bombing in Laos was a politically sensitive issue, as the Johnson administration had to maintain the appearance of respecting the 1962 Geneva Agreements while combating the NVA/Viet Cong, which also operated in Laos despite the accords. Moreover, the United States did not want its involvement in Laos to provoke a Chinese or Soviet response that might expand the war.

In April 1965, to better serve the air campaign in Laos, the United States divided air operations in Laos in two, with BARREL ROLL covering the northern area and STEEL TIGER covering the southern area. All missions in BARREL ROLL were henceforth restricted to a predefined area on the strategic Plaines des Jars in northern Laos.

OPERATIONS STEEL TIGER AND TIGER HOUND

The interdiction of the Ho Chi Minh Trail complex in MR III and MR IV was an early priority for the United States in Laos. Several thousand small roads, trails, waterways, and footpaths through Laos and Cambodia linked North Vietnam and the NVA/Viet Cong troops fighting in South Vietnam against the RVN and U.S. forces. Operation STEEL TIGER, which commenced on April 3, 1965, was designed to complement Operation ROLLING THUNDER, which had begun in March 1965, by targeting the Ho Chi Minh Trail in Laos. In 1965, STEEL TIGER missions averaged approximately 1,000 per month and achieved limited success against the NVA/Viet Cong. The air campaign was hampered by the command-and-control relationship that had developed between Ambassador Sullivan and the USAF and MACV. Because target selection was largely political, missed opportunities resulted from delays in the authorization of missions. There were instances when a target was located but not bombed because of the need for authorization. By the time authorization was given, the target was no longer available.

The United States combined day and night bombing during Steel Tiger to keep the NVA/Viet Cong off balance. Older World War II-era bombers, such as the B-57 and A-26, complemented newer F-4, F-100, and F-105 in dominating the daytime sky while the AC-47, AC-119, and AC-130 gunships worked with reconnaissance aircraft, such as the O-1 and OV-10, to attack trucks and supply depots at night. When the USAF and USN failed to locate a target, they would bomb known trails and roads to raise obstacles. Damage was temporary but provided some psychological benefit to the pilots in an often-frustrating campaign. It was estimated that 4,500 NVA troops per month and 300 tons of supplies per day entered South Vietnam from the Steel Tiger area in October and November 1965.

Ironically, the flow of traffic down the Ho Chi Minh Trail and through the Steel Tiger area of operation increased after the bombing campaign commenced. The strategic importance of southern Laos to the DRV in its struggle against the RVN made the area a high priority and resulted in an escalation of the conflict. In mid-November the northern forces made contact with the U.S. 7th Cavalry in the first major engagement of the war in the Ia Drang valley.[3] While Steel Tiger would continue until December 1968, the flow of personnel and supplies and the Battle of Ia Drang prompted General Westmoreland to request control of the eastern section of Steel Tiger. He sought to better coordinate air and ground assets against the NVA/Viet Cong along the Ho Chi Minh Trail in Laos. The division of Steel Tiger was not without controversy as Ambassador Sullivan strongly disagreed with the decision. Sullivan worried that Westmoreland would ignore the political sensitivities involved in conducting a military campaign in a country with which the United States also needed to maintain a political alliance during a war with its neighbor. The ambassador maintained that he was in a better position to assess the military situation in Laos and coordinate the air strikes for maximum gain. Military necessity in South Vietnam outweighed Laotian political concern in this instance, and Westmoreland's request was granted.

Because many of the Steel Tiger air sorties were conducted at night, the need for night vision was desperate. After some experimentation, the United States developed equipment that enabled American and allied crewmen to see at night. With the introduction of the starlight scope, which captured all available light and made night vision possible, sortie effectiveness improved dramatically. In Steel Tiger a comparison of the dry season air campaign (December to April) from 1966–67 to 1967–68 showed the improvement.

STEEL TIGER Results, 1965–1967

	1965 Targets	*1966 Targets*	*1967 Targets*
Destroyed	173	1,692	3,445
Damaged	141	737	595

Source: CHECO Report, C. William Thorndale, "Interdiction in Southeast Asia, November 1966–October 1968—Continuing Report," 153.

The starlight scope and improved Air Force tactics accounted for the impressive increase.

Westmoreland's new operation, begun on December 6, 1965, and named TIGER HOUND, covered the area from the 17th parallel to the southern border of Laos and Cambodia. TIGER HOUND was designed to be an extension of the war in South Vietnam that allowed for better coordination with the interdiction campaign against the North along the DMZ and ground operations in I CTZ. Westmoreland was also more liberal than Sullivan in target selection and authorization, allowing a greater number of sorties against potential threats to Laos and South Vietnam. The campaign called for unlimited armed reconnaissance sorties along all Lao roads without preapproval, although targets beyond 200 yards of the road had to be preapproved. Westmoreland compromised with Ambassador Sullivan by not striking villages or built-up areas without approval from the embassy or the RLAF and by refraining from using napalm.

Westmoreland had two simple objectives for TIGER HOUND: interdict NVA/Viet Cong transportation and supply, and create bottlenecks on the Trail complex to provide for more lucrative targets. He hoped to slow the rate of NVA/Viet Cong entering South Vietnam through Laos and give the U.S. military an opportunity to build up its forces in South Vietnam to meet the threat. In organizing TIGER HOUND, Westmoreland worked with the 2nd Air Division, whose expertise and organization were better suited to the operation's requirements than were MACV's.

Another component of TIGER HOUND was the use of C-123 aircraft from the 309th Air Commando Squadron's Special Aerial Spray Flight in RANCH HAND missions. These sorties sought to defoliate the vegetation cover along the Trail complex, used by the NVA/Viet Cong to hide their routes and supplies. Two C-123s flew fifty-six sorties in December 1965 to spray 42,375 gallons of Agent Purple in the TIGER HOUND area. One C-123 could spray an area fourteen kilometers by eighty meters in one pass at a rate of three gallons of defoliant per acre. By May 1966 there had been over 250 sorties along the major transportation routes, which had denied the NVA most of its jungle camouflage.[4]

Early TIGER HOUND results were not too impressive, but as the defoliants took hold during the first few months of spraying, the sorties became more effective. By January 12, 1966, fifty-two of the sixty-nine targets selected had been struck in over 1,850 sorties. Another factor that improved the bombing results of the air campaign was the introduction of USAF O-1 forward air controllers. As the FAC pilots learned the terrain in their areas of operation, they were better able to call in air strikes with effect. Through 1966, TIGER HOUND began to affect the NVA/Viet Cong operating out of Laos and into South Vietnam. Infiltration numbers were lower according to U.S. intelligence estimates.

Weather also played a major role in the lower numbers, although the American ability to strike at the NVA/Viet Cong bases within Laos increased with greater familiarity with the terrain and better intelligence. The USAF accounted for the majority of sorties during TIGER HOUND, with the USMC and USN following in order. ARC LIGHT missions conducted by B-52 bombers (see chapter 2) were also included in the bombing area when targets of opportunity presented themselves.

The United States used air power in ways other than the more traditional bombing sortie to stop the flow of supplies through Laos. One project, called Popeye, sought to seed clouds over Laos to cause an early beginning to, and extension of, the monsoon season. It was hoped that this weather modification program would hamper ground transportation. On September 1, 1966, the JCS authorized the project, which began after ten days of reconnaissance over the Se Kong watershed. From September 29 through October 28 the USAF seeded the clouds. A review of fifty-six cases of cloud seeding showed positive results in 85 percent of the samples.[5] The United States continued to try to influence the weather, including cloud rainout over the ocean to reduce precipitation over American and allied troops and cloud dissipation to improve visibility. While the project showed some positive results, it did not stop the flow of supplies through Laos and into South Vietnam.

An extension of TIGER HOUND was Operation TALLY HO, which covered the area from Dong Hoi to the DMZ in North Vietnam. TALLY HO interdiction sorties were designed to complement TIGER HOUND and allow for continuity between the interdiction campaign in Laos and the southern part of North Vietnam. The TALLY HO headquarters were located at Tan Son Nhut in Saigon, with a forward operating site in Da Nang and O-1 forward locations at Dong Ha and the Special Forces camps at Khe Sanh, Kham Duc, and Kontum—all along the Laotian-South Vietnamese border. Operation TIGER HOUND continued through 1968 and was effective in harassing the NVA/Viet Cong supply lines, although the DRV was able to adapt to the intensity of the air campaign by increasing the quantity of supplies going through Laos to compensate for losses resulting from TIGER HOUND. The air campaign may have slowed down the DRV—or at least required more forces to maintain the supply routes—but it never stopped supplies from reaching those troops fighting in South Vietnam.

OPERATION BARREL ROLL

In May 1964 the Pathet Lao attacked neutralist forces under General Kong Le on the Plaines des Jars, which prompted the United States to respond on May 19 with photographic reconnaissance missions. Also, on June 19 the first USAF jet, a F-105 from Da Nang, attacked an air defense site in northern Laos. Less than two months later the Gulf of Tonkin incident escalated the war in Vietnam and began a new chapter in the air war over Southeast Asia. General Kong Le had been allied with the DRV and Pathet Lao during the August 1960 coup d'état that overthrew the pro-Western government, but he became discouraged by NVA involvement in Laos and by 1963 raised an army to combat the NVA and Pathet Lao on the Plaines des Jars. The Royal Laotian Government was in danger of losing the northern half of its country to the Pathet Lao. If this occurred, it would be only a matter of time before the NVA/Pathet Lao forces overthrew the RLG led by Prime Minister Souvanna Phouma.

The loss of Laos to the Pathet Lao would mean the unhampered flow of DRV personnel and materials from North to South Vietnam through Laos and the loss of the RVN. President Johnson authorized a new air campaign against the NVA/Pathet Lao in northern Laos, but he restricted it because of political concerns. There was a constant fear that the Chinese and DRV would overtly intervene in the war in Laos if the United States overtly disregarded the 1962 Geneva Agreements. While the U.S. military had proof that the Chinese were involved in Laos, based upon reconnaissance flights and intelligence reports, Johnson did not believe that this warranted American ground troops in the country, especially when his administration was focused on Vietnam. Unlike his predecessor, John F. Kennedy, Johnson did not really understand the strategic value of Laos and its relationship with Vietnam. In addition to supporting the RLA and irregular forces, the United States concentrated on creating and maintaining the RLAF to defend Laos. The first combat sorties began in Laos in June 1964 in the northern territory of MR II, in support of the RLG and local guerrilla forces under Vang Pao.

Concurrent with STEEL TIGER and TIGER HOUND, Operation BARREL ROLL continued until 1973. The Pathet Lao, with the assistance of the NVA, controlled the easternmost area of MR II in northern Laos and had been involved in heavy fighting with the RLA and Vang Pao's guerrillas throughout the region, especially on and around the strategic Plaines des Jars bordering North Vietnam. The air war over northern Laos during BARREL ROLL kept the same pattern as the monsoon. During the dry season, from November to April, U.S. aircraft targeted NVA/Pathet Lao forces concentrating for attack as well as newly established depots supplying the offensive while Vang Pao's forces holed up in mountain and outcrop strongholds called Lima Sites. American aircraft supported Vang Pao's wet season offensives, from April to November, with tactical air support and airlift of troops to areas where ground transportation was hampered by the weather. The concentration of Vang Pao's irregular forces in the wet season allowed them to even the odds against the NVA/Pathet Lao forces that were scattered and unable to easily reinforce one another.

A significant part of BARREL ROLL and the USAF effort in Laos was training and equipping the RLAF. In 1964, under Project Waterpump, the USAF sent Detachment 6, 1st Air Combat Wing, to assist in the training. Four T-28 aircraft and their crews set up camp behind the Air America hangar in Udorn, Thailand, and set to work immediately. While the United States trained the RLAF, Thai pilots under Project Firefly helped to fill the American sortie requirements, and Air America pilots took on Combat Air Patrol and SAR responsibilities. Training the RLAF was at times frustrating. For example, one T-28 was declared Not Operationally Ready-Supply because the RLAF crew believed that it was possessed by evil spirits. The USAF had the plane exorcised: "The cost was $7.62 covering the cost of candles and herbs for the ceremony and Salem cigarettes, toothpaste, and soap for the monks. This was considered a small price to pay for the continued utilization of a $181,000 aircraft."[6]

More serious concerns in the training and maintenance of the RLAF were corruption, smuggling, and inefficiency. The U.S. military constantly battled these obstacles in forming the RLAF. While there were several setbacks along the way, the RLAF was able to conduct its first military sorties, alone, in May 1968 in MR IV. Its crews would later prove themselves capable during BARREL ROLL in 1969 and 1970, but the problems with the USAF's training of the RLAF remained throughout the war. While the Americans developed tactical efficiency in the RLAF, they never were able to instill self-sufficiency. The main aircraft used by the RLAF were the T-28 fighter and the AC-47 gunship. The United States flew a combination of F-4, F-105, and A-1 aircraft with AC-119 and AC-130 gunships to support the war in northern Laos. FAC pilots with the call name Raven manned O-1, T-28, and U-17 aircraft while other FACs called in air and artillery support with OV-1 and OV-10. Throughout the air campaign over northern Laos, U.S. aircraft were deployed from bases in the RVN and Thailand.

C-47 Skytrain, nicknamed the Gooney Bird. *Douglas Pike Collection, The Vietnam Archive, Texas Tech University*

The air campaign over Northern Laos presented the United States with a unique set of challenges. An evaluation of the air campaign covering the 1969–70 period concluded that "USAF FACs were flying secretly from Laos, under control of the Air Attaché for a Meo [Hmong] ground commander advised by the Central Intelligence Agency, to direct strikes by USAF planes based in Thailand under control of a command center in Vietnam."[7] The most intense fighting in Laos occurred from 1967 to 1969 when RLA and Vang Pao's guerrillas pushed back the Pathet Lao to near the DRV border only to suffer a serious setback as the Pathet Lao and NVA, supported by Soviet-made tanks, retook most of the area. The two forces moved back and forth on the Plaines des Jars with increased numbers of BARREL ROLL operations offsetting Soviet-made tanks and heavy artillery.

T-28 Nomad, the workhorse of the Royal Laotian Air Force. *Douglas Pike Collection, The Vietnam Archive, Texas Tech University*

When the United States adopted the strategy of Vietnamization—the policy of handing the war over to ARVN and withdrawing from Southeast Asia—the air war over northern Laos suffered. It was further negatively affected by the concentration of available air assets over the Ho Chi Minh Trail at the expense of BARREL ROLL. During the critical year of 1970, when U.S. and ARVN forces entered Cambodia to attack and eliminate NVA/Viet Cong bases, only thirty sorties per day were authorized over northern Laos. The U.S. miliary continued to develop new techniques and strategies to offset this limitation. In 1970 the "hunter-killer" concept was created in Laos as part of BARREL ROLL. Acting as the "hunter," the OV-1 would seek targets of opportunity such as trucks and supply depots. Using side-look airborne radar or infrared heat-detecting devices, the OV-1 would direct AC-119 gunships that acted as the "killer." The AC-119, with its four 7.62mm mini-guns and two 20mm Vulcan Gatling guns, proved to be an effective weapon in this type of mission. The addition of the Forward Looking Infrared and Night Observation Device allowed the pilot's gunsight to guide the guns to the appropriate target.

In May 1970 the United States created a Quick Reaction Force of F-4 aircraft based in Udorn. The QRF had the capability to respond to FACs when a target of opportunity presented itself. The time of notification of the target to the delivery of ordnance was usually under one hour. The QRF carried an assortment of weapons depending on the target, although the typical load included six 500-pound bombs and four CBU-24. In 1970 a new version of the cluster bomb, the CBU-38, was developed that could cover an 800-by-100-foot area with bomblets. A usual QRF mission began when a Raven discovered a target and relayed the information to the Airborne Battlefield Command and Control Center, or Cricket, which then passed on the information to the 7th Air Force Command Post (Blue Chip). Once the QRF mission was approved, the F-4 would fly toward the target as the sortie information was passed back down to the Raven, which remained on station the entire time and waited to direct the QRF to its target.[8]

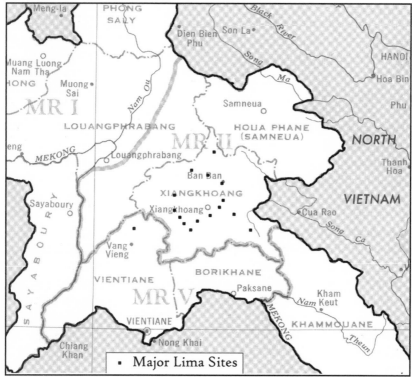

Another technique introduced into northern Laos in 1970 was Hotspot, a form of Combat Skyspot that had been used in the ROLLING THUNDER campaign. Hotspot used radar to guide aircraft to their targets and then provided a countdown for bomb release. During the wet season, Hotspot was often the only way to complete bombing sorties. Initially, the technique had several disadvantages. It suffered from antenna site problems and poor mapping of northern Laos, which resulted in pilots not being able to see where their bombs hit. Hotspot, however, allowed the air war to continue with a reasonable degree of accuracy during severe weather conditions.

The battlefield in northern Laos differed greatly from conventional battlefields. On the Plaines des Jars, strategic control of the battlefield meant maintaining the Lima Sites. These mountaintop strongholds with their airstrips changed hands continually in hand-to-hand fighting. Control of a Lima Site did not mean control of the surrounding jungle, which caused continuous frustration for both sides as they attempted to hold the Plaines des Jars. The fluid nature of battle meant temporary victory and defeat, but it also allowed for a greater familiarization with the battlefield terrain. During the heaviest contact with the NVA/Pathet Lao, U.S. air sorties increased to meet the demand while Air America sorties played a significant role in keeping Van Pao's force mobile, supplied, and supported.

During the dry season of 1970–71, NVA/Viet Cong forces threatened Long Tieng and the four major Lima Sites (15, 20, 72, and 108). Only the coordinated efforts of Raven and FACs and a series of Designated Bombing Areas prevented the collapse of Vang Pao's forces. The RLAF also played a significant role in the dry season offensive in 1970 and 1971 as it coordinated T-28 and AC-47 sorties in meaningful attacks against the NVA/Pathet Lao, thus offsetting the decreased number of U.S. sorties. RLAF AC-47 gunships had a reputation for losing sight of their Forward Air Guide, firing their complement of 21,000 rounds of ammunition into a tree line, and returning to base. The gunship crews would then sell the scrap ammunition shells and divide the money with the base officials. These AC-47 sorties would always expend their entire munitions package, whether engaged with the enemy or not. The result was increased gun barrel deterioration, which required excessive repair and replacement, and ammunition depletion. During the dry season offensive of 1970–71, with the inclusion of an American AC-47 adviser, the RLAF began to change their earlier, wasteful practices as fire discipline came into place.

OPERATION COMMANDO HUNT

When President Johnson announced a halt to bombing north of the 19th parallel on November 1, 1968, the move freed U.S. air assets for other operations in Southeast Asia. This shift benefited the air war over Laos. Operation COMMANDO HUNT began on November 15 and covered the area over Laos between the 16th and 18th parallels. The main objective of the air campaign was the interdiction of DRV supplies traveling through the area and especially through the mountain passes of Nape, Mu Gia, and Ban Karai.

The 7th Air Force Command Center was responsible for the campaign and, with Task Force Alpha, used the Igloo White system of sensors to determine when and where the NVA moved within the COMMANDO HUNT area. The majority of COMMANDO HUNT sorties were interdiction along the Ho Chi Minh Trail. Attacks on truck parks and storage facilities also were given high priority as were air defense systems. Aircraft in COMMANDO HUNT ranged from the F-4 used in truck-killing operations during the day to A-26, A-1, and B-57 aircraft and AC-123 and AC-130 gunships used at night on missions. The United States also deployed C-123 aircraft in Operation RANCH HAND to defoliate the heavy vegetation that covered the roads and pathways.

The first phase of the COMMANDO HUNT campaign lasted until the end of 1968 and was considered a success. U.S. intelligence indicated that the air campaign had reduced the flow of supplies into South Vietnam as well as extended the time it took for materials to transit from the DRV to RVN via Laos. Air sorties averaged 124 per day and forty at night. Intelligence reports estimated that the first phase of COMMANDO HUNT doubled the time it took for trucks to move through the passes. The NVA reacted to the U.S. air power concentration on the passes by creating a series of bypasses around the natural choke points as well as stationing maintenance crews nearby to make quick repairs. The United States responded to the NVA move by initiating the second phase of COMMANDO HUNT. Rather than apply a strict targeting list to the bombing sorties, as in the first phase, the second phase allowed for changing target priorities based upon Pathet Lao/NVA movement. The Americans also targeted stockpiles of war materials in the COMMANDO HUNT area that had been gathered as the result of bottlenecking the supply route in phase one. Military planners and policymakers also relaxed the rules of engagement for air strikes and designated Special ARC LIGHT Operating Areas in which B-52 sorties were not required to obtain additional permission to restrike the area. With Igloo White identifying possible convoys in these special areas, immediate reaction was now possible.

Phase three of COMMANDO HUNT improved with additional intelligence from the Igloo White technology, which allowed for greater accuracy in target selection and more bomb damage. The United States began to use special munitions packages for various sorties. Antivehicle and antipersonnel munitions were more effective when used against the targets for which they were designed. During the first three phases of COMMANDO

HUNT, from November 1968 through April 1969, 67,094 tactical air and 3,811 ARC LIGHT sorties were flown.[9] It was estimated that 4,300 trucks were destroyed and 1,600 damaged. A more significant result was an estimated arrival rate into South Vietnam of only 18 percent of the supplies that had originated in North Vietnam and traveled through the COMMANDO HUNT area. It was the effectiveness of COMMANDO HUNT in early 1969 that allowed ARVN troops the opportunity to train as the program of Vietnamization commenced. Despite the early success of COMMANDO HUNT, it did not stop the flow of supplies. NVA troops continued to function in South Vietnam and regroup in Laos and Cambodia. While COMMANDO HUNT made living conditions difficult for the NVA, it did not force them to the negotiating table. COMMANDO HUNT bought time for the United States to begin Vietnamization and for ARVN to regroup and train after the three phases of Tet 1968. It would not change the outcome of the war nor would it succeed in denying NVA/Viet Cong troops access to the Ho Chi Minh Trail to supply their forces for the largest offensive of the war in 1972.

LAM SON 719

The success of the May 1970 Cambodian incursion made the southern part of Laos more strategic to the survival of the NVA/Viet Cong.[10] With the sea supply route interdicted with Operation MARKET TIME and the land supply route cut in Cambodia, all materials to the DRV troops fighting in South Vietnam came through Laos. The NVA/Pathet Lao captured the strategic cities of Attopeu and Saravane on the RLG side of the cease-fire line demarcated after the 1962 Geneva Agreements. These troops threatened to expand their area of control in southern Laos and destroy the RLG forces. The Americans and South Vietnamese decided to follow up the Cambodian operation with a similar one in Laos, a continuation of the strategy of cutting the NVA infiltration routes into the South. As a result of the Cambodian incursion, the U.S. Congress prohibited the use of ground troops outside of South Vietnam, but it did not exclude air assets in conducting similar operations. The U.S. military took advantage of this window of opportunity by developing a military operation for 1971, named Lam Son 719, to cut the Ho Chi Minh Trail and destroy the numerous supply depots in and around the Tchepone area. A successful Lam Son operation would also provide much-needed time for the Vietnamization program, as it would disrupt the NVA timetable for its next offensive into South Vietnam and allow ARVN forces to continue training and equipping themselves.

Lam Son 719 was divided into four phases:

- *Phase I*: The area in South Vietnam to the east of Lam Son 719, including the old base at Khe Sanh and all of route 9, would be secured. During this time the USAF would redeploy by air almost 10,000 ARVN troops to a staging area along the border. This phase of the attack was called Dewey Canyon II. As phase I ended, the USAF would intensify its AAA suppression sorties around Tchepone.
- *Phase II*: A coordinated ground and air assault was designed to take Tchepone in two or three days. ARVN Rangers would establish blocking positions to the north of route 9, and ARVN Marines would conduct operations to the south of route 9.
- *Phase III*: After the capture of Tchepone, ARVN forces would sweep through base area 604 in search-and-destroy operations to locate and eliminate any NVA personnel and supplies.
- *Phase IV*: As ARVN forces withdrew from Laos, any remaining NVA personnel or supplies in base area 604 or base area 611 would be taken care of in search-and-destroy operations.

The Laotian operation required U.S. air support because the NVA had developed sophisticated air defense systems throughout the Tchepone area, designated base area 604. The VNAF did not have enough trained pilots or equipment to confront these defenses. The USAF conducted tactical air support sorties against the NVA air defenses as well as engaged NVA forces by air when they were located. Air power also supported ARVN ground troops and suppressed and interdicted the movement of NVA and Pathet Lao forces. Army helicopters furnished airlift capabilities to ARVN troops. Indeed, helicopters played a pivotal role in whether the operation would have a successful outcome.

While phase I finished successfully, phase II was hampered by poor coordination and a change in plans by South Vietnamese president Nguyen Van Thieu and ARVN commander General Hoang Xuan Lam. Thieu and Lam changed the objective from Tchepone to a clearing operation around Ban Dong. The operation was further hindered by the inability of the United States Army and Air Force to coordinate the movement of helicopters and fixed-wing aircraft. This failure resulted in a high number of helicopters destroyed or damaged at landing zones because the

Air Force was not included in the planning for the operation and did not launch preemptive air strikes to clear the areas of NVA personnel. The high loss of helicopters during phase II resulted in forced cooperation between the Army and Air Force but demoralized the ARVN troops who were conducting the operation. ARVN forces formed defensive perimeters instead of striking out against the NVA, which allowed NVA soldiers to surround and attack these positions with artillery and mortar fire. ARVN troops captured an abandoned Tchepone but failed to open route 9 from South Vietnam into Laos.

The hollow victory of capturing an empty Tchepone was reversed when the NVA counterattacked and forced ARVN troops to withdraw early and in disarray back to South Vietnam. Lam Son 719 produced the haunting image of ARVN troops hanging on to helicopter skids in a desperate attempt to be evacuated. In the eyes of the North Vietnamese and the American civilian population watching the war on television, Lam Son 719 ended in failure. While most ARVN troops eventually made it back to South Vietnam, the general conclusion in the United States was that had it not been for U.S. air assets in the operation, ARVN forces would have suffered much greater casualties and Vietnamization would have been set back several years. Air power saved the situation in Lam Son 719 from becoming a total disaster.[11]

The intelligence estimates of Lam Son 719 suggest that the offensive ended with mixed results. The NVA lost 13,600 personnel during the operation as well as 217,000 gallons of POL, 7,000 weapons, and 20,000 tons of ammunition. Bomb damage assessments estimated ninety-nine tanks destroyed with another thirty-four damaged and over 2,700 trucks either damaged or destroyed. It was difficult to confirm these statistics during the operation due to the nature of the offensive. The USAF provided these numbers based on conservative readjustments of the intelligence gathered during and after the operation. The USAF and USN flew over 9,100 sorties (plus another 1,358 B-52 sorties) and dropped over 20,000 tons of bombs with the loss of only seven planes. Helicopter losses exceeded 100, with some 600 damaged (ninety of which were beyond repair). In the end, ARVN troops failed in their original objective but wreaked considerable harm on base area 604. The NVA survived the operation and was able to rebuild the base area in time for the 1972 Eastertide Offensive.

The Eastertide Offensive directed much of the attention as well as the air assets away from Laos. With the remaining American and ARVN troops engaged in defeating the invading NVA, more and more sorties were diverted to South Vietnam. Operation LINEBACKER II concluded with a resumption of the peace negotiations and eventual cease-fire agreement, signed in Paris on January 27, 1973. The Laotian campaign became an added burden to the war-weary United States while the struggle against the NVA/Pathet Lao became another casualty of the Vietnam War. The United States signed a cease-fire agreement with the Pathet Lao on February 21, a month after a similar agreement was signed with the DRV. The last BARREL ROLL mission concluded two months later. As the DRV rolled into South Vietnam in 1975, so did Pathet Lao forces into RLG territories in Laos. Without the Americans to support the RLA forces in the field, the RLG fell. The Pathet Lao occupied the whole country by August and in December proclaimed the Lao People's Democratic Republic.

One of the great failures of the air campaigns in Laos was the Americans' inability to train the RLAF to fight its own war. Although the RLAF was trained to be tactically superior, it did not attain self-sufficiency that would allow for continued success. Additionally, air power over the Ho Chi Minh Trail complex in Laos did not achieve its primary goal. Despite a concerted effort of interdiction, the NVA/Viet Cong were able to keep the supply routes open through Laos to support their forces in South Vietnam. In fact, the use of U.S. air power in Laos compelled the DRV to commit a larger number of troops to keeping the Trail open, which, in turn, increased instability in the region and made it more difficult for the RLG to succeed in eliminating the Pathet Lao forces. Alone, the Laotian theater was a difficult and complex area in which to wage a war. With the conflict in Vietnam on its eastern border, the situation became even more strategic, difficult, and complex.

NOTES

1. CHECO Report, C. William Thorndale, "Interdiction in SEA—November 1966–October 1968—Continuing Report" (June 30, 1969), 64–66.

2. CHECO Report, Lucius D. Clay Jr., "USAF Operations in Laos, 1 January 1970–30 June 1971" (May 31, 1972), 100.

3. For more on the battle in the Ia Drang valley, see Harold G. Moore and Joseph L. Galloway, *We Were Soldiers Once . . . and Young: Ia Drang—The Battle that Changed the War in Vietnam* (New York: Random House, 1992).

4. CHECO Report, Melvin F. Porter, "TIGER HOUND—Continuing Report" (September 6, 1966), 43–44.

5. CHECO Report, Lee Bonetti, "The War in Vietnam—January–June 1967—Semi-Annual Report" (April 29, 1968), 123–24.

6. CHECO Report, John C. Pratt, "The Royal Laotian Air Force—1954–1970—Special Report" (September 15, 1970), 45–46.

7. CHECO Report, Harry D. Blout, "Air Operations in Northern Laos—1 April–1 November 1970—Continuing Report" (January 15, 1971), 5.

8. Ibid., 20–23.

9. CHECO Report, Kenneth Sams et al., "The Air War in Vietnam—1968–1969" (April 1, 1970), 43.

10. See chapter 5 for more information on the 1970 Cambodian incursion.

11. CHECO Report, Lucius D. Clay Jr., 187–234.

CHAPTER Five

NIXON'S OTHER WAR
THE AIR CAMPAIGN IN CAMBODIA, 1969–1975

THE DRV USED THE SEA AS A MAJOR SUPPLY ROUTE DURING THE WAR. Because South Vietnam had an extensive coastline and not enough resources to defend it, the North Vietnamese took advantage of the opportunity to move a majority of its supplies by water. Smaller sampans and junks from North Vietnam dotted the coastline while larger 100-ton steel-hulled trawlers landed unopposed on South Vietnamese beaches to offload valuable equipment for the NVA/Viet Cong fight in South Vietnam. When the United States entered the war, it challenged this unfettered access with a naval blockade. Operation MARKET TIME, which began on March 11, 1965, effectively cut off the sea route. A combination of air and sea assets stopped the flow of DRV personnel and materials entering South Vietnam by sea. This halt forced North Vietnam to explore other options in order to continue its support of the war. Two solutions to the problem emerged: the land route through Laos (examined in the previous chapter) and the sea route from the DRV to Sihanouk-ville, the major port in Cambodia, and then along land routes through Cambodia to the NVA/Viet Cong bases along the border. The effectiveness of MARKET TIME made Cambodia even more strategic to the DRV as it became a major resupply route for the NVA/Viet Cong operating in III and IV CTZs.

Cambodia, under the leadership of Prince Norodom Sihanouk, chose neutrality in the war between North and South Vietnam but failed to live up to that neutrality. After the implementation of MARKET TIME, the North Vietnamese contacted Sihanouk and worked out an agreement whereby transport ships loaded with munitions and other war supplies could offload their cargoes at Sihanoukville for transport overland and through Cambodia to the NVA/Viet Cong bases in eastern Cambodia, bordering on South Vietnam. The Sihanouk government looked the other way in this obvious violation of Cambodia's neutrality in the war, while the DRV rewarded these indiscretions financially and restrained the NVA/Viet Cong forces in their Cambodian bases from moving west and threatening the capital, Phnom Penh.[1] The DRV established the Hak Ly Company in Sihanoukville as a front to move supplies from the port along highway 4 to Kampong Speu, where the materials were divided into two logistic depots. One of the depots was run by the NVA/Viet Cong while the other belonged to the Cambodian army at Lovek. The materials were then moved by smaller vehicles to the NVA/Viet Cong bases that formed a line parallel to the Cambodian-South Vietnam border. These bases, with a new and plentiful source of resupply from Sihanoukville, allowed the NVA/Viet Cong to operate from a position of safety while threatening III CTZ and IV CTZ in South Vietnam.

By 1969 the NVA/Viet Cong had put in place training areas, rest and relaxation camps, hospitals, forward bases, and a series of bunker complexes from which the NVA/Viet Cong conducted operations into South Vietnam. It is estimated that 40,000 NVA/Viet Cong troops were in Cambodia during 1969, many of whom were showing more aggressive signs against the government by collecting taxes from the locals and conscripting them to build their roads, camps, and other facilities used in the war against South Vietnam. The NVA/Viet Cong promoted a black market for rice by paying a higher-than-market value for it, which also helped to undermine the Cambodian economy. The NVA/Viet Cong threat was furthered by their support of the Khmer Rouge, a small but growing Communist insurgency in Cambodia, which sought to overthrow the government. Despite repeated requests by the Americans and South Vietnamese, Sihanouk continued to ignore the NVA/Viet Cong in his country. It was not until 1969, when it was obvious that the NVA/Viet Cong had begun to cast their eyes west toward Phnom Penh, that Sihanouk took action.

When Richard Nixon entered the White House in January 1969, he recognized that the NVA/Viet Cong threat in Cambodia required immediate and forceful action. The NVA/Viet Cong had launched attacks against U.S. and allied troops throughout the war from sanctuaries in

Cambodia, and in 1969 they conducted an offensive designed to over-throw the Saigon government. While this offensive was smaller than Tet in 1968, it raised the question of Cambodia's neutrality. Recognizing the NVA/Viet Cong threat to South Vietnam from Cambodia, General Creighton Abrams, who assumed command of MACV in July 1968, re-quested authorization to launch air operations designed to eliminate the NVA/Viet Cong bases. Nixon approved a new air campaign, Operation MENU, with air missions named Breakfast, Lunch, Supper, Dessert, and Snack. Operation MENU lasted from March 18, 1969, to May 26, 1970, with over 120,000 tons of bombs delivered on known NVA/Viet Cong base areas. MENU, a secret operation over a country that still publicly pro-claimed its neutrality, sought to disrupt the NVA/Viet Cong's 1969 offen-sive, eliminate their threat in Cambodia, and give ARVN forces more time to train during the Vietnamization period. MENU remained secret for over one year until, on May 2, 1970, the *New York Times* ran a story on the air sorties over Cambodia. By this time the political instability in Cambodia had come to the surface, and the need for greater U.S. military involvement became clear.

In March 1969, Sihanouk announced that the NVA/Viet Cong were using his country as a base of operations against South Vietnam. He be-gan to restrict the shipment of weapons from Kampong Speu and Lovek to the NVA/Viet Cong base areas along the South Vietnamese border. In August, under increasing political pressure, Sihanouk organized the Sal-vation Government under Lon Nol, the former army commander in chief who served as prime minister, and Prince Sisowath Sirik Matak, who served as deputy prime minister. Lon Nol strongly opposed the presence of NVA/Viet Cong troops in Cambodia. Because Cambodia was central to Hanoi's war against South Vietnam, Hanoi pressured Sihanouk to re-lax his position and return to the status quo that favored NVA/Viet Cong troops in Cambodia in return for a significant monetary profit. By Sep-tember, Sihanouk had reached an accord with the DRV to release nearly 5,000 tons of materials. In return for this guarantee, the DRV agreed to limit the use of the base areas in Cambodia, vacate a base area as the need for it declined, and terminate assistance to the Khmer Rouge. This deal did not sit well with Lon Nol and added to his frustration in running the government. He departed for France in October 1969, after a 30-day-mourning leave of absence following the death of his wife, and did not re-turn to Cambodia until February 18, 1970. In the interim the relationship between Sihanouk and Matak deteriorated as Matak's role in the government, and his desire to end Cambodia's relationship with the NVA/Viet Cong, increased. When Sihanouk left the country for Europe on January 6, 1970, for health reasons, the anti-DRV forces in Cambodia took advantage of the situation.

When Lon Nol returned to Cambodia in February, the forces sympathetic to his anti-DRV stance began to conspire against Sihanouk, and public demonstrations took place on March 8 against the NVA/Viet Cong in several of the border towns. The protestors then ransacked the embassies of the DRV and Provisional Revolutionary Government of South Vietnam, which was the political arm of the Viet Cong. On the heels of this demonstration, Lon Nol announced that Cambodia would return to strict neutrality and ordered the NVA/Viet Cong forces to vacate the country by March 15. In France, Sihanouk voiced opposition to this new policy. His opposition to the withdrawal of the NVA/Viet Cong led Lon Nol and Matak to call for Sihanouk's removal from office. On March 18 the Cambodian national assembly voted in secret to replace Sihanouk as the chief of state, which allowed Lon Nol and Matak to take over the reins of government. Sihanouk called for the dissolution of the Lon Nol regime and broadcast a call to arms to the Cambodian people on Radio Peking. In April he aligned himself with the Indochinese People's United Front, a Communist coalition from Vietnam, Cambodia, and Laos, and on May 5 declared that the Royal Government of National Union was the legitimate government of Cambodia.

During the growing crisis from March to May 1970, the NVA/Viet Cong stepped up their activity along the border but focused west into Cambodia instead of east into Vietnam. NVA/Viet Cong cadres organized pro-Sihanouk rallies and infiltrated organizations supporting Lon Nol and Matak. Their forces also expanded their control into Cambodia from a 3- to 15-mile corridor and spearheaded pushes toward Phnom Penh with the intent of isolating the capital and aiding in the overthrow of Lon Nol. For the first time in the history of the Vietnam War, Cambodian troops— Forces Armées Nationales Khmer (FANK)—fought in set battles against NVA/Viet Cong elements. On April 13, Lon Nol issued an appeal to all nations to come to Cambodia's aid in its fight against communism. He abandoned his neutralist attitude and adopted a decidedly pro-United States position with the expectation that the U.S. military would assist Cambodia as it had South Vietnam against North Vietnam.

With the fall of Sihanouk and on the heels of Operation MENU, the United States began planning for an operation to eliminate the NVA/Viet Cong base areas along the border with South Vietnam. Washington officials hoped that the elimination of these concentrations of personnel and supplies would ease the pressure in III and IV CTZ and provide ARVN forces with valuable time to complete additional training. This attention on so-called enemy sanctuaries in Cambodia coincided with the American policy of Vietnamization, which resulted in fewer U.S. combat forces available for action in Southeast Asia.

On March 27, during a MACV strategy conference on Cambodia, the 7th Air Force recommended a complete photograph reconnaissance of potential objectives in Cambodia and the use of ARVN airborne units and air strikes to block the NVA/Viet Cong in known base areas. Neither recommendation made the March 29 MACV plan sent to the JCS, who decided that the 7th Air Force had enough assets available in Southeast Asia to support the incursion into Cambodia. Reasoning that aircraft could be diverted from Operation STEEL TIGER in southern Laos, where the monsoon season had caused a decrease in sortie rates, they increased the number of sorties per aircraft per day. During the incursion, the number of sorties in I CTZ actually rose by 200 per week while IV CTZ maintained the pre-incursion rate. In many cases, VNAF sorties took over USAF preplanned sorties in the four CTZ areas. By April the United States had formulated a plan—an incursion into Cambodia—to destroy the NVA/Viet Cong while limiting the incursion to appease international and domestic critics who feared that the United States was permanently invading the country. At the end of April 1970, President Nixon stated in a televised message that the United States had three options for Cambodia: do nothing, provide massive military assistance, or eliminate the sanctuaries and the NVA/Viet Cong threat. Shortly before Nixon made his announcement, U.S. and ARVN forces secretly began their execution of the third option around the area of the Fishhook while ARVN forces had earlier attacked the Parrot's Beak, a salient of Cambodian territory approximately thirty kilometers from Saigon that pointed directly toward the city.[2]

This incursion, as it would be known, was the first real test of Vietnamization and gave U.S. air power an opportunity to play an even more active and significant role in the elimination of the NVA/Viet Cong threat in the Mekong Delta. The USAF was not formally ordered to begin planning for the incursion until April 27, two days before the first ARVN troops entered Cambodia. Operational information was kept at a very high level to limit leaks to the press until after Nixon's speech. Despite the two days of planning time, air assets were ready and coordinated for the incursion. The USAF divided its air power into two main categories: air

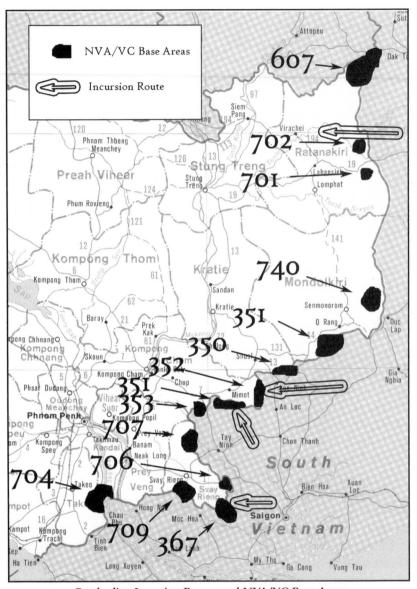

Cambodian Incursion Routes and NVA/VC Base Areas

support for the ground troops, and interdiction of the NVA/Viet Cong who were in and entering the battlefield.

There were twelve named operations during the Cambodian incursion. On April 29, the first day, ARVN forces initiated Operation TOAN THANG 42 against the Parrot's Beak. The main targets were the NVA/Viet Cong's base areas 367 and 706, from which they could easily threaten Saigon and split III CTZ from IV CTZ. The VNAF flew 166 sorties during the first day and a total of 1,604 during the operation, achieving a 5:1 ratio to American sorties. TOAN THANG 42 was strictly an ARVN operation with U.S. forces and air power in a supporting role. The Americans, however, took the lead in TOAN THANG 43, a move against the Fishhook. The United States sent four A-1 aircraft from Nakhon Phanom and two HH-3E helicopters from Da Nang to Bien Hoa to support SAR operations and placed one AC-130 gunship at Tuy Hoa in case of emergency or a lucrative target. Because the area of operations was limited, it was necessary to coordinate rigidly the air assets over the battlefield. An O-2 FAC, designated Head Beagle, orbited south of the Parrot's Beak over South Vietnamese territory and coordinated the FAC pilots and bombing sorties supporting the ground operations. This strategy allowed for greater flexibility in response to the fluid ground situation. Preplanned operations had been scheduled throughout the incursion, but Head Beagle had the authority to override them to match air power to the situation. This flexibility occurred with greater frequency as the incursion progressed. Head Beagle also monitored the weather and the flow of sorties per FAC in order not to overload any one FAC with too many sorties at one time.

Air power played a significant role in supporting the troops on the ground in Cambodia even though the air and ground campaigns were hampered by a lack of accurate intelligence, some of which was outdated by as much as six months. During TOAN THANG 43, American intelligence suggested that U.S. forces would meet 7,000 NVA/Viet Cong troops in the Fishhook.[3] From this assessment the plan was for massive air strikes around landing zones and objectives. FAC pilots and artillery officers created and plotted 381 targets and then prioritized them in the following order: 1) antiaircraft and automatic weapon sites, 2) strong points, 3) headquarters, 4) base camps, 5) bunkers, and 6) supply depots. Six air strikes of six B-52 ARC LIGHT sorties started the operation on May 1 with an additional 148 tactical air strikes scheduled for the first day. The United States also began psychological warfare on May 3 by dropping leaflets over NVA/Viet Cong areas.

The United States also launched four COMMANDO VAULT missions, where 15,000-pound BLU-82 bombs cleared four helicopter landing zones used for troop insertion. An additional twenty COMMANDO VAULT operations were launched during the incursion. As the 11th Armored Cavalry Regiment, 3rd Brigade, and 3rd ARVN Airborne set up a corridor around the Fishhook, United States Army hunter-killer teams of light observation helicopters and Cobra gunships closed the encirclement. TOAN THANG 43 produced only limited contact and small engagements with the NVA/Viet Cong. As a result, the number of preplanned operations decreased and were diverted to immediate needs. By the end of the second day, reconnaissance flights showed the NVA/Viet Cong retreating to the northeast from the area of operation. The United States responded by airlifting the 2nd Brigade (ARVN) to block their avenue of escape. The new, expanded area of operation almost tripled the size from the original plan, which relieved the air traffic congestion handled through Head Beagle but also made it more difficult to locate NVA/Viet Cong forces.

This change in operations was responsible for the lower number of preplanned air strikes as the fluidity of the battlefield increased. The initial small area of operation posed significant problems for the coordination of air power. There were a few incidents of short rounds (munitions expended short of the target) and friendly fire casualties (men accidentally struck by their own aircraft), although the quick thinking and skill of FAC pilots prevented many accidents. By May 5 the area of operation was firmly established, and the need for FAC pilots decreased with fewer targets of opportunity available. The FAC pilots returned to their usual duties the next day, and Head Beagle was dissolved.

American military planners designed the incursion as a search-and-destroy operation aimed at NVA/Viet Cong camps and material depots. While the NVA/Viet Cong refused to concentrate and confront the U.S. and ARVN forces, they left small bands of troops in the area to disrupt the allied operations and screen the main forces' escape into South Vietnam or north to Laos. This tactic was enhanced by the American intelligence failure as the U.S. and ARVN troops had few sources that indicated where they might expect to find the main force of the NVA/Viet Cong. Air operations followed along the same lines as TOAN THANG 43 for the remainder of the incursion. As U.S. forces established their area of operation, air sorties would diminish in numbers with typical missions designed to cover ground troop movement or reconnaissance. During ARVN-led missions the VNAF would carry out air duties with USAF support and advice. While VNAF FACs did not perform as well as their American counterparts, they were able to coordinate adequately air strikes based on priority. During BINH TAY I, the northernmost operation during the incursion, American and ARVN troops combined to assault base area 702 after a series of B-52 strikes. In all of the operations, air assets provided the extra firepower that gave the American and ARVN forces the advantage. It was estimated that the NVA/Viet Cong lost 11,562 soldiers compared to 1,147 allied killed-in-action, a ratio of 10:1.

U.S. and VNAF Air Strikes during the 1970 Cambodian Incursion

		U.S. Air Strikes			VNAF Air Strikes	
	Preplanned	Immediate	Gunship	Flareship	Strikes	Gunship
TOAN THANG 42	130	180	11	0	1,604	126
TOAN THANG 43	2,322	678	71	15	364	30
TOAN THANG 44	360	78	8	3	4	0
TOAN THANG 45/46	1,495	395	68	19	37	2
BINH TAY I	476	101	11	2	148	0
BINH TAY II	170	37	3	1	73	4
BINH TAY III	171	130	13	2	198	0
CUU LONG I	18	25	6	0	168	14
CUU LONG II	30	50	1	0	86	8
CUU LONG III	48	18	0	0	218	4

Source: CHECO Report, David I. Folkman Jr. and Philip D. Caine, "The Cambodian Campaign—April 29–June 30, 1970—Special Report" (September 1, 1970). Statistics for the various operations are found throughout the report.

Intensity in the Cambodia incursion increased on May 6 when the United States and ARVN launched Operations TOAN THANG 44, 45, 46, and 500 into NVA/Viet Cong base areas. Again, the NVA/Viet Cong eluded contact although major stores of ammunition and weapons were captured. CUU LONG I commenced on May 9 with the objective of capturing the Prey Veng ferry and evacuating over 35,000 refugees from northern Cambodia, where the NVA/Viet Cong and Khmer Rouge were firmly entrenched. In mid-May, CUU LONG II, predominately involving ARVN, moved toward Kampong Speu and was merged with CUU LONG III, which continued beyond the U.S. withdrawal from Cambodia on June 30.

In the BINH TAY and CUU LONG operations, where ARVN took the lead, USAF FACs served many roles in addition to assisting their counterparts with air strikes. These FACs located civilians and refugees caught in the fighting and passed on the information to the military and political advisers to avoid unnecessary casualties. They provided reconnaissance for ARVN troops entering unknown territory. Throughout the incursion, American pilots were praised for their actions. By the end of June the

United States ceased its operations in Cambodia, and by July only Cuu
Long III continued with VNAF air support.

Operation Freedom Deal

   As the NVA/Viet Cong withdrew from their threatened border base areas alongside South Vietnam, they consolidated in the northeastern
provinces of Cambodia, east of the Mekong River and north of route 13,
and continued to apply pressure on Phnom Penh. The FANK weapons depot at Kratie fell on May 6, and NVA/Viet Cong forces captured the northern city of Stung Treng on May 18. The NVA/Viet Cong continued to pressure FANK forces in the northeast. To the south the provincial capital of
Kampong was seriously threatened after the fall of Ton Le Bet, directly
across the Mekong River and midway between Kratie and Phnom Penh.
FANK reinforced Kampong instead of the cities in the northeast. To deal
with the NVA/Viet Cong pressure in the northeastern provinces, Secretary
of Defense Melvin Laird asked the JCS to develop a plan to counter the

new threat. The JCS plan called for an air interdiction program based on the assumption that the NVA/Viet Cong would consolidate in the northern provinces. This area had a higher level of importance for the NVA/Viet Cong as the northeast corridor was the only way to move personnel and resupplies to South Vietnam. FREEDOM DEAL would be the last significant air operation in Cambodia.

FREEDOM DEAL covered the geographic area of greatest concern for the United States and FANK, which started from a line 200 meters west of the Mekong River at the Laotian border to Kratie and along route 3/13 to the border of South Vietnam. It was seen as an extension of STEEL TIGER. Air sorties in Operation FREEDOM DEAL concentrated on interdiction, supported FANK troops under fire, and provided reconnaissance with a special emphasis not to strike at monuments, temples, or historic sites. The United States went to great pains to avoid cultural artifacts and distributed detailed grid coordinates on maps and photographs of individual sites. As American troops began to leave Cambodia, after the objectives of the incursion were met, FREEDOM DEAL focused on supporting the forces of Lon Nol and disrupting both the land and sea NVA/Viet Cong supply lines through Cambodia. The first strikes occurred on May 30 when U.S. aircraft flew beyond the 30-kilometer limit set for American forces in Cambodia. Interdiction resumed on June 4 but was not officially announced until June 6. Because interdiction was a significant aspect of FREEDOM DEAL, MK-36 mines were placed in the Se Kong and Se San rivers to limit use of the waterways as a viable enemy supply route. Reconnaissance missions expanded beyond the FREEDOM DEAL area to include all of Cambodia except around Phnom Penh.

As more intelligence was gathered about NVA/Viet Cong movement and base areas, the United States recognized the need for the deployment of more air power. On June 18, General Abrams requested that the original area of operations for FREEDOM DEAL be expanded to include the territory immediately south and that B-52 strikes be launched. This new area, known as FREEDOM ACTION, added the stretch from route 3/13 to route 7. Additional O-1, O-2, and OV-10 were introduced to coordinate FAC responsibilities and air strikes between the U.S. military, VNAF, and FANK. The first FREEDOM ACTION strikes took place on June 20 under the same guidelines and restrictions as FREEDOM DEAL and ended on the last day of June, when all American troops withdrew from Cambodia. Operation FREEDOM DEAL and its extension, FREEDOM ACTION, hindered the NVA/Viet Cong's ability to freely roam and consolidate its power in northeastern Cambodia.

The results of the incursion were mixed. American and ARVN forces were never able to engage the NVA/Viet Cong in a large-scale battle. Except for the early periods of TOAN THANG 42 and BINH TAY I and II, all contact was sporadic and small. Despite the American and ARVN inability to destroy NVA/Viet Cong personnel, the incursion did succeed in wrecking a significant amount of war materials. It is estimated that the supplies captured or destroyed included enough rice to feed almost 38,000 soldiers one pound each per day for one year as well as a cache of individual weapons to supply fifty-five Viet Cong infantry battalions. Also captured were enough crew-served guns for thirty-three Viet Cong infantry battalions and 18,500 mortar, rocket, and recoilless rifle rounds. Both American and ARVN troops discovered and destroyed extensive NVA/Viet Cong bunker complexes, including full hospitals, training bases, and sophisticated logistical centers. Intelligence estimates suggested that the incursion disrupted NVA/Viet Cong plans for a 1970 offensive and forced the expansion of the Ho Chi Minh Trail through Laos after the sea and land routes via Cambodia were effectively cut off. Placing the burden on the Laotian trails and cutting off Cambodia strained the NVA/Viet Cong, who needed to move the 10,000 tons per year necessary to support the war in South Vietnam. The incursion provided additional time for ARVN to train as U.S. forces left the region through the policy of Vietnamization. The incursion was successful in these results based in great part on the role of air power.[4]

Air power also provided cover for sea and land supply convoys to Phnom Penh. In 1971 the United States used air power in an offensive role to interdict roads to the capital during an NVA/Viet Cong offensive. The Khmer Rouge had been remarkably successful in late 1970, taking over more than 50 percent of the Cambodian territory; and, despite U.S., ARVN, and FANK efforts, the Communists were able to maintain their hold on most of the country in 1971 and 1972. Because of the political climate in the United States, the 7th Air Force ordered its crews to report all combat support sorties as interdiction—based on the assumption that any air strike that ultimately helped to slow down the NVA/Viet Cong or Khmer Rouge was a form of interdiction. These missions continued through 1973, although Cambodia (renamed the Khmer Republic in October 1970 by Lon Nol) remained a low priority in bombing operations in the Southeast Asian theater. The exception to this trend was the December 1971 FANK offensive, Chenla II, and the COMMANDO HUNT VII campaign that crossed the border from southern Laos to northeastern Cambodia. When the North Vietnamese invaded South Vietnam in March 1972, the

U.S. military reduced the number of sorties in Cambodia to dozens. During this time, USAF A-37, F-4, A-7 aircraft (beginning in October 1972) and AC-130 gunships took part in the majority of the sorties in support of FANK forces. The USMC flew A-4s in Cambodia beginning in May 1972, and the VNAF flew A-1, A-37, and F-5 aircraft and AC-119 gunships, which supported ARVN cross-border attacks against the NVA/Viet Cong. All of these air assets complemented the Khmer (Cambodian) Air Force, whose aircraft numbered slightly over 100 during this period. The workhorse of the Khmer Air Force was the T-28, as it was in Laos, as well as the O-1 and AC-47.

U.S. Air Strike Sorties, 1972–1973

		Air Strikes (Tactical)			Air Strikes (Support)	
	B-52	USAF	VNAF	USMC	USAF	VNAF
1971						
TOTAL	1,324	16,550	11,824	14	18,460	11,631
1972						
January	109	785	560	0	839	1,292
February	180	943	4,668	0	761	1,511
March	256	871	671	0	787	732
April	48	406	3,374	0	725	75
May	27	239	131	4	563	9
June	196	445	390	106	699	10
July	148	415	353	85	385	1
August	190	708	448	211	268	0
September	307	327	194	166	237	0
October	223	185	381	224	184	1
November	167	218	20	126	233	0
December	49	223	130	156	161	2
TOTAL	1,900	5,765	11,320	1,078	5,842	3,633
1973						
January	201	283	156	344	187	0
February	65	337	0	12	93	0
March	1,254	3,716	0	24	1,475	0
April	1,934	3,425	0	334	3,267	0
May	1,672	4,998	0	426	4,026	0
June	1,170	4,535	0	383	2,529	0
July	1,200	5,596	0	464	4,716	0
August	620	2,930	0	277	2,575	0
TOTAL	8,116	25,820	156	2,264	18,868	0

Source: CHECO Report, Major Paul W. Elder, "Air Operations in the Khmer Republic—1 December 1971–15 August 1973" (April 15, 1974), 75.

A-37 Dragonfly. *Douglas Pike Collection, The Vietnam Archive, Texas Tech University*

On January 28, 1973, as a result of the Paris peace talks, a cease-fire went into effect in Vietnam. One stipulation of the cease-fire was the end of foreign military activities in Cambodia and the total withdrawal of armed forces, weapons, and war materials from the country. In response to the cease-fire agreement, Lon Nol declared a suspension of FANK of-fen-sive action starting on January 29. In the spirit of the move toward peace, the U.S. military decreased its air strikes within Cambodia. While FANK stopped, the Khmer Rouge did not. With logistical and military support from the NVA/Viet Cong, the Khmer Rouge was able to apply continuous pressure on FANK forces throughout Cambodia. On March 18, as Khmer Rouge forces threatened Phnom Penh, Lon Nol declared a state of siege. U.S. air power engaged the Khmer forces and stopped them from marching into the capital.

While the Khmer Rouge pressured FANK forces, the NVA/Viet Cong took advantage of the conflict to move additional troops through Cambo-dia and into South Vietnam in preparation for their final push toward Saigon. U.S. air power increased dramatically over the following months to meet this activity, but war weariness in the United States took its toll. The American public was tired of the war. It saw the air war in Cambodia as an expansion of the war in Southeast Asia at a time when President Nixon's policy of Vietnamization was supposed to be extracting the United States from the conflict. While the air strikes continued in Cambodia, FANK forces withstood the Khmer Rouge. When the air strikes ceased, it was only a matter of time before Lon Nol's government fell.

With the war in Vietnam over for the United States in January 1973, Congress started to apply pressure to end American involvement in Cambodia. In June 1973, Nixon vetoed a bill that would have prohibited funding of U.S. operations. He compromised with Republican leaders in the House of Representatives to delay similar legislation that would have ended the air campaign immediately, for an extension of air operations until August 15. Nixon signed Public Law 93-53 on July 1, 1973. With this bill the United States hoped to provide a six-week window of opportunity to force the Khmer Rouge to the negotiating table.

Recognizing that the Nixon administration was ending its military commitment to Cambodia, the Khmer Rouge disengaged from FANK and waited until after August 15. With the United States completely out of Cambodia in mid-August, the Khmer Rouge was able to begin the consolidation of its power. In April 1975 it launched an offensive that brought its soldiers to the capital, forcing the surrender of Lon Nol's troops on April 17. FANK continued the fight, although the loss of Phnom Penh and the imminent withdrawal of the Americans from Southeast Asia demoralized the remaining troops. Gerald Ford, who had replaced Richard Nixon after his impeachment and resignation from office, was not able to come to the aid of the Cambodians because of congressional restraints. Cambodia fell, just as South Vietnam would fall at the end of April 1975, without American aid or assistance to stave off defeat. Before the final collapse of Phnom Penh and Saigon, there would be one last major air campaign that would call into question the use of air power in Southeast Asia earlier in the Vietnam War, fueling debate for scholars of the air war to this day.

NOTES

1. CHECO Report, David I. Folkman Jr. and Philip D. Caine, "The Cambodian Campaign—April 29–June 30, 1970—Special Report" (September 1, 1970), 1–4.
2. Ibid., 4–7.
3. Ibid., 15.
4. Ibid., 29–33. Statistics for the various operations are found throughout the report.

CHAPTER Six

A YEAR OF DECISION, 1972

T HE AIR WAR OVER NORTH VIETNAM EXPERIENCED A THREE-AND-one-half-year lull after the November 1, 1968, bombing halt. Occasional strikes south of the 20th parallel against DRV targets represented a real threat to the U.S. armed forces in the form of either a concentration of supplies or air defense systems that had attacked reconnaissance aircraft over North Vietnam. In June 1969, as noted, the United States implemented Vietnamization, the process of handing over the war to the South Vietnamese as American troops began to withdraw. By the end of 1971, U.S. forces numbered approximately 184,000 while ARVN had increased to over 1.1 million soldiers. Many of the latter, however, still needed time to train as units. This phase of Vietnamization made South Vietnam particularly vulnerable, as ARVN forces were not organized enough to defend the entire country and the remaining American combat troops were too few to repulse an invasion. To compensate for the withdrawal of American ground troops, the USAF and USN remained at a high state of readiness. USAF personnel participated in the withdrawal even though military planners relied on air power to compensate for the loss of U.S. military potential. American intelligence estimates anticipated a DRV offensive in 1972, although one as intense as Tet 1968 was not expected. When the offensive finally began on the night of March 29, 1972, the role of air power changed dramatically in

Khammouane
(Thakhek)

Dong Hoi

Demarcation Line·

Séno

Sépone

Quang Tri

Savannakhet

Hue

Da Nang

Ubon
Ratchathani

Saravane

Warin
Chamrap

Paksé

Ah

Kontum

Pleiku

An Nhon

14 -

Stung Treng

n Reap

C A M B O D I A

TONLE
SAP

Me Kong

Kratie

Ban Me
Thuot

Da Lat

IOM PENH
pong
ieu

Kom ng
Cha

S O U T H

ukville

Kampot

Svay Rieng

V I E T N A M

Bien Hoa

SAIGON

Phan Thiet

Long
Xuyeu

My Tho

Vinh
Long

Vung Tau

HU QUOC
etnam)

Can
Tho

Quan
Long

Bac
Lieu

10 -

SOUTH

CHINA

SEA

CON SON

SOUTH

CHINA

NVA Invasion
Route

The North Vietnamese 1972 Eastertide Offensive

response to the coordinated and massive attack by the North Vietnamese against South Vietnam.

The 1972 Eastertide Offensive was a three-pronged attack against the DMZ in I CTZ, Pleiku and Kontum in II CTZ, and An Loc in III CTZ. Initiated by an estimated 120,000 NVA troops supported by Soviet-built tanks and artillery with 80,000 reserves, the offensive was designed to cut South Vietnam in two along highway 19, force the surrender of ARVN troops in I CTZ, and establish the seat of a permanent revolutionary government at An Loc. The DRV had timed the invasion to coincide with the change in the monsoon from the northeast to the southwest. Typically, during this time the northern part of Vietnam had continual cloud cover, fog, or drizzle. The DRV wanted to take advantage of the weather conditions to negate the overwhelming American air superiority. The U.S. military had removed a majority of its combat troops from South Vietnam and was not in a position to reinsert troops to help in the defense of the South. The United States did have air assets left in Southeast Asia, although at a much lower level than at the peak of ROLLING THUNDER. It was U.S. air power that reinvigorated ARVN troops who had initially suffered significant losses in the offensive. Moreover, the implementation of Operation LINEBACKER I, a major air campaign, eventually turned back the Eastertide Offensive.

All military intelligence leading up to the Eastertide Offensive suggested that the NVA would launch an attack around the DMZ and, with support from NVA/Viet Cong forces in Quang Tri province, would attempt to take the province and defeat and demoralize ARVN troops charged with the defense of the northern border. The NVA started the attack on March 30 and within a week captured the string of fire support bases that created a barrier between the DMZ and the rest of South Vietnam. In what would become typical of the offensive, many of the ARVN troops withered under intense NVA rocket and mortar fire and, as a result of poor command and control, failed to halt the initial assault. Not all ARVN troops failed; there were several examples of unit cohesion and fighting spirit, notably in the Vietnamese Rangers and Marine Corps.

American air power was not effective in the opening weeks of the offensive because of poor weather conditions. The loss of the fire support base line resulted in a new defensive perimeter around the city of Quang Tri, during which time the USAF, USN, and USMC were able to use air power to some effect when weather permitted. Despite this assistance, ARVN troops were unable to retain Quang Tri and abandoned the city on

May 1. During May the weather improved dramatically, allowing the U.S. military to stabilize the situation by the end of the month. South Vietnamese president Nguyen Van Thieu fired the I CTZ commander, Lieutenant General Hoang Xuan Lam, and replaced him with Lieutenant General Ngo Quang Truong, who had been in charge of IV CTZ (the Mekong Delta). Truong's leadership and a resumption of full-time ARC LIGHT attacks, tactical air sorties, and naval gunfire allowed ARVN forces to regroup north of Hue and halt the NVA/Viet Cong momentum. ARVN forces, with U.S. air power, fought their way north toward the fire support base line and retook a majority of Quang Tri province by October 1972. Despite early failures, ARVN had proven itself capable of fighting the NVA/Viet Cong with the assistance of U.S. air power.

During the operation, B-52 attacks were very successful as were the USAF aircraft (A-1, F-4, and F-5), the USN aircraft (A-4, A-6, A-7, and F-4), and the VNAF's A-1 and A-37. The American FACs, who flew in O-2 and OV-10 aircraft, were invaluable as they coordinated attacks and brought in air power as needed. While these slow-moving aircraft were easy targets, the NVA/Viet Cong shot down only nine over I CTZ between April and June. The North Vietnamese attacked using conventional tactics, coordinating armor, infantry, and artillery. The army that attacked South Vietnam in 1972 was very different from the one that fought during the 1960s. While the tanks (T-34, T-54, and PT-76) rolling during the offensive were effective in the early days, U.S. air power was able to counter them once the weather cleared and helped to stabilize ARVN forces. These factors, combined with new and dynamic Vietnamese leadership, were decisive in the recovery of the ground lost in the opening months of the offensive.

The NVA had moved a number of air defense weapons into I CTZ, including 23mm, 37mm, 57mm, and 100mm antiaircraft artillery, to challenge American air power. There were also incidents of SA-2 firings from north of the DMZ and the Tchepone region in Laos. The North Vietnamese reintroduced another SAM during the offensive that proved threatening, if not lethal. The SA-7 (the Strela, designated by NATO as the Grail) was a handheld, lightweight, and easy-to-operate SAM that utilized a heat-seeking guidance system. It was launched with some effect in the years preceding the offensive but was truly battle-tested during Eastertide. The limited-range SA-7 had little effect against fast-moving aircraft such as the F-4 but posed a threat to helicopters and the propeller-driven FAC aircraft. It could be moved anywhere on the battlefield. The SA-7 was most effective when fired at the rear of an aircraft, allowing it to lock onto the hot exhaust trail of the engine.

The battle for the central highlands in II CTZ remained relatively quiet as the fighting raged in Quang Tri (I CTZ) and around An Loc (III CTZ). In mid-April the NVA/Viet Cong attacked the Tan Canh-Dak To area (designated the B-3 Front by the Viet Cong) and forced the 22nd ARVN to surrender Pleiku. The battle for Kontum began in mid-May, and with it came a threat that South Vietnam would be divided along QL 19, the highway from Pleiku to Qui Nhon. In defense of Kontum was the 23rd ARVN and U.S. air power. In the early days of the offensive in II CTZ, American aircraft held their traditional role of ground support and enemy interdiction. They also had the added task of destroying equipment abandoned by ARVN forces as they fled. During the battle for Kontum, air power again was seen as the decisive factor in the outcome. The USAF flew a combination of gunships (AC-119 and AC-130) and aircraft (F-4, A-1, A-37, and B-52) to keep the NVA/Viet Cong off balance.

**Sorties Flown over II Corps
Tactical Zone (CTZ), March 28–June 30, 1972**

VNAF	USMC	USN	ARC LIGHT	Gunships	TACAIR	U.S. Total
3,517	1,351	1,870	2,297	297	3,466	9,281

Source: CHECO Report, Peter A. W. Liebchen, "Kontum: Battle for the Central Highlands, March 30–June 10, 1972—Special Report" (October 27, 1972), 90–93.

During the worst of the offensive in II CTZ, South Vietnamese president Nguyen Van Thieu relieved the II Corps commander, Lieutenant General Ngo Dzu, and replaced him with Nguyen Van Toan. Major General Toan reorganized his staff and, with American assistance, turned back the NVA/Viet Cong from Kontum on May 14. For the next two weeks the NVA/Viet Cong continued the attack only to be repulsed by ARVN defenders supported by massive U.S. air strikes and TOW-missile-equipped antitank helicopters. On May 28 the tide of battle shifted, and ARVN conducted a house-to-house counterattack to clear the enemy from the city.

In the most southern push of the Eastertide Offensive against Binh Long province, the NVA/Viet Cong hoped to capture An Loc, the provisional capital, and establish its own revolutionary capital to pave the way for entry into, and capture of, Saigon. The NVA/Viet Cong were able to overrun Loc Ninh in early April and set siege to An Loc after a failed attempt to overrun the city on April 19. Again, American aircraft played a decisive role in the defense of An Loc during the critical months at the beginning of Eastertide. FAC pilots organized and coordinated nearly continuous bombing missions over the battlefield. They directed AC-130 and AC-119 gunships against tank formations, troop concentrations, and points of attack. The USAF also deployed the B-52, A-1E, and F-4 to great effect to strike against an exposed enemy. The initial NVA/Viet Cong attack stalled on April 23 but resumed on May 11, although it failed to gain its objective. The siege of An Loc also required air resupply of the city after the NVA/Viet Cong overran the airfield at Quan Loi and QL13, the highway leading into the city from the south. Aerial resupply presented a challenge to the USAF as the drop zone was consolidated into a 200-by-200-meter area. On many of these missions, each participating C-130 transport suffered damage but was still able to release its load. With some revision in drop techniques, the majority of supplies reached the beleaguered ARVN and U.S. advisers defending the city. ARVN forces finally cleared An Loc on July 11, thus ending the 95-day battle.

During the siege of An Loc the USAF lost eleven aircraft, most of which were shot down by gunfire. The NVA/Viet Cong moved a number of AAA batteries (most were 23mm and 37mm) as well as the SA-7 into the area to defend against air attack. During the siege the SA-7 forced the USAF to revise the use of the AC-119 and AC-130, both of which were slow moving and required secure skies from which to operate. The SA-7 was credited with shooting down only one USAF aircraft, an O-2, although it was suspected that two additional O-2s were shot down by the SA-7. Despite the heavy concentration of AAA fire and the SA-7, air power over An Loc was the primary reason the city did not fall and ARVN was able to regain the initiative in the area and drive the NVA/Viet Cong into Cambodia. While American and ARVN forces countered the NVA/Viet Cong attacks in the south with the assistance of air power, the U.S. military also began an impressive air campaign over the DRV.

The air campaign over North Vietnam to counter the invasion of South Vietnam had the primary objective of reducing the DRV's ability to wage war against South Vietnam. To accomplish this goal, the USAF and USN drew up three tasks:

- Destroy the war materials stockpiled in the DRV
- Stop external war materials and support from reaching the DRV
- Stop or slow down the movement of personnel and war materials into Laos and South Vietnam

While the USAF made contingency plans to interdict DRV personnel and supplies from reaching south of the 17th parallel and to eliminate war materials used in support of the offensive, it also worked toward increasing its air capabilities in support of ARVN and American ground troops. In early February 1972 the Tactical Air Command (TAC) Operational Plan 100, named Constant Guard, brought about the largest tactical air power deployment in history.[1]

Constant Guard had three phases in which the USAF augmented its existing aircraft. Constant Guard I brought two squadrons of F-4E (thirty-six aircraft) and one squadron of F-105G (twelve aircraft) to airfields in Thailand and Vietnam. The F-105 arrived between April 10 and April 12 and was put into immediate action, as were the F-4 squadrons that had come earlier, on April 8. The USAF also deployed an additional eight EB-66 for ECM in ARC LIGHT missions. On the heels of Constant Guard I, Constant Guard II added two more squadrons of F-4E to Udorn, Thailand, on May 2. The final phase of Constant Guard included the entire 49th Tactical Fighter Wing (TFW), consisting of four squadrons of F-4 aircraft. B-52 bombers, with KC-135 support aircraft from SAC, flew out of Thailand and Guam to augment the Constant Guard aircraft. The USMC redeployed the 1st Marine Air Wing to Da Nang, and the USN maintained four aircraft carriers at Yankee Station in the Gulf of Tonkin that could launch up to 2,100 sorties per carrier per month in emergency conditions.

By the end of Constant Guard, the American strike force in South Vietnam stood at 182 aircraft with an additional 443 in Thailand and eighty-six B-52 bombers in Guam. The influx of aircraft as well as the fluid nature of the initial stage of the DRV offensive caused some confusion and organizational problems for the USAF. A few of the Constant Guard squadrons arrived without basic supplies, while the airfields suffered from overcrowding; they were not prepared for such large numbers of aircraft. The overcrowding forced the USAF to redistribute its air assets quickly, and the ingenuity of USAF personnel limited the potential for hardships caused by a lack of supplies.

By June the Eastertide Offensive had stalled as ARVN troops, with American aircraft, held the line and began taking back lost territory. As the shift in the battlefield occurred, the USAF, USN, and USMC also began redeploying their aircraft from South Vietnam to Thailand—even during the offensive the U.S. military continued to withdraw ground troops from Vietnam. This policy placed the USAF in a difficult position as it had to continue the number of sorties while decreasing its available manpower. During the LINEBACKER missions the 7th Air Force headquarters reduced its staff from 1,200 to 500 while conducting and coordinating the air campaign over North and South Vietnam. On June 1, SAC created the 17th Strategic Aerospace Division at U-Tapao, Thailand, which consolidated all of the equipment and personnel necessary for the maintenance and operation of the B-52 sorties over Vietnam. By the end of July there were some 850 aircraft and 50,000 personnel stationed in Thailand and supporting the air campaign over Vietnam and Laos. Through these measures the United States was able to organize for one of the most intense air campaigns of the war after peace negotiations in Paris became mired in quibbling.

OPERATIONS FREEDOM TRAIL AND LINEBACKER I

The Eastertide Offensive did not come as a surprise to the United States. In December 1971 the USAF had launched a preemptive strike, named PROUD DEEP ALPHA, against large concentrations of war materials being stockpiled near the DMZ. In February 1972 the American military developed a plan to counter the impending offensive, which called for maximum effort to support the VNAF. This plan included an increase in B-52 sorties to 1,200 per month and a less restricted targeting scheme over North Vietnam. When the DRV struck on March 30, 1972, President Richard Nixon ordered the return of F-4 squadrons to Vietnam and augmented the B-52 forces at the Guam and U-Tapao airfields, as well as instructed the USN carrier force on its way back to the United States to return to Vietnam.

On April 6, with available air assets, the U.S. military initiated Operation FREEDOM TRAIL, which marked the first sustained bombing of the DRV since 1968. FREEDOM TRAIL sorties were concentrated south of the 20th parallel, although north of the 20th parallel a few targets were struck, including the Petroleum Products Storage (PPS) around Haiphong with 35 percent of the facility destroyed. In less than two weeks, FREEDOM TRAIL sorties managed to hit nearly 50 percent of the PPS in Hanoi and Haiphong. Unlike ROLLING THUNDER and the U.S. escalation in the mid-1960s, the response of 1972 was not gradual. The 1972 air campaign would follow a different set of guidelines and have less political restraint in determining targets of opportunity. From April 6 through May 7, FREEDOM TRAIL sorties struck at the DRV's major POL storage and transportation facilities, lines of communication, railways, bridges, and other infrastructure aiding the invasion of South Vietnam.

For several years the United States had plans for an air campaign to counter a North Vietnamese invasion of South Vietnam and had continuously updated them to reflect the changing political climate, weapons technology, and military might of the DRV. One constant in the planning was the two-part strategy over North Vietnam to cut off the flow of all war materials entering the DRV and to disrupt the lines of supply to the invading forces. After the initial invasion began on March 30, FREEDOM TRAIL deployed all available air assets to support ARVN forces under attack.

When enough American aircraft were in place, President Nixon announced a new air campaign, named LINEBACKER. In contrast to the political and military restrictions of ROLLING THUNDER, there were only two significant limitations placed on the air campaign. The United States established a no-strike zone within twenty-five to thirty nautical miles of the Chinese border, and the JCS had to approve air strikes within ten nautical miles of Hanoi. Operation LINEBACKER began on May 9 with the mining of Haiphong harbor as well as other minor DRV harbors at Cam Pha, Hon Gai, Vinh, and Thanh Hoa. This step had not been taken during the Johnson administration, which considered the action politically risky because it might serve as a catalyst for Chinese or Soviet overt intervention. By 1972 the likelihood of such outside interference had diminished, and Nixon was able to authorize the mining of the harbors. As a result, reconnaissance flights noted that no large transports attempted to enter or leave those harbors. The sea route, one of the two major supply lines into the DRV, was cut off. On May 10, in what was known at the time as Operation ROLLING THUNDER ALPHA, USAF aircraft struck at targets near Hanoi while USN aircraft hit targets at Haiphong. By the end of the day the air campaign was renamed Operation LINEBACKER.

With the sea route blocked and DRV war supplies under attack, the second supply route—the rail lines from China—became the next target. There continued to be political considerations in designating bridges and railways on the Chinese border, and selected targets required JCS approval. The major difference between ROLLING THUNDER and LINEBACKER was that the JCS was freer to authorize the sorties without presidential orders. Operation LINEBACKER sorties were still instructed to avoid religious sites, civilian structures, hospitals, schools, and Third Country shipping. To limit the collateral damage of the LINEBACKER missions, the U.S. military took advantage of new guidance technology that ensured better accuracy.

Advances in American weapons technology made precision bombing more of a reality during LINEBACKER. Three technologies employed during LINEBACKER distinguished it from ROLLING THUNDER: guided bombs, precision navigation, and a new fighter-bomber. The United States introduced the first guided bomb, the AGM-62 (Walleye), into Vietnam in 1967.[2] The Walleye, an electro-optically guided bomb (EOGB), did not become plentiful in Vietnam until shortly before Lyndon Johnson announced the March 1968 bombing restrictions, and it was never fully battle tested there. The Walleye was perfect for hard targets such as buildings, bridges, and bunkers as it had the ability to penetrate up to eighteen inches of steel-reinforced concrete. Aircraft personnel could guide the weapon to its target from up to 40,000 feet away. The United States also had developed a laser-guided bomb (LGB), named the Paveway I, in August 1968. It, too, was put into only limited action before Johnson ordered the cessation of bombing over the DRV in November 1968. The Paveway I was an extremely efficient weapon for its time, with a high accuracy rate and a circular error probable (area in which the weapon contacted at least 50 percent of the time) of zero feet.

The effect of the guided bombs was apparent from the first strikes. On May 10 and 12, six bridges in the Hanoi-Haiphong perimeter were destroyed or damaged. American aircraft achieved a more impressive result on May 13 when three F-4 flights in a combination of fifteen MK-84 (EOGB), nine M-118 (LGB), and forty-eight MK-52 (500-pound conventional bombs) made the Thanh Hoa bridge unserviceable. In one day, with twenty-four guided bombs (conventional bombs were not effective), the USAF did what the combined air assets in ROLLING THUNDER had not been able to do in three and one-half years. In addition to the successful destruction of the major bridges linking the forces engaged against South Vietnam, the U.S. flights also struck at the major railways between the DRV and China. Using LGB and EOGB weapons, American forces interdicted the northwest and northeast transportation corridors leading to China and stopped all but a few supply convoys from getting through to resupply Hanoi and points south.

During the air campaign, in many of the sorties against the railways and their bridges, there was almost complete cloud cover. The LGB and EOGB were affected by the poor weather conditions over the DRV. Through the middle of July, priority determined target selection while weather remained secondary. As LINEBACKER progressed, weather forecasting became more important, and weather reconnaissance determined the target lists. Weather forecasters rose in prominence during the air campaign while the LGB and EOGB became less effective as weather conditions deteriorated. By mid-July the forecasters played a significant role in determining whether a mission was to be continued, delayed, or cancelled, or whether an alternative target was to be hit. Both EOGB and LGB were also susceptible to smoke, dust, and rain, but these factors did not deter their use. Advances in weather forecasting along with the new weapons technology played an important part in the success of the LINEBACKER missions over the DRV. More sorties succeeded in destroying their targets while limiting civilian damage.

In December 1971, during PROUD DEEP ALPHA, the USAF began employing long-range navigation (LORAN)-assisted bomb deliveries. LORAN enabled the USAF to determine the location of aircraft flying over North Vietnam and, in theory, allowed for greater accuracy in bombing missions. It measured the difference in radio signal time between the moving aircraft and three stationary receiving facilities located in Vietnam and Thailand. By triangulating the signal time differences between the station and aircraft, the USAF could determine the exact location of the aircraft and guide it to its target. LORAN did not work as well as the U.S. military had hoped during the air campaigns in 1972. It was affected by weather, human and mechanical error, and the threat of air defense weapons. Aircraft employing LORAN needed to fly in relatively straight patterns in order not to lose contact. It was estimated that a 30-degree bank turn resulted in 50 percent LORAN signal strength loss while a 45-degree bank turn resulted in 70 percent loss. LORAN missions flew over a target once to minimize aircraft vulnerability to AAA and SAM targeting, resulting in a lower level of bombing accuracy. While this technology had promise for future air campaigns, it did not test well in Vietnam.

One technological advance that also held promise was the F-111, a low-level, night-capable, all-weather fighter-bomber. It was first introduced to Southeast Asia in 1967 and brought back toward the end of LINEBACKER. Because the F-111 could conduct single sortie missions (it had the capability of flying alone), it was an effective weapon of surprise. Unlike other missions that required chaff, MiG Combat Air Patrol, and ECM support aircraft, the F-111 could do it all. The DRV had few responses to the F-111, and through October 22 only one suffered damage from seventy SA-2 illuminations over North Vietnam. The F-111 attacked truck parks and supply and storage areas with good results during LINEBACKER.

While the USAF and USN air strikes focused on bridges and railways, LINEBACKER missions also targeted the concentration of war supplies stored by the DRV throughout the country. The United States struck the

PPS during FREEDOM TRAIL, and these targets continued to receive attention throughout LINEBACKER. In addition to the PPS, the U.S. military targeted port and truck facilities, SAM and AAA sites, and military supply depots. The LGB hit Hanoi's electrical transformer station, the Son Tay storage area, the Bac Giang power plant, and other sites that supported military operations. In June, U.S. air strikes destroyed the Dang Chi hydroelectric power plant, which supplied a majority of the electricity to the DRV's industries, and the remaining supply depots in the DRV. These attacks resulted in a significant reduction of supplies flowing south and created a desperate situation for the NVA soldiers involved in the Eastertide Offensive: "They hadn't eaten in three days; they were down to one clip each for their AK-47s. We captured a young lieutenant at Quang Tri. He had come down from the North and was briefed on the situation in Quang Tri City. He was told he would be issued his sidearms and other weapons when he got into the city. There weren't any available. And when he got there, he discovered that the issue consisted of finding a weapon from a dead body."[3]

During LINEBACKER, the USAF and USN worked toward gaining air superiority over North Vietnam, which had one of the finest air defense systems in the world. In the years between the end of ROLLING THUNDER and the beginning of FREEDOM TRAIL/LINEBACKER, the DRV had been able to set up a series of air defense rings around its strategic areas. The USAF and USN used a combination of chaff and ECM to confuse the DRV radar-guided air defense weapons as well as an early warning system to detect MiG fighters (called Teaball), which was introduced in September 1972. It was with this technology that the United States had its first aces (someone who has shot down at least five enemy aircraft) of the war, USN Lieutenant Randall Cunningham and his radar intercept officer, Lieutenant (jg) William Briscoll. In the early phases of LINEBACKER, the United States suffered a .47:1 loss ratio against the DRV. After the introduction of Teaball with its integration of chaff, ECM, and early warning technology, the ratio was reversed to 3.8:1. A few of the losses during Teaball resulted from malfunctions in the system. During LINEBACKER the USAF and USN shot down forty MiG fighters, including eleven on the first full day of the air campaign. A total of sixty-three American aircraft were lost (twenty-two to MiGs, twenty to SAMs, and twenty-one to AAA).

Chaff and ECM did not always mean a safe bombing run. There were occasional malfunctions of the ECM, and wind played havoc with chaff. A combination of these anomalies resulted in the loss of the first B-52 to enemy fire during the war. From June 1965 to November 1972 the B-52 flew over 112,000 sorties without a single loss to enemy fire. SA-2 struck five B-52s, but the aircraft suffered only minimal damage. On November 15, two waves of nine B-52s were on a mission over Vinh to destroy supplies destined for South Vietnam. The fifth B-52 in the lead strike, flown by Captain Norbert J. Ostrozny, was supported by four F-4s who laid out a chaff corridor and three EB-66s who were providing electronic jamming, as well as by other F-4s in a MiG Combat Air Patrol role and two F-105s for SAM suppression. The flight was normal until just before the target when two SA-2s were spotted heading toward the aircraft. The first missed, but the second hit the right wing and forced the aircraft down. The B-52 made it over the Mekong River into Thailand, and all six crew members survived. The fifteen B-52s lost in December during the tail end of LINEBACKER and LINEBACKER II were not so fortunate.

On September 1, 1972, Admiral Noel Gaylor replaced Admiral John S. McCain Jr. as Commander in Chief, Pacific (CINCPAC) with over-all theater control of Operation LINEBACKER. The change in leadership did not affect the air campaign. All B-52 strikes continued to require JCS approval, as did any targets within a designated restricted zone. Gaylor set up a CINCPAC joint committee to validate targets selected by the Air Force to ensure that they did not accidentally strike a civilian area or cause any undue civilian casualties (say, by damaging a dike or irrigation dam). Gaylor continued to target industry, electric power, and shipping facilities in addition to military command-and-control centers. The successful destruction of these targets also required continued pressure on the DRV's air defense system. Another series of targets proposed during this time were in the previously restricted buffer zone near the Chinese border. There were several railways and bridges between China and the DRV still in use. The United States had been very successful in disrupting the rail lines outside the restrictive zone, but that did not deter the Chinese from continuing their support. On September 3 the JCS approved plans to strike at the previously forbidden targets, code-named Prime Choke. The air campaign was not able to achieve its results as weather and a change in the DRV position at the Paris peace talks took precedence.

The Paris peace talks suffered a severe setback with the Eastertide Offensive. It was not until the fall of 1972, after the military situation in South Vietnam stabilized, that the DRV gave any indication it was willing to come back to the negotiating table and discuss peace in earnest.[4] On October 11, CINCPAC instructed the USAF and USN to cease air operations within ten nautical miles of Hanoi. The number of sorties over route packages 5 and 6 also decreased during the period of October

U.S. Sorties over North Vietnam, 1972–1973

	May 1972	June 1972	July 1972	Aug. 1972	Sept. 1972	Oct. 1972	Nov. 1972	Dec. 1972	Jan. 1973
USN attack	3,920	4,151	4,175	4,746	3,937	2,674	1,716	1,383	863
USAF attack	1,919	2,125	2,310	2,112	2,297	2,214	1,606	1,548	716
USMC attack	23	34	8	38	102	84	79	119	50
B-52	1	271	308	572	411	616	846	1,381	535
TOTAL ATTACKS	5,862	6,310	6,493	6,896	6,336	4,972	3,401	3,050	1,629
TOTAL SORTIES*	10,983	12,392	13,187	13,888	13,644	11,984	9,755	9,275	7,266

Sources: CHECO Report, Melvin F. Porter, "LINEBACKER: Overview of the First 120 Days" (September 27, 1973); and CHECO Report, Calvin R. Johnson, "LINEBACKER Operations—September–December 1972" (December 31, 1978).

*U.S. Armed Forces: no breakdown

16–22. On October 23, President Nixon ordered the cessation of air operations north of the 20th parallel. The United States used the restriction and reduction as a sign of good faith toward the peaceful resolution of the American involvement in the war. The U.S. military continued to strike at targets south of the 20th parallel in its effort to maintain the interdiction of war materials destined for the North Vietnamese forces engaged with ARVN, even though all three prongs of the DRV Eastertide Offensive had been turned back. Air operations were reduced during this period as long as the peace negotiations were making progress. When, in early December, it became clear to both Nixon and National Security Adviser Henry Kissinger that the DRV was stalling for time, the president ordered the resumption of bombing. From December 18 through December 29 an intensive bombing campaign, referred to as LINEBACKER II or the Christmas Bombings, was launched over the DRV.

OPERATION LINEBACKER II

On December 15, 1972, the JCS sent a message to Admiral Gaylor that air assets in Southeast Asia should be prepared for a three-day intensive bombing campaign against North Vietnam. Beginning on December 18 and lasting for twelve days, the U.S. military conducted an air campaign, Operation LINEBACKER II, against North Vietnam that was unlike any previously carried out. A maximum effort was made to destroy all major targets in and around Hanoi, Haiphong, and the lesser strategic military facilities in North Vietnam. American military strategists identified six types of targets:

- HANOI TARGET COMPLEX: Radio station, power plant, railroad yards, repair shops, port, and Bac Mai Airfield
- HAIPHONG TARGET COMPLEX: Power plant, railroad yard, warehouses, shipyards, naval base, and airfield
- ELECTRIC POWER FACILITIES: Thermal power plants at Uong Bi, Thai Nguyen, and Bac Giang
- RADIO COMMUNICATION FACILITIES: International radio transmitter at Hanoi and radio communications transmitters at Hanoi and Lang Truoc
- AIR DEFENSE TARGETS: Phuc Yen, Kep, Yen Bai, and Hoa Lac
- TRANSSHIPMENT POINTS: Bac Giang[5]

The objective of LINEBACKER II was clear—to force the DRV to the negotiating table for the final peace by bringing to bear the full might of the USAF, USN, and USMC against North Vietnam. The air campaign was designed to show the vulnerability of the DRV in the face of unleashed American air assets. The USAF divided the missions into day and night operations with almost 2,700 sorties during the course of the air campaign. There were 729 B-52 and 143 F-111 nighttime sorties. A total of twenty-seven aircraft were lost during LINEBACKER II (six for the USN and USMC and twenty-one for the USAF), all but one the result of DRV air defense. The B-52 suffered the greatest losses, at fifteen, while the newer F-111 was shot down only twice.

The original phase of LINEBACKER II began on December 18 and lasted for the three days initially planned by the JCS. It was a maximum effort campaign that included 314 B-52 sorties. The first strikes occurred on the night of December 18 when sixteen targets in the Hanoi-Haiphong area were struck by three waves of B-52 bombers (thirty-six aircraft). Over the course of the first day of bombing, the United States lost five aircraft (three B-52s), four of which were shot down by SA-2 SAMs. It could not be determined what happened to the fifth one. No aircraft were lost during the second day, although another six B-52s were shot down on December 20, all by SA-2 missiles. The high loss rate of the B-52 forced the USAF to reformulate its LINEBACKER II strategy as the United States could not afford to continue such losses and keep up its pressure on the DRV.

The second phase lasted four days, starting on December 21 when 120 B-52 sorties struck at Haiphong and joined F-111, F-4, and USN A-7 aircraft in striking lower-priority targets. Only seven aircraft were lost (two B-52s and one EB-66c to engine failure) despite almost 600 combat sorties. By this time the DRV had expended a large part of its SA-2 missiles. The SA-2 and MiG had been the primary threat during the air campaign. Approximately 1,300 SAMs were fired, with 1,032 aimed at B-52 aircraft. SAM gunners had a 68.8:1 ratio during LINEBACKER II. The MiG threat never materialized, and SAM suppression (IRON HAND) helped to limit the number of SAM-related losses to two during this phase. Antiaircraft artillery and automatic weapons fire did account for at least two downed aircraft. LORAN was used because of poor weather conditions, and LGB was employed on December 21, 27, and 28—days when the weather permitted. Air operations were suspended on Christmas Day not only to observe the holiday but also to prepare for the third, and final, phase of the air campaign.

The third phase began on December 26. The bombing missions were redirected to Hanoi and Haiphong, with over 800 (295 B-52s) sorties and the loss of nine aircraft (four B-52s) during the period. On December 30, President Nixon ordered the suspension of bombing north of the 20th parallel as a good-faith response to indications that the DRV was ready to resume negotiations in Paris. Serious talks started on January 8, 1973. On January 15, Nixon ordered the end of all bombing over North Vietnam as a condition of the final cease-fire agreement, which was signed in Paris on January 27, 1973. When asked on January 24 whether LINEBACKER II had played the key role in reaching the final agreement, Nixon adviser and chief negotiator Henry Kissinger replied that the air campaign had broken the deadlock and made the peace possible.

After the war many military and civilian leaders argued that LINE-BACKER I and LINEBACKER II were prime examples of how air power, if unrestricted, could have won the war in Vietnam. The proof offered is that LINEBACKER I resulted in the defeat of the Eastertide Offensive while LINE-BACKER II sent the DRV back to the peace table in Paris, where they signed the cease-fire agreement. The LINEBACKER campaigns are often compared to ROLLING THUNDER to bolster the argument because there were significant differences between the 1965–1968 and 1972 air campaigns. In 1965 the Johnson administration faced a legitimate threat of Chinese or Soviet intervention if the air war became too intense, while this threat had mostly disappeared with Nixon's overtures to the People's Republic of China in 1972. In 1965, Vietnam was a country unknown to the United States, and American strategy and tactics suffered from limited and poor intelligence about the people and culture of Vietnam. In 1972, Nixon and his military leaders faced a different war and were better prepared to conduct the air campaign. The LINEBACKER I campaign was unlike any other ever experienced. The U.S. aircraft involved in the operation were able to target known forces that relied on equipment vulnerable to air attack. The success of LINEBACKER I came not only from a new set of strategy and tactics but also from a different battlefield, one on which the DRV fought a conventional war with conventional weapons. It was an ideal situation for the employment of American air power.

Likewise, LINEBACKER II achieved its ultimate goal, although some have argued that the air campaign was designed as much to influence Saigon as it was Hanoi. On the one hand, President Thieu was not cooperative in accepting the final Paris Peace Agreement because of the difficult position in which it placed South Vietnam. The United States, on the other hand, recognized that its time was over in Southeast Asia. In the end, American insistence won out as the January agreement was very near the one proposed in October.[6] In the postwar period, Socialist Republic of Vietnam officials would claim that LINEBACKER II was America's Dien Bien Phu, in reference to the loss of the fortress in 1954 that ended French involvement in Indochina. This analogy has always been considered a strange one as U.S. forces inflicted significant and serious damage on North Vietnam with minimal losses. The similarity, and perhaps the most important aspect of the two events—the battle for Dien Bien Phu and LINEBACKER II—was the final result. While the French had been defeated and left Vietnam, the Americans were not defeated in the air campaign but still left Vietnam. For the Vietnamese people it did not matter who won the battle as long as the war was over and the U.S. military was removed from Vietnam.

After the signing of the cease-fire agreement, it would take two years for the DRV to overrun South Vietnam and capture Saigon, thus ending the war on April 30, 1975. The United States did not intervene in the final moments, despite the desperate situation of the South Vietnamese. It had already ended its war. For the USAF and air assets of the USN and USMC, the last battle was won even if the war was lost. LINEBACKER II was a great, though hollow, victory as its only significant achievement was the end of U.S. involvement in the war and the final defeat of South Vietnam. In this context it is difficult to see how LINEBACKER II indicated that the United States would have won, especially when the air campaign also demonstrated that the Americans continued to misunderstand and underestimate the North Vietnamese until the very end.

NOTES

1. CHECO Report, Charles A. Nicholson, "The USAF Response to the Spring 1972 NVN Offensive: Situation and Redeployment—March–July 1972—Special Report" (October 10, 1972), 38–51.

2. For a history of the guided bomb, see CHECO Report, Melvin F. Porter, "LINEBACKER: Overview of the First 120 Days" (September 27, 1973), 19–33.

3. Mel Porter interview with General John W. Vogt Jr., Commander, 7th Air Force, Tan Son Nhut Air Base, RVN, November 12, 1972, in ibid., 42–43.

4. For more on the U.S. and DRV negotiations in Paris, see Larry Berman, *No Peace, No Honor: Nixon, Kissinger, and Betrayal in Vietnam* (New York: Free Press, 2001).

5. CHECO Report, Calvin R. Johnson, "LINEBACKER Operations—September–December 1972" (December 31, 1978), 57–58.

6. Jeffery P. Kimball, *Nixon's Vietnam War* (Laurence: University Press of Kansas, 1998).

Conclusion

Assessing whether the air war over Southeast Asia was a success or failure is an invitation to a never-ending debate. On either side of the argument are veterans, historians, and scholars who have pointed to events or operations during the conflict as well as to postwar U.S. military action as proof for their evaluations of this most contentious of questions. There is no single answer that satisfies everyone. This book seeks to understand the total role of U.S. air assets in Southeast Asia. The air war was larger than Operation ROLLING THUNDER and the LINEBACKER campaigns, although both were a significant part of military and diplomatic strategy, just as the air war was more than the campaigns over North and South Vietnam. To assess the air war and its effectiveness, one must include all the air campaigns in Southeast Asia as well as all the combat and noncombat sorties. This examination does not offer a definitive answer, but it does provide more data from which to draw conclusions.

Was the air war successful? Yes. American and allied aircraft flew a number of different types of missions that allowed the military and politicians to proceed with their strategy and tactics. There could have been no American involvement, let alone success, in South Vietnam without the combined efforts of the air assets of U.S. Armed Forces. Government troops in Laos and Cambodia would never have survived as long as they did against the North Vietnamese and the insurgency movements without American aircraft and their personnel, nor would South Vietnam have experienced a government not under colonial or Communist rule. The U.S. and allied aircraft flew the missions assigned and fought the war presented to them. The number of sorties that successfully completed their missions is staggering, and there is no doubt that advances in technology and tactics developed at a rapid rate during the war, although this is often the case in modern warfare.

Was the air war a failure? Yes. American air campaigns failed to convince the North Vietnamese that their intervention in South Vietnam would risk the destruction of their infrastructure. Few in American circles believed that the North Vietnamese could withstand such an assault, although this number grew as the war progressed. Air power in South Vietnam, Laos, and Cambodia multiplied the firepower of the ground troops but did not determine the military and political course of the war. It is true that the air campaigns against North Vietnam prior to 1972 were restricted, but an analysis of the bomb damage assessments confirms that nearly all targeted objectives were destroyed—many to be rebuilt faster than the United States had anticipated.

This campaign was doomed from the start because Washington officials failed to appreciate the perspective of North Vietnam. In a country that had suffered exploitation and destruction during 100 years of French rule, the bombings did not deter its people's focus—they only strengthened it. The 1972 LINEBACKER II campaign is often presented as the exception to the rule. As the argument goes, with the use of unrestricted air power (this book shows there were still restrictions), the United States was able to achieve its objective of forcing the North Vietnamese to the peace table. The argument continues that if ROLLING THUNDER had been like the LINEBACKER campaigns, the North Vietnamese would have been forced to capitulate.

As discussed in chapter 6, the NVA's Eastertide Offensive was a modern campaign vulnerable to air power. While it is true that North Vietnam suffered tremendous losses as a result of U.S. and allied air power, the December 1972 decision to sign the peace accords in January 1973 favored the North Vietnamese. While LINEBACKER II did bring about the peace negotiations, it was a move favored by the North Vietnamese, who took advantage of the American withdrawal to rebuild their forces and conquer South Vietnam. LINEBACKER II achieved military success, but the political future had already been determined. The air campaigns in Laos and Cambodia gave the armed forces of those countries the upper hand over their adversaries, but they did not guarantee victory. Air power, alone, was not enough.

These observations will not change the minds of those die-hards on either side of this "argument without end"—a phrase coined by former Secretary of Defense Robert McNamara.* The Vietnam War was a war of perspective, and the study of the war and other conflicts in Southeast Asia should follow this model. There is no right answer to any of its aspects and most certainly to the air war, whose legacy continues to divide veterans,

*Robert S. McNamara et al., *Argument without End: In Search of Answers to the Vietnam Tragedy* (New York: Public Affairs, 1999).

scholars, and politicians. In examining the air war, this work takes on an American perspective but widens that perspective to include all aspects of the war.

The legacy of the air war over Southeast Asia is equally as interesting as the debate surrounding the employment of air power during the conflict. The lessons learned and the technological breakthroughs as a result of the American experience in Vietnam, Laos, and Cambodia are stunning. The technological gains have vaulted the United States to unchallenged supremacy of the skies. During the major engagements since the Vietnam War, such as the Persian Gulf, Americans controlled the air space over Iraq and Kuwait from the first day by using advanced technology and military tactics with restrictions different from those during the Vietnam War. For critics who point to the Persian Gulf War of 1991 as an example of how the Vietnam air war should have been fought, there should be a cautious reminder that the two wars have very few similarities. Stealth technology allowed the U.S. aircraft to launch preemptive strikes against Iraqi AAA and SAM sites around the capital of Baghdad that were as formidable as those around Hanoi in 1967. Other aircraft, such as the F-15 Eagle and F-16 Fighting Falcon, provided the firepower once reserved for the F-4 and F-105, although these planes were also equipped with precision missiles and bombs.

The advances in technology led to a major lesson learned: for air power to be effective, it had to be accurate. The old laser-guided bombs of the Vietnam War were improved to the point where the pilot could place his weapon exactly over the target with minimal danger to the aircraft and its crew. These weapons, developed in the Vietnam War, allowed the United States to inflict a maximum amount of damage with a minimum amount of ordnance and risk to nonmilitary targets. The lack of collateral damage—it did exist during the Persian Gulf War but nowhere near the level of Vietnam—allowed President George H. W. Bush to authorize his generals to identify and strike targets of opportunity that were the foundation of Saddam Hussein's war machine. While the political concern for civilian casualties existed in Iraq, President Bush did not have to anguish over the air campaign to the extent that President Johnson had done during ROLLING THUNDER. Additionally, there was no China on the Iraqis' northern border ready to come to their aid.

After the first phase of the air war in the Persian Gulf was complete, U.S. air power focused on the Iraqi military. Modern aircraft including the A-10 Warthog, the next generation of the A-1, combined with Vietnam-era aircraft, most notably the B-52 bomber, were able to inflict such damage on the Iraqi military that American troops faced little opposition when the ground war commenced. In Vietnam, pictures of bomb damage required multiple 40-foot containers to relay photographic reconnaissance to the United States, while the Gulf War was the first real-time conflict. Scanners, satellites, and other wireless communication provided timely intelligence and immediate access to information over the battlefield and throughout the United States. The advance of technology, stemming from the Vietnam War, is one of the most positive legacies for the military in the postwar period.

Another notion tested in Vietnam was the need for more than air power to decide the conflict. While air power was significant in the outcome, it was not the only factor to defeat the enemy. Committing the American and allied armed forces to a mutual goal yielded better results in Iraq than in Southeast Asia. Air power in Iraq destroyed the enemy instead of acting as a political tool to bring an end to the war. This recognition of how and when to use American aircraft in combat, based upon the Vietnam experience, was one of the greatest legacies of the lessons learned.

During the 2003 Iraqi war, American air power once again reasserted itself with impressive results. Stealth technology and cruise missiles disabled most of Iraq's air defense system while guided munitions resulted in the most accurate bombing in modern warfare. The military and political results were outstanding. The Iraqi armed forces had no response to allied air power and were unable to halt the momentum of the ground invasion. International criticism of the air campaign failed to sustain their assault as few munitions strayed from the careful paths chosen to minimize civilian deaths and damage. President George W. Bush, like his father, followed the advice of his military leaders to once again learn one of the valuable lessons of the Vietnam War.

Lessons learned are more effective when the conflicts share similar characteristics. The U.S. Armed Forces have yet to experience another war like the one in Southeast Asia and, with luck, may never again. In the years that followed Vietnam, the United States employed its air power in a limited role, except during the Persian Gulf War where the air war was quite different. In the opening years of the new millennium, the Armed Forces again find themselves faced with a military and political situation in Iraq, after having successfully flexed their air-power muscle in Afghanistan. In this confrontation, with technology and air assets so different from the 1960s, the skies over Southeast Asia have taught us that no two wars are the same. Military strategy and tactics should be determined by the present situation and available technology. The air war over Southeast Asia was a massive undertaking, which experienced both success and failure. Its legacy is a part of the larger Vietnam War legacy—one in which acrimony and disagreement continue to dominate the debate.

Bibliographical Essay

The war over Vietnam has remained a controversial topic for those military and political leaders directly involved in the air campaigns, as well as for military and Vietnam War scholars who have tried to measure the impact and effect of these campaigns against the North Vietnamese and Viet Cong. In the aftermath of the fall of the RVN, many involved in the air war tried to reconcile their parts in it with the failure of the United States to keep South Vietnam free from Communist domination.

For those whose background requires some general overviews of the wars in Southeast Asia, there are a few good starting points. Ronald B. Frankum Jr. and Stephen F. Maxner, *The Vietnam War for Dummies* (New York: Wiley, 2002), serves as a solid reference without too much analytical review, while Spencer C. Tucker, ed., *The Encyclopedia of the Vietnam War: A Political, Social, and Military History* (New York: Oxford University Press, 1998), provides a hands-on reference to the many layers of the war. David A. Anderson, *Columbia Guide to the Vietnam War* (New York: Columbia University Press, 2002), is also very useful and presents a good introduction to the war. George Herring's *America's Longest War: The United States and Vietnam, 1950–1975* (New York: McGraw-Hill, 1979, 2002) offers an easy-to-read overview. In the debates that followed the final collapse of South Vietnam, the air war over Southeast Asia has become a focal point for discussion, debate, and incrimination, as the quantity and quality of books and resources indicate.

The Air Force Historical Research Agency at Maxwell Air Force Base has made available a number of reports on the air war in Southeast Asia. The Contemporary Historical Examination of Current Operation Reports of Southeast Asia, 1961–1975, better known as the CHECO Reports, covers all aspects of the air war. Project CHECO began in 1962 with the goal of collecting and analyzing data on the U.S. air war in Southeast Asia. The CHECO Reports were designed to provide current analyses of the major components of the air campaigns in an effort to use contemporary lessons learned during the war. The declassification of the CHECO Reports gave scholars access to a rich source for USAF analyses of the air campaigns. When supplemented with the air war's secondary literature, the CHECO Reports are an incredibly rich resource for understanding the air war. Among the several hundred CHECO Reports available, those interested in the air war over Southeast Asia should begin with the series that chronicles the American effort from 1965 to 1969. Included in these studies are Wesley R. C. Melyan, "The War in Vietnam— 1965—Semi-Annual Report" (January 25, 1967); Wesley R. C. Melyan and Lee Bonetti, "The War in Vietnam—1966" (October 23, 1967); Lee Bonetti, "The War in Vietnam—January–June 1967—Semi-Annual Report"(April 29, 1968); Lee Bonetti et al., "The War in Vietnam— July–December 1967—Semi-Annual Report" (November 29, 1968); and Kenneth Sams et al., "The Air War in Vietnam—1968–1969" (April 1, 1970). These CHECO Reports examine all aspects of the air war and reference U.S. air campaigns in Laos and Cambodia.

How were the North Vietnamese able to overcome the series of air campaigns against the North that should have destroyed the country? One theory emerged that the failure of the air war in North Vietnam was not a failure of the military—USAF, Army, and USN air assets—but rather, it was a result of an overzealous civilian and political sector that hampered the ability of those involved to exert maximum force. While Operation ROLLING THUNDER (March 2, 1965–October 31, 1968) is seen as the prime example of this failed policy that allowed civilians to overmanage the air war, proponents of this theory point to Operation LINEBACKER I (May 10, 1972–October 23, 1972) and Operation LINEBACKER II (December 18, 1972–December 29, 1972) as examples of what the Air Force could have done had it not been restrained by the civilians and politicians.

This school of thought, which originated within military circles, was articulated by Admiral Ulysses S. G. Sharp in *Strategy for Defeat: Vietnam in Retrospect* (Novato, CA: Presidio Press, 1978, 1998). In this work, Admiral Sharp argues that the Johnson administration, rather than allowing the Air Force to destroy the industrial, economic, and political infrastructure of North Vietnam, used Operation ROLLING THUNDER to persuade the North Vietnamese to cease their support of the war by taking the conflict directly to the North. American politicians, and Lyndon Johnson specifically, believed that the DRV would falter at the prospect of a prolonged air war and lose its will to resist. As W. Hays Parks argued in "Rolling Thunder and the Law of War," *Air University Review* 33(2) (1982), the American air operations over the North were designed as a diplomatic "slow squeeze" signaling device rather than a coordinated air campaign, as in World War II, that would destroy the enemy's ability to wage war and break their will to resist. Others would follow Sharp and Parks in questioning the role of the civilians and politicians who were attempting to run a military campaign.

James Clay Thompson, *Rolling Thunder: Understanding Policy and Program Failure* (Chapel Hill: University of North Carolina Press, 1980), and Zalin Grant, *Over the Beach: The Air War in Vietnam* (New York: W. W. Norton, 1986), both provide evidence to support the notion that the U.S. military had its hands tied in the air war, causing its failure. Thompson, who served as an intelligence analyst during the Johnson administration and staff member for the Office of the Assistant Secretary of Defense, International Security Affairs, analyzes the role of the U.S. government in running the air war and how foreign policy concerns overrode military necessity. Grant served both in the military and as a journalist for *Time* and *The New Republic* in Vietnam. While his book focuses on the history of a squadron of F-8 Navy pilots from the USS *Oriskany*, he reiterates the frustration perceived by those who participated in the air war when missions designed by military strategists were amended by civilians to further political aims. John Schlight, *The War in South Vietnam: The Years of the Offensive, 1965–1968* (Washington, DC: Office of Air Force History, USAF, 1988), reinforces the notion that civilian and political considerations shaped the way the war was fought in Vietnam, although he also examines the internal debate in the Air Force and its negative effect on the conduct of the air war. Schlight argues that instead of driving Air Force tactics during the war, strategy and internal policy were governed by them, which resulted in dangerous situations and failure.

At the approach of the 1990s a response to the idea that civilian and political leaders hamstrung the military emerged, as scholars reevaluated the strategic thinking of the military and expanded the debate to include America's former enemy. Mark Clodfelter, *The Limits of Air Power: The American Bombing of North Vietnam* (New York: Free Press, 1989), examines the three major air campaigns against North Vietnam and effectively argues that Air Force strategy—undertaking a strategic bombing campaign similar to the one conducted during World War II—did not match the wartime realities of Vietnam. Clodfelter was not the first to argue this point. J. William Gibson, *The Perfect War: Technowar in Vietnam* (New York: Vintage Press, 1986), argues along similar lines; his study helped to shape the debate over the next decade.

Clodfelter, moreover, maintains that the first air war over North Vietnam—Operation ROLLING THUNDER—did not have the capability, despite the tonnage of bombs dropped, to stop the North Vietnamese supply lines to the insurgents in the South. Thus, the outcome was less a failure of Johnson's and his advisers' management of the air war than it was related to the nature of the guerrilla war conducted by the North Vietnamese and Viet Cong. Clodfelter argues that with the use of air power as a primary weapon in the war, there was never a chance for a lasting victory for the United States. He also states that the success of Operations LINEBACKER I and LINEBACKER II resulted not because President Richard Nixon unleashed the Air Force over North Vietnam but because the North Vietnamese change in strategy and tactics—more like a traditional World War II offensive—left their forces in the open and vulnerable to American air power. In examining the bombing of the Ho Chi Minh Trail, John F. Guilmartin Jr., "Bombing the Ho Chi Minh Trail: A Preliminary Analysis of the Effects of Air Interdiction," *Air Power History* 38:4 (1991), argues that the campaign was a tactical success in that it drew considerable resources from the North Vietnamese to maintain the flow of personnel and equipment down the Trail. The campaign, however, was not decisive. The flow of supplies necessary for the North Vietnamese and Viet Cong forces to operate was sustained throughout the war.

Earl H. Tilford Jr., *Crosswinds: The Air Force's Setup in Vietnam* (College Station: Texas A&M University Press, 1991, 1993), argues that the primary cause of failure in the air war over Vietnam was an ill-suited Air Force doctrine that relied on the concept of strategic bombing regardless of the type of conflict. Tilford suggests that Air Force officials did not have the intellectual capacity to formulate an air campaign suited to the situation in Vietnam because they relied on the strategy successfully employed in World War II and sufficiently employed during the Korean War. He also maintains that those within the Air Force establishment became entranced with quantifying the air war (missions flown, items destroyed, bombing tonnage), just as Secretary of Defense Robert McNamara quantified the ground war, to measure success in statistics. This line of reasoning received support from a number of scholars, including Larry Cable, *Unholy Grail: The U.S. and the Wars in Vietnam, 1965–1968* (London: Routledge, 1991), and Jon M. Van Dyke in a very early study, *North Vietnam's Strategy for Survival* (Palo Alto, CA: Pacific Books, 1972).

While Tilford revises the notion that civilian and political leaders were to blame for the Air Force failures, he holds to the concept that the Air Force had the capability to destroy North Vietnam even though wartime realities eliminated the possibility. Operation LINEBACKER II was a success but not because it "brought Hanoi to its knees." Tilford sees it as a return to the strategic bombing campaigns of World War II and cites its psychological impact on the North Vietnamese government. The operation managed to destroy North Vietnam's air defense system and compelled the North Vietnamese to return to the peace table for meaningful negotiations. This assessment is slightly different from Clodfelter's, who saw the success of the LINEBACKER operations not in their approach but rather as a result of changed North Vietnamese strategy and tactics.

The debate about the air war over the North continues among historians, although recent scholarship has not concentrated on the air campaigns over North Vietnam. Ser Hwee Quek, *Before Tet: American Bombing and Attempts at Negotiation with North Vietnam, 1964–1968* (Ph.D. diss., University of Washington, 1995); Marshall Michel, *Clashes: Air Combat over North Vietnam, 1965–1972* (Annapolis, MD: Naval Institute Press, 1997); John T. Smith, *The Linebacker Raids: The Bombing of North Vietnam, 1972* (London: Arms and Armour, 1998); Dennis M. Drew, *Rolling Thunder, 1965: Anatomy of a Failure* (Maxwell Air Force Base, AL: Air University Press, 1998); and Wayne Thompson, *To Hanoi and Back: The United States Air Force and North Vietnam, 1966–1973* (Washington, DC: Smithsonian Institution Press, 2000), have all weighed in to the debate surrounding the question of civilian versus military control of the air campaign over North Vietnam and assessing who is to blame for the air war failures. The bombing campaign over North Vietnam accounted for a small percentage of the sorties flown by the USAF, USN, USMC, and Army. It is estimated that Operation ROLLING THUNDER flew nearly 307,000 sorties over North Vietnam and dropped 643,000 tons of bombs while Operations LINEBACKER I and LINEBACKER II account for an additional 48,000 tons. Still, almost 75 percent of the sorties flown in the Southeast Asian theater over South Vietnam were in support of ground troops, on interdiction raids, on search-and-rescue, and on other operations. Fifteen percent flew over Laos and 3 percent over Cambodia.

Several CHECO Reports provide valuable information on the role of the USAF and USN during ROLLING THUNDER and LINEBACKER. These reports supply chronological details that are not always evident in the secondary works. For Operation ROLLING THUNDER, the CHECO Reports of value include "ROLLING THUNDER—March–June 1965—Continuing Report," prepared by SEA CHECO Team (March 28, 1966); Wesley R. C. Melyan and Lee Bonetti, "ROLLING THUNDER—July 1965–December 1966—Continuing Report" (July 15, 1967); James B. Overton, "ROLLING THUNDER—January 1967–November 1968—Continuing Report" (October 1, 1969); and Robert Leo Vining, "ROLLING THUNDER—17 November 1968" (November 17, 1968). When North Vietnam invaded South

Vietnam in 1972, it offered the United States another chance to employ air power against the NVA. The CHECO Reports for the 1972 invasion are divided into two categories—the air campaign over North Vietnam under Operation LINEBACKER and the air campaign over South Vietnam to repel the invasion.

One report, Charles A. Nicholson, "The USAF Response to the Spring 1972 NVN Offensive: Situation and Redeployment—March–July 1972—Special Report" (October 10, 1972), discusses the initial U.S. reaction to the invasion. Two CHECO Reports that deal with the northern air campaigns essentially divide the two LINEBACKER operations: Melvin F. Porter, "LINEBACKER: Overview of the First 120 Days" (September 27, 1973), and Calvin R. Johnson, "LINEBACKER Operations—September–December 1972" (December 31, 1978). Reports on the air response to the invasion are divided by region into I, II, and III CTZ: David K. Mann, "The 1972 Invasion of Military Region I: Fall of Quang Tri and Defense of Hue" (March 15, 1973); Peter A. W. Liebchen, "Kontum: Battle for the Central Highlands—March 30–June 10, 1972—Special Report" (October 27, 1972); and Paul T. Ringenbach and Peter J. Melly, "The Battle for An Loc—5 April–26 June 1972" (January 31, 1973). While these CHECO Reports do not provide the intense analyses found in postwar scholarship, they are important to an understanding of the status, role, and achievements of U.S. air assets in their most challenging battle of the war.

The secret air war over Laos has received attention in recent years with the publication of Perry L. Lamy, *Barrel Roll, 1968–1973: An Air Campaign in Support of National Policy* (Maxwell Air Force Base, AL: Air University Press, 1996); Timothy N. Castle, *One Day Too Long: Top Secret Site 85 and the Bombing of North Vietnam* (New York: Columbia University Press, 1999); John Prados, *The Blood Road: The Ho Chi Minh Trail and the Vietnam War* (New York: Wiley, 1999); Jacob van Staaveren, *Interdiction in Southern Laos, 1960–1968* (Washington, DC: Center for Air Force History, 1993); and Jan Churchill, *Classified Secret: Controlling Airstrikes in the Clandestine War in Laos* (Manhattan, KS: Sunflower University Press, 2000). This phase of the campaign brought with it much controversy during the war when its true nature was revealed, and it remains controversial not only in substance but also in method. The CHECO Reports are very valuable to an understanding of the air campaigns over Laos. These reports, as with others in the series, are designed to serve as lessons learned and to offer a unique perspective of the wartime analysis of air campaigns. John C. Pratt, "The Royal Laotian Air Force—1954–1970—Special Report" (September 15, 1970), and Peter A. W. Liebchen, "MAP Aid to Laos—1959–1972" (June 25, 1973), provide overviews of the development of the RLAF and American assistance to its growth. Kenneth Sams, John C. Pratt, C. William Thorndale, and James T. Bear examine the start of the air war in 1968 in "Air Support of Counterinsur-gency in Laos—July 1968–November 1969—Special Report" (November 10, 1969).

For those interested in the BARREL ROLL campaign, the reports by Kenneth Sams, John C. Pratt, and John Schlight, "Air Operations in Northern Laos—1 November 1969–1 April 1970" (May 5, 1970); Harry D. Blout, "Air Operations in Northern Laos—1 April–1 November 1970—Continuing Report" (January 15, 1971); Harry D. Blout and Melvin F. Porter, "Air Operations in Northern Laos—1 November 1970–1 April 1971—Continuing Report" (May 3, 1971); and Richard R. Sexton and William W. Lofgren Jr., "Air Operations in Northern Laos—1 April–30 November 1971" (June 22, 1973), provide a detailed account of the operation and the stalemate that ensued. The Lam Son 719 operation and the events leading up to the South Vietnamese invasion into Laos under U.S. air protection are covered by Lucius D. Clay Jr., "USAF Operations in Laos, 1 January 1970–30 June 1971" (May 31, 1972), and J. F. Loye Jr., Leo J. Johnson, G. K. St. Clair, and John W. Dennison, "Lam Son 719—30 January–24 March 1971—The South Vietnamese Incursion into Laos" (March 24, 1971). While there is some discussion of the failure of the Lam Son 719 operation, the most informative section of these reports is the analysis of ARVN failure and its rescue by U.S. air power. Warren A. Trest, "LUCKY TIGER: Combat Operations" (June 15, 1967), and Melvin F. Porter, "TIGER HOUND—Continuing Report" (September 6, 1966), are two interesting reports on some of the other operations that affected Laos during the war.

There has been very little written on the air war over Cambodia. If the Laotian campaign is the "secret" war, then the Cambodian campaign is the forgotten war. Four CHECO Reports chronicle the air campaigns over Cambodia and are worth examining for those interested in learning more about that facet of the war: David I. Folkman Jr. and Philip D. Caine, "The Cambodian Campaign—April 29–June 30, 1970—Special Report" (September 1, 1970), discusses the U.S. incursion into Cambodia in May 1970 and supplies some background to this military move; Philip D. Caine and J. F. Loye Jr., "The Cambodian Campaign—1 July–31 October 1970—Special Report" (December 31, 1970); Charles A. Nicholson, "Khmer Air Operations—November 1970–November 1971" (June 15, 1972); and Paul W. Elder, "Air Operations in the Khmer Republic—1 December

1971–15 August 1973" (April 15, 1974), examine the role of the United States and its allies over Cambodia until the end of the conflict by congressional decree on August 15, 1973. A recent book by Richard Wood, *Call Sign Rustic: The Secret Air War over Cambodia, 1970–1973* (Washington, DC: Smithsonian Institution Press, 2002), examines the role of forward air controllers in Cambodia and is a fine addition to the literature of the Cambodian campaigns. There are two available Congressional Reports on hearings conducted as a result of the Cambodian air campaigns: *Bombing in Cambodia* (Washington, DC: Government Printing Office), which chronicles the hearings before the Senate Armed Services Committee on July 16–August 9, 1973, and *Statement of Information*, Book XI, *Bombing of Cambodia* (Washington, DC: Government Printing Office), which chronicles the hearings before the House Judiciary Committee in 1974. Both are informative and supplement the CHECO Reports.

ARC LIGHT missions and the role of the B-52 are examined extensively in the CHECO Reports. There are four CHECO Reports that detail B-52 strikes: Kenneth Sams, "ARC LIGHT B-52 Strikes, June–December 1965" (October 9, 1966); Wesley R. C. Melyan, "ARC LIGHT, 1965–1966—Continuing Report" (September 15, 1967); "ARC LIGHT, January–June 1967—Continuing Report" (March 22, 1968); and James B. Pralle, "ARC LIGHT, June 1967–December 1968—Continuing Report, Volume 1" (August 15, 1969). A good overview of SAC operations, from which the ARC LIGHT missions originated, is in CHECO Report, Warren A. Trest, "USAF SAC Operations in Support of SEAsia—Special Report" (December 17, 1969).

The evolution of airmobility and the rise of the helicopter played a significant role in American military strategy and tactics. The CHECO Reports by Robert Leo Vining, "Air Operations in the Delta—1962–1967—Special Report—Volume 1" (December 8, 1967); Bernell A. Whitaker and L. E. Paterson, "Assault Airlift Operations—January 1961–June 1966—Continuing Report" (February 23, 1967); Ernie S. Montagliani, "Army Aviation in RVN—A Case Study—11 July 1970—Special Report" (July 11, 1970), provide a good foundation from which to begin studying the role of air assault. The history of the Air Cavalry in Vietnam is represented in Lawrence H. Johnson III, *Winged Sabres: The Air Cavalry in Vietnam* (Harrisburg, PA: Stackpole Books, 1990), and Shelby L. Stanton, *Anatomy of a Division: The 1st Cavalry in Vietnam* (Novato, CA: Presidio Press, 1987).

A number of first-person accounts deal with helicopter and airmobility, including Chuck Carlock, *Firebirds: The Best First-person Account of Helicopter Combat in Vietnam Ever Written* (New York: Bantam Books,

1995, 1997); Matthew Brennan, *Brennan's War: Vietnam, 1965-1969* (Novato, CA: Presidio Press, 1985); James L. Estep, *Comanche Six: Company Commander, Vietnam* (Novato, CA: Presidio Press, 1991); Colonel Kenneth D. Mertel, *Year of the Horse—Vietnam* (New York: Bantam Books, 1990); and Dominick Yezzo, *A G.I.'s Vietnam Diary, 1968-1969* (New York: Franklin Watts, 1974). The first major U.S. air assault in the Ia Drang Valley in November 1965 has garnered some attention. Lieutenant General Harold G. Moore and Joseph L. Galloway, *We Were Soldiers Once . . . and Young: Ia Drang—The Battle that Changed the War in Vietnam* (New York: Random House, 1992), is a good starting point; Colonel Moore commanded the 1st Battalion, 7th Regiment Cavalry in the battle. J. D. Coleman, *Pleiku: The Dawn of Helicopter Warfare in Vietnam* (New York: St. Martin's Press, 1988), gives another perspective on the airmobility operation.

Several subcategories of the air war, such as intervention, tactical airlift, and SAR, have received limited coverage. C. William Thorndale authored two CHECO Reports on interdiction, "Interdiction in SEA—November 1966–October 1968—Continuing Report" (June 30, 1969), and "Interdiction in Route Package One—1968—Special Report" (June 30, 1969), that discuss the importance of stopping the flow of personnel and supplies from North to South Vietnam. The CHECO Report on tactical airlift, Ronald D. Merrell, "Tactical Airlift in Southeast Asia, 1969–November 1971—Continuing Report" (February 15, 1972), addresses aerial supply in Southeast Asia. Ray L. Bowers, *Tactical Airlift* (Washington, DC: Office of Air Force History, USAF, 1983), is an extensive study on tactical airlift, and David K. Vaughan, *Runway Visions: An American C-130 Pilot's Memoir of Combat Airlift Operations in Southeast Asia, 1967-1968* (Jefferson, NC: McFarland, 1998), offers a firsthand account of air transportation during the war.

Three CHECO Reports chronicle the reconnaissance effort in Southeast Asia. Mark E. Smith, "USAF Reconnaissance in Southeast Asia—1961–1966—Continuing Report" (October 25, 1966); Edward P. Brynn, "Reconnaissance in SEAsia—July 1966–June 1969—Continuing Report" (July 15, 1969); and Robert F. Colwell, "USAF Tactical Reconnaissance in Southeast Asia—July 1969–June 1971" (November 23, 1971), examine how American air assets gathered intelligence in the DRV on the NVA and Viet Cong and on the location of an elusive enemy. Other CHECO Reports, such as two by C. William Thorndale, "Visual Reconnaissance in I Corps—January–August 1968—Special Report" (September 30, 1968), and "Tactical Recon Photography Request/Distribution—

1966–1968—Special Report" (February 15, 1969), discuss the various techniques used to gather information and ensure its dissemination to the appropriate military officials. There are a few firsthand accounts of reconnaissance pilots, including Taylor Eubank, *Alone, Unarmed, and Unafraid: Tales of Reconnaissance in Vietnam* (Jefferson, NC: McFarland, 1992). An interesting account of reconnaissance drones is William Wagner, *Lightning Bugs and Other Reconnaissance Drones* (Fallbrook, CA: Armed Forces Journal International and Aero Publishers, 1982).

Search-and-rescue played a significant psychological role as well as an important asset preservation role in the air war. SAR operations saved a number of American and allied pilots and crews who had been shot down. Six CHECO Reports chronicle SAR operations: B. Conn Anderson, "USAF Search and Rescue (SAR) in Southeast Asia, 1961–1966—Continuing Report" (October 24, 1966); Richard A. Durkee, "USAF Search and Rescue (SAR) in SEA—July 1966–November 1967—Continuing Report" (January 1968); James B. Overton, "USAF Search and Rescue (SAR) in SEA—November 1967–June 1969—Continuing Report" (July 30, 1969); Walter F. Lynch, "USAF Search and Rescue (SAR) in SEA—1 July 1969–31 December 1970—Continuing Report" (April 23, 1971); Leroy W. Lowe, "Search and Rescue Operations in SEA—January 1971–March 1972—Continuing Report" (October 17, 1972); and David G. Francis and David R. Nelson, "Search and Rescue OPS in SEA—1 April 1972–30 June 1973" (November 27, 1974). A good overview of SAR operations is Earl H. Tilford Jr., *Search and Rescue in Southeast Asia* (Washington, DC: Center for Air Force History, 1992). George J. Marrett, *Skyraiders Low and Slow: Combat Rescues in Laos and Vietnam* (Washington, DC: Smithsonian Institution Press, 2002), offers a unique look at the A-1 Skyraider and the preference for its use as combat support aircraft for SAR operations. Firsthand accounts of medical evacuations, or Dustoffs, have contributed to the literature. Two works of note are John L. Cook, *Rescue under Fire: The Story of Dust Off in Vietnam* (West Chester, PA: Schiffer, 1998), and Michael J. Novosel, *Dustoff: The Memoir of an Army Aviator* (Novato, CA: Presidio Press, 1999).

While defoliation operations and the effects of Agent Orange have caused a tremendous amount of postwar controversy, the air campaign that sprayed the defoliants has received little attention. There are two CHECO Reports on RANCH HAND: Charles V. Collins, "Herbicide Operations in Southeast Asia—July 1961–June 1967—Special Report—Volume 1" (October 11, 1967), and James R. Clary, "RANCH HAND: Herbicide Operations in Southeast Asia—1967–1971" (July 13, 1971). The official

USAF monograph by William A. Buckingham Jr., *Operation Ranch Hand: The Air Force and Herbicides in Southeast Asia, 1961–1971* (Washington, DC: Office of Air Force History, USAF, 1982), offers a reasonably objective analysis of defoliant spraying; and Paul Cecil, *Herbicidal Warfare: The* RANCH HAND *Project in Vietnam* (Westport, CT: Praeger, 1986), provides a perspective from one of the RANCH HAND participants who supported the role of the UC-123 and the spraying missions. Two CHECO Reports discuss the ever-present issues and challenges of the command-and-control structure: Kenneth Sams, "Command and Control—1965—Continuing Report" (December 15, 1966), and Robert M. Burch, "Command and Control—1966–1968—Continuing Report" (August 1, 1969), show the difficulties of organization as the air war expanded to meet the escalation of the ground war. An often-mentioned but under-examined aspect of the air war was topography and climate. The CHECO Report by Louis Seig, "Impact of Geography on Air Operations in SEA—Special Report" (June 11, 1970), supports the notion that weather was one of the greatest adversaries of the Americans during the air war.

Thousands of books have been published on the Vietnam War and the conflicts in Laos and Cambodia, and more scholars and veterans are focusing on specific air campaigns or individual air missions. The result is a tremendous amount of literature with many conflicting ideas and notions. Further examination of specific air campaigns and missions is needed. As the literature on the air war in Southeast Asia continues to grow, a greater understanding of its successes and failures as well as its challenges and triumphs is sure to follow.

Appendix
Aircraft Flown in Southeast Asia

A-1   The A-1 Skyraider, built by Douglas, was a modified version of the AD-6 Skyraider. It was renowned in Southeast Asia for its ability to loiter over a target area for a considerable time. It carried four 20-mm cannons, but its armament also could include rockets, CBUs, bombs, mines, grenades, flares, and smoke depending upon the mission. The Skyraider flew all types of missions but was most noted for its work in SAR and its ability to sustain damage and continue to fly. It was also the principal aircraft of the VNAF.

A-4   The A-4 Skyhawk, built by McDonnell Douglas, was used as a short-range attack fighter during the war. The aircraft carried two internally mounted 20-mm cannons and a payload of 2,040 pounds of ordnance. The USMC used the aircraft in a number of operations including ground support, target bombing, and escort.

A-6   The A-6 Intruder, built by Grumman, was an all-weather medium attack aircraft with a crew of two. It had a maximum speed of 648 mph and carried a wide assortment of ordnance. During the war, it also was modified for reconnaissance and electronic warfare.

A-37   The A-37 Dragonfly, built by Cessna, was a light attack aircraft that was also used for armed reconnaissance. It could carry up to 3,000 pounds of bombs and had a 7.62 mini-gun and the option for additional guns, rocket pods, or CBUs. It had a crew of one.

AC-47   The AC-47 Spooky, built by Douglas, served as a gunship during the war. It had three 7.62 mini-guns that could fire as fast as 6,000 rounds per minute. It was also used as a flare ship to light up the night sky over besieged villages and fire support bases. It had a crew of seven.

AC-130   The AC-130 Spectre, built by Lockheed, was based on the
          C-130 Hercules with armament modifications, including two
          7.62 mini-guns, two 20-mm and two 40-mm cannons, and one
          105-mm cannon. The gunship, along with the AC-47 and AC-
          119, was one of the most effective against NVA/Viet Cong ve-
          hicles and exposed troops. It had a crew of up to fourteen.

AH-1   The AH-1 Cobra, built by Bell, was an attack helicopter used
          in close combat support and against armored vehicles. It had
          one 7.62 mini-gun capable of firing between 2,000 and 4,000
          rounds per minute and a 40-mm grenade launcher. Its primary
          weapons were the 26-round rocket pods on either side of its
          stubbed wings. The Cobra was also equipped from time to time
          with a 20-mm cannon. It had a crew of two.

B-26   The B-26 Invader, built by Martin, served in Southeast Asia
          early in the air war as both a bomber and armed reconnais-
          sance aircraft. It carried .50 caliber machine guns and up to
          11,000 pounds of bombs.

B-52   The B-52 Stratofortress, built by Boeing, was the primary
          heavy bomber of the USAF. It could carry up to 70,000 pounds
          of ordnance, including all the types in the U.S. arsenal, and had
          an unlimited range because of its ability to be refueled aerially
          by the KC-135. The B-52 was the one aircraft that struck fear
          in the Vietnamese people as it could deploy its ordnance from
          such a high altitude that it could not be seen. Typically, it had
          a crew of five.

B-57   The B-57 Canberra, built by Martin and originally designed in
          England, was primarily a bomber. It had a large bombing ca-
          pacity and could stay over its target for a long period of time.
          The B-57 was also used to destroy DRV air defense weapons
          and to perform reconnaissance during the war.

B-66   The EB-66 Destroyer, built by Douglas, provided ELINT and
          ECM aircraft for bombing sorties over North Vietnam. The
          RB-66 also conducted reconnaissance missions. It had a crew
          of three.

C-7   The C-7 Caribou, built by DeHavilland, served as a light trans-
          port aircraft. The Caribou was able to take off and land on
          short runways, of which there were many in Vietnam. It could
          carry about 6,000 pounds of equipment and had a crew of
          three.

C-46   The C-46 Commando, built by Curtiss, served as a transport aircraft. This older plane saw service in Southeast Asia as part of the Air America fleet. The C-46 carried more than the C-47 Skytrain but was more difficult to maintain.

C-47   The C-47 Skytrain, nicknamed the Gooney Bird and built by Douglas, had diverse roles. Although primarily a transport, it doubled as a surveillance and electronics aircraft and was also modified as a gunship. It had a crew of six.

C-119   The C-119 Flying Boxcar, built by Fairchild, served as a transport during the war and was modified as a gunship (AC-119) with the capability of firing 6,000 rounds per minute from its 7.62 mini-guns.

C-123   The C-123 Provider, built by Fairchild, was initially designed as a short-range assault transport with the ability to take off and land on short runways. The C-123, designated the UC-123 in RANCH HAND operations, gained its fame in Southeast Asia as the primary aircraft for defoliation missions. It had a crew of either three or four.

C-124   The C-124 Globemaster, nicknamed Old Shakey and built by Douglas, provided airlift support for the United States in Southeast Asia. It could transport up to 200 soldiers or 125 medivac patients in its double-deck cabin. With a maximum range of 2,175 miles, it was suitable for the transpacific journey.

C-130   The C-130 Hercules, build by Lockheed, served primarily as a transport, although it had a number of different roles during the war, including electronic surveillance (EC-130) and control aircraft for SAR (HC-130). The C-130 carried a complement of five depending on the type of mission.

C-141   The C-141 Starlifter, built by Lockheed-Georgia, was a long-range troop and cargo transport. It had a maximum payload of 175,000 pounds and a range of 2,500 miles. The C-141 had a crew of six.

CH-21   The CH-21 Workhorse, built by Vertol, served as a SAR helicopter. It could carry up to twenty troops or eleven medivac patients. It had a crew of two.

CH-46   The CH-46 Seaknight was a medium-lift assault helicopter, built by Boeing and used by the USN and USMC to move troops. It had a load capacity of approximately 13,000 pounds and a crew of five.

CH-47   The CH-47 Chinook was a medium-lift helicopter, built by Boeing and used by the Army to move troops around the battlefield. With a load capacity of approximately 27,000 pounds, it had a crew of two.

CH-53   The CH-53 Sea Stallion was a heavy-lift helicopter, built by Sikorsky and used in SAR operations by the USN and USMC to move troops. It had a load capacity of approximately 36,000 pounds and a crew of two, with an additional number of crewmen depending on the type of mission.

CH-54   The CH-54 Skycrane was a heavy-lift crane helicopter, built by Sikorsky to move heavy equipment and for use in recovery efforts. It had a crew of three. It could carry a payload of 20,000 pounds and often replaced the CH-47 Chinook when payloads required it. The Skycrane also carried 10,000-pound cratering bombs.

DC-4   The DC-4 Skymaster, built by Douglas, was a 1930 transport aircraft used by Air America in Laos and Cambodia to perform such duties as airlift and psychological warfare. It was later modified into the C-54.

EC-121   The EC-121 Constellation, built by Lockheed, was a modified C-121 transport that conducted electronic surveillance and ELINT for American fighters engaged with MiGs over Southeast Asia. It could carry over 12,000 pounds of electronic equipment. The EC-121 also assisted in directing aerial refueling and SAR. The number of crew members depended on the type of mission.

F-4   The F-4 Phantom, built by McDonnell Douglas, was a much-used aircraft during the war. It was a durable and fast jet fighter that flew most types of missions over Southeast Asia, notably MiG Combat Air Patrol and Reconnaissance sorties. It could carry up to 16,000 pounds of ordnance, including rockets, missiles, and bombs in addition to 20-mm cannons. It had a crew of two.

F-5   The F-5 Freedom Fighter, built by Northrop and initially designated the T-38, served as a fighter. It provided the VNAF with a low-cost, fast option for their fleet. The F-5 could carry a maximum payload of 5,500 pounds and had two 20-mm guns for air combat.

F-100   The F-100 Super Sabre, built by North American, was the first supersonic fighter used by the Air Force. With a crew of one

| | and a cruising speed of 600 mph, it flew MiG Combat Air Patrol, Reconnaissance, and FAC missions. It had four 20-mm cannons and could carry forty-two 2.75-inch rockets or up to 5,000 pounds of munitions. |

F-101   The F-101 Voodoo, built by McDonnell and flown at a maximum speed of 1,000 mph, served as an Air Strike and Reconnaissance aircraft. It had four 20-mm cannons and could carry approximately 1,600 pounds and a crew of one.

F-102   The F-102 Delta Dagger, built by Convair, was used as an interceptor over North Vietnam. With a maximum speed of 810 mph it could outfly the MiGs but was less maneuverable than the modern MiGs. It carried twenty-four 2.75-inch rockets and six guided missiles. It had a crew of one.

F-105   The F-105 Thunderchief, built by Republic, was a fighter, interceptor, and bomber that conducted a majority of the air strikes over North Vietnam in the 1960s. It flew at over 2.2 Mach (approximately 1,500 mph) and was armed with one 20-mm cannon in addition to 14,000 pounds of ordnance. It had a crew of one.

F-111   The F-111, built by General Dynamics, had the unofficial nickname of Aardvark. It was designed as an all-weather, day-and-night fighter-bomber with built-in ECM. Essentially, it was designed to do everything the USAF needed in one aircraft. It was armed with a 20-mm cannon and a variety of bombs. The F-111, with its crew of two and maximum speed of 1,450 mph, saw the most action during the December 1972 air campaign.

HC-130   The HC-130 King, built by Lockheed, coordinated SAR operations between the helicopter and support aircraft and the downed pilot. The HC-130 carried a crew of seven, including two pilots, a navigator, a radio operator, two flight engineers, and a loadmaster. This four-engine, fixed-wing aircraft was equipped with High Frequency (HF), Very High Frequency (VHF), Ultra High Frequency (UHF), and Frequency Modulated (FM) radios in its role as mission control. The HC-130 was also equipped with search gear and served as the refueling tanker for the HH-53 helicopters.

HH-3   The HH-3, nicknamed the Jolly Green Giant and built by Sikorsky, served as a SAR helicopter. It had been designed initially as a medium assault helicopter and designated the CH-3. It could carry two .50-caliber machine guns as well as equipment needed for rescue and recovery operations. The USN used the SH-3, a version of the HH-3, for SAR missions in the Gulf of Tonkin and along the coast. The SH-3, with a crew of four, had a maximum speed of 100 knots and a radius of 250 nautical miles. It also had a 150-foot hoist cable.

HH-43   The HH-43 Pedro, built by Kamen, had been flown in Southeast Asia for most of the air war. It carried a crew of four, including either two pilots or two firefighters, one medical technician, and one crew chief. Daylight flying, under Visual Flight Rules, required only one pilot, although nighttime flight and Instrument Flight Rules required two. The HH-43 had a 217-foot jungle penetrator cable but, because it could not be aerially refueled, was limited in range. It had a top speed of 105 knots and was capable of achieving twenty knots backward and sideways. After the introduction of the HH-53, the HH-43 was used for combat rescue missions and backed up the Jolly Green Giants. These helicopters also provided crash fire suppression. Two versions of the HH-43 were employed in Southeast Asia: the B and F models, which had similar characteristics, except that the F model was equipped with armor to protect the crew and vital machinery and with more sophisticated communication systems.

HH-53   The HH-53 Buff or Super Jolly Green Giant, built by Sikorsky, carried a crew of five, including a pilot, copilot, flight engineer, and two pararescue personnel, and could hold up to forty passengers. It had an Automatic Flight Control System, a 240-foot jungle penetrator cable that could hoist 600 pounds, armor plating for the crew, and three 7.62 mini-guns. The HH-53 had a range of 290 nautical miles without aerial refueling and a top speed of 170 knots. It could move at thirty knots backward and thirty-five knots to either side.

JU-52   The JU-52, built by Junkers, was used by the German Luftwaffe during World War II as a bomber and was shaped like the C-47. The French deployed captured JU-52 during the First Indochina War (1945–1954) to fight the Viet Minh. It had four 7.9-mm machine guns.

KC-135   The KC-135 Stratotanker, build by Boeing, served as the primary aerial refueling aircraft. With a crew of four, it had a range of over 11,000 miles and could transfer up to 120,000 pounds of fuel.

MiG-15   The MiG-15 Fagot, built by Mikoyan-Gurevich, was in the North Vietnamese Air Force at the beginning of the war. It carried two 23-mm cannons and one 37-mm cannon in addition to rockets or 2,000 pounds of bombs. With a maximum speed of 670 mph and a range of 500 miles, it was not a great threat to U.S. fighters.

MiG-17   The MiG-17 Fresco, built by Mikoyan-Gurevich, was in the North Vietnamese Air Force during the war. It carried two 23-mm cannons and one 37-mm cannon in addition to sixteen rockets or 1,100 pounds of bombs. It had a maximum speed of 711 mph and a range of 510 miles, slightly better than the MiG-15 and with better maneuverability.

MiG-19   The MiG-19 Farmer, built by Mikoyan-Gurevich, was the first supersonic fighter in the North Vietnamese Air Force. It had three 30-mm cannons. With a maximum speed of 903 mph and a range of 1,243 miles, it was a formidable threat to the American bomber force over North Vietnam.

MiG-21   The MiG-21 Fishbed, built by Mikoyan-Gurevich, was the most advanced aircraft in the North Vietnamese Air Force. It had one 30-mm cannon and two air-to-air missiles. It had a maximum speed of 1,300 mph but only a 400-mile range.

O-1   The O-1 Bird Dog, built by Cessna, was an observation and FAC aircraft. It was originally designated the L-19. It carried no weapons, although it could deploy smoke to identify targets of opportunity for fighters and bombers. It had a crew of two.

O-2   The O-2 Skymaster, built by Cessna, was an observation and FAC aircraft. It had a unique tractor-pusher propeller that allowed it to sustain greater ground fire than the O-1. Four wing pylons carried rockets, flares, smoke, or 7.62 mini-gun pods. The O-2 also flew psychological warfare missions. It had a crew of two.

OH-6   The OH-6 Cayuse, built by Boeing, was a light observation helicopter used in "hunter-killer" teams with the AH-1 Cobra. The OH-6 would serve as bait for the NVA/Viet Cong who, after exposing their position, would become a target for the Cobra.

OV-1   The OV-1 Mohawk, built by North American, was the primary surveillance aircraft in Southeast Asia. There were three models, each with unique characteristics for gathering intelligence about the NVA/Viet Cong. The OV-1A had a KA-30 camera in its belly for vertical and angled photographs of the countryside as well as a KA-60 in its nose for 180-degree photographs of the area in front of the aircraft. The OV-1B was equipped with side-look airborne radar that mapped the terrain by means of pulses that bounced off objects on the ground and translated the data into photographic images. The OV-1C used infrared, or Red Haze, coverage to detect objects on the ground. The equipment registered temperature variations that transferred the data onto film in the aircraft. All of the techniques had unique advantages and were dependent on weather and other environmental conditions.

OV-10   The OV-10 Bronco, built by North American, was a twin-engine propeller-driven aircraft. It flew observation, escort, armed reconnaissance, and FAC sorties. It was armed with four 7.62-mm machine guns and up to 3,600 pounds of ordnance or gun pods. The OV-10 could carry up to 3,200 pounds of equipment, five troops, or two litters and a medic.

SR-71   The SR-71 Blackbird, built by Lockheed-Martin, served as a reconnaissance aircraft over North Vietnam. A long-range aircraft, it had the ability to refuel in midair as well as the advantage of high-altitude (85,000 feet) flight. The SR-71 was equipped with sophisticated instruments for intelligence gathering. It had a crew of two.

T-28   The T-28 Trojan, built by North American, was used primarily as a trainer. The T-28D Nomad entered the Southeast Asian theater as both a trainer and fighter for forces in Vietnam and Laos. It had two .50-caliber guns and could externally carry 1,800 pounds of bombs or rockets. It had a crew of two.

U-2   The U-2 Dragon Lady, build by Lockheed, was a high-altitude reconnaissance aircraft with a 70,000-foot ceiling and a maximum speed of 528 mph. It provided both day and night reconnaissance over North Vietnam during the war. It had a crew of one.

UH-1   The UH-1 Iroquois, built by Bell, was a utility helicopter in its initial design. The UH-1B/C, nicknamed Huey, was a utility helicopter with two primary weapons subsystems: a 7.62 mini-gun, capable of firing 2,400 rounds per minute; and a seven-round rocket pod mounted on each side of the helicopter. For the UH-1B/C without the mini-gun, a nineteen-round rocket pod replaced the seven-round rocket pod and a 40-mm grenade launcher at the helicopter's nose. The UH-1B/C also had the option of an M-60 machine gun anchored at the cargo doors on either side of the helicopter for more firepower and additional sets of eyes.

Index

Radar: FANSONG, 96; ground sites,
64; radar-guided bombs, 36
Radford, Arthur, 5
RB-26 aircraft, 10
RB-57 aircraft, 10, 97
RB-66 (ELINT) system, 31
Reconnaissance. *See* Air
reconnaissance
Red River Delta, 38
Republic of Korea, 105, 107
Republic of Vietnam (RVN): air
mobility in, 67, 79–84; creation of,
6; defoliation in, 68, 88–92; ground
support in, 67–72, 74–79;
interdiction in, 67, 84–88;
objectives of air power in, 69, 70,
74, 84–86; relations with United
States, 6, 18, 20–21, 104, 165;
search-and-rescue missions in, 101.
See also Army of the Republic of
Vietnam (ARVN); Republic of
Vietnam Air Force (VNAF)
Republic of Vietnam Air Force
(VNAF), 69–70, 74; air
reconnaissance by, 10, 93–94,
97–98; American military advisers
to, 2, 6, 8–11, 18, 75, 93–94, 99,
107; during Cambodian incursion,
137, 139–42; creation of, 6–8; in
CTZ IV, 75, 76; defoliation
missions by, 89; during Eastertide
Offensive, 145, 152, 156;
helicopters used by, 6, 7–8, 11–12,
89; during Lam Son 719, 129;
during Operation FARM GATE,
10–11, 99, 104; during Operation
FLAMING DART, 17, 18; during
Operation ROLLING THUNDER,
20–26, 30, 31; planes flown by, 10,
12, 17, 70, 89, 145, 152; and
Project Fire Brigade, 104–5; and
Vietnamization, 97–98
RF-4C aircraft, 97
RF-101 aircraft, 93–94, 97
Ron, 41
Route 13, 89
Route 15, 87–88

Route 137, 87–88
Route packages: creation of, 35; route
package 1, 43, 46, 49–51, 54,
60–62, 64, 72, 86–88, 93; route
package 2, 43, 51, 61, 93; route
package 3, 61, 93; route package 4,
61; route package 5, 38, 50–51, 57,
58, 61, 161; route package 6, 38,
50–51, 57, 58, 61, 161
Rusk, Dean, 21, 29
Ryan, John D., 55
Ryan Aeronautical Company, 96

Saigon, 17, 106–7; Brinks Hotel in,
15; fall of, 147; during Tet
Offensive, 72
Saravane, 128
Satellite transmission, 97
Sather, Richard, 15
Search-and-destroy operations, 70,
103–4, 129; Cambodian incursion
(1970), 124, 128, 137, 139–42,
144
Search-and-rescue (SAR), 68, 79, 92,
98–101, 108; composition of crews,
99–100; in DRV, 100–101; in Laos,
18, 99, 100–101, 103, 122;
restrictions on, 101; in RVN, 101;
and tactical airlifts, 104
Search-Locate-Annihilate-Monitor
operations, 71, 115
2nd Advanced Echelon (ADVON), 9
2nd Aerial Port Group, 106
2nd Air Division, 9, 119
2nd Bombardment Wing, 76
Se Kong river, 143
Se San river, 143
7th Air Force, 43, 50, 56, 64, 86, 96,
101, 116, 125, 127, 144, 156
7th Cavalry, 118
17th Strategic Aerospace Division, 156
74th Tactical Wing, 75
Sharp, Ulysses S. G., 24, 35, 43,
46–49, 51–52
Sihanouk, Prince Norodom, 134,
135–36
Sihanoukville, 133, 134

V I E T N A M

AMERICA IN THE WAR YEARS

SERIES EDITOR

David L. Anderson

University of Indianapolis

The Vietnam War and the tumultuous internal upheavals in America that coincided with it marked a watershed era in U.S. history. These events profoundly challenged America's heroic self-image. During the 1950s the United States defined Southeast Asia as an area of vital strategic importance. In the 1960s this view produced a costly American military campaign that continued into the early 1970s. The Vietnam War was the nation's longest war and ended with an unprecedented U.S. failure to achieve its stated objectives. Simultaneous with this frustrating military intervention and the domestic debate that it produced were other tensions created by student activism on campuses, the black struggle for civil rights, and the women's liberation movement. The books in this series explore the complex and controversial issues of the period from the mid-1950s to the mid-1970s in brief and engaging volumes. To facilitate continued and informed debate on these contested subjects, each book examines a military, political, or diplomatic issue; the role of a key individual; or one of the domestic changes in America during the war.

VOLUMES PUBLISHED

Melvin Small. *Antiwarriors: The Vietnam War and the Battle for America's Hearts and Minds* (2002). Cloth ISBN 0-8420-2895-1
Paper ISBN 0-8420-2896-X

Edward K. Spann. *Democracy's Children: The Young Rebels of the 1960s and the Power of Ideals* (2003). Cloth ISBN 0-8420-5140-6
Paper ISBN 0-8420-5141-4

Ronald B. Frankum Jr. *Like Rolling Thunder: The Air War in Vietnam, 1964–1975* (2005). Cloth ISBN 0-7425-4302-1